Selected Poems of

ROBERT
PENN
WARREN

Selected Poems of
ROBERT PENN WARREN

EDITED BY JOHN BURT

LOUISIANA STATE UNIVERSITY PRESS

BATON ROUGE   2001

Typeface: Times Roman
Printer and binder: Thomson-Shore, Inc.

Library of Congress Cataloging-in-Publication Data
Warren, Robert Penn, 1905–
      [Poems. Selections]
      Selected poems of Robert Penn Warren / edited by John Burt.
           p.   cm.
      Includes index.
      ISBN 0-8071-2686-1 (cloth : alk. paper)
      I. Title: Robert Penn Warren. II. Burt, John, 1955–.   III. Title.
PS3545.A748 A6 2001
811'.52—dc21   00-053457

CONTENTS

from Eleven Poems on the Same Theme

from Selected Poems 1923–1943

from Brother to Dragons

from Promises

from You, Emperors, and Others

from Tale of Time

from Incarnations

Audubon: A Vision

from Or Else

from Can I See Arcturus From Where I Stand?

from Now and Then

from Being Here

from Rumor Verified

from Chief Joseph of the Nez Perce

from Altitudes and Extensions

INTRODUCTION

The first poet laureate of the United States, and twice winner of the Pulitzer Prize for poetry (in 1957 for *Promises* and again in 1979 for *Now and Then)*, Robert Penn Warren is nevertheless more widely known as a novelist than as a poet. In this, as in many other things, he resembles Thomas Hardy, who also won fame as a novelist but thought of himself, first and last, as a poet.

Warren might have been neither, for his ambition as a precocious high-school student from Guthrie, Kentucky, was to attend the U.S. Naval Academy at Annapolis and become the Commander of the Pacific Fleet. After graduating two years early from high school, and attending an extra year of school in nearby Clarksville, Tennessee, he did win an appointment to Annapolis, but a freak accident during the summer before he was to enroll cost him the use of one eye and cost the navy a brilliant admiral-to-be. At the last minute, his parents were able to arrange for his admission to Vanderbilt University, where fate gave him John Crowe Ransom and Donald Davidson as teachers, and Allen Tate and Cleanth Brooks as friends. In Nashville, Warren fell in with a loosely structured circle of intellectuals, only some of them connected with Vanderbilt (which thought of them then as an embarrassment), who gathered at the house of Sidney Mttron Hirsch to discuss philosophy and poetry, a circle now known as the Fugitives after the short-lived literary magazine they published (under Warren's editorship) from 1922 to 1925, *The Fugitive.*

It would be a mistake to think of the Fugitives as being of one mind either about poetry or (after the thinking of some took a political turn during the early years of the Depression) about politics. But they were mad for poetry, both for writing it and for reading it, and especially for the most avant-garde poetry of that era, the work of T. S. Eliot and Ezra Pound. Indeed, this group of literary amateurs in what was then a somewhat provincial city were far more attuned to contemporary poetry, and to the writing of poetry, than the academic literary scholars Warren was later to study under as a graduate student at the University of California, at Yale, and as a Rhodes scholar at Oxford. Something of this poet's-eye view, this practitioner insight into how poems are put together, was to inform the work of Brooks and Warren as literary critics and to motivate the pedagogical style associated with New Criticism. (It's not for nothing that New Criticism as a pedagogy grew up not in the scholarly bastions of the Ivy League but in the sophomore poetry survey course in the state university of one of the poorest states in the Union.) The poetry that Warren, at the age of seventeen, began to publish in *The Fugitive*, in that other great, short-lived periodical of the awakening South, *The Double Dealer*, and elsewhere, shows him reaching beyond adolescent influences (Edgar Allan Poe and the Pre-Raphaelites) to the work of Eliot on the one hand (most evident in the hallucinatory 1931 poem "The Return:An Elegy"), and to the work of Thomas Hardy, A. E. Housman, and the traditional balladeers on the other. At its best, this early poetry has a feel for the stark, nonhuman alienness and grandeur of the natural world, a world that (to paraphrase a famous formulation from Warren's later *Audubon: A Vision*) does not know pity, or if it did, we should not be worthy of it. Here, for instance, is Warren's 1928 poem "Rebuke of the Rocks," from the sequence "Kentucky Mountain Farm," whose ethos, if not whose style, is a part of Warren's poetry early and late.

Now on you is the hungry equinox,
O little stubborn people of the hill,
The season of the obscene moon whose pull
Disturbs the sod, the rabbit, the lank fox,
Moving the waters, the boar's dull blood,
And the acrid sap of the ironwood.

But breed no tender thing among the rocks.
Rocks are too old under the mad moon,
Renouncing passion by the strength that locks
The eternal agony of fire in stone.

Then quit yourselves as stone and cease
To break the weary stubble-field for seed;
Let not the naked cattle bear increase,
Let barley wither and the bright milkweed.
Instruct the heart, lean men, of a rocky place
That even the little flesh and fevered bone
May keep the sweet sterility of stone.

After Warren's first chapbook, *Thirty-Six Poems* (1935) (issued by the same press that published Wallace Stevens's *Ideas of Order*), Warren's poetry began to absorb new influences, most especially from Andrew Marvell and John Donne. *Eleven Poems on the Same Theme* (1942) gathers most of these new poems, which are darker and more self-consciously formal that the poems of the twenties and early thirties. The theme mentioned in the title is that of human fallenness — not just the fallenness of original sin, but the fallenness of finding one's self thrown into a world in which one feels the demand of having a metaphysical purpose but can't find any that are not already somehow shot through with fakery.

The world of these poems is a world in which one is shadowed by an unplaced sense of guilt, a guilt that is unplaceable because it originates not from concrete wickedness but from rootlessness and disillusion. If one could account for that guilt (by remembering, for instance, some sin worth the candle) one would at least have a story or a destiny, if a dark one; perhaps, indeed, one ought to hazard doing something really evil, since then at least one would know reality for what it is, and would no longer be adrift on a foggy sea of the unreal. It would be a mistake to think of the darkness of these poems as a kind of late Calvinism, for Calvinism is at least able to match the experience of original sin with the experience of grace, but Warren's poetry of this period is able only to match its sense of fallenness with a deeper and still more confusing draft of the knowledge of good and evil. In the moral world of these poems, one feels the urgent demand that one give an account of how one's life looks in the harsh light of absolute meaning, yet at the same time one feels that that meaning not only always escapes one but never even presents itself at all except in ways that are already fatally qualified by self-deceit and wishful thinking. The moral predicament outlined in these poems is like that faced by the dark fanatics of Warren's novels — by Percy Munn of *Night Rider* (1939) or Jeremiah Beaumont of *World Enough and Time* (1950) — characters who do the evil deeds of fanatics not because they are maddened, as true fanatics are, by the pure Idea, but because in their despair and emptiness they hope that if they do the fanatic's violence they might at least come to some portion of the fanatic's conviction.

The politics of Warren's poem "Terror" may have embarrassed him later (the poem ridicules those who, led by a fear of emptiness and by a hunger for a life-justifying — or rather death-justifying — conviction, fight first for the Left in Spain and then for the Right in Finland), but its moral universe is Warren's to the end of his life, despite profound changes in his concrete politics. As "Kentucky Mountain Farm" is echoed in the later "Evening Hawk," so we find in the later "Rumor Verified" echoes of these sentiments from "Terror":

So some, whose passionate emptiness and tidal
Lust swayed toward the debris of Madrid,
And left New York to loll in their fierce idyll
Among the olives, where the snipers hid.
And now the North — to seek that visioned face
And polarize their iron of despair,
Who praise no beauty like the boreal grace
Which greens the dead eye under the rocket's flare.
They fight old friends, for their obsession knows
Only the immaculate itch, not human friends or foes.

Nietzsche says that we would rather have the void as our purpose than be void

of purpose. Something of this self-annihilating version of Pascal's wager —
which the speaker at once ironically condemns and is ineluctably drawn toward
— informs not only the *Eleven Poems*, but also the most ambitious poem of War-
ren's early phase, the long, multivoiced narrative "The Ballad of Billie Potts,"
the principal new poem in his 1943 *Selected Poems*.

The body of the poem recounts, in a ballad-like style, a folktale Warren had
heard in his youth from a relative. Big Billie Potts and his wife run an inn in the
region between the Cumberland and Tennessee Rivers, "The Land Between the
Rivers." When wealthy travelers stay with them, they arrange for the travelers
to be ambushed and murdered. Their son, Little Billie, sent to contact the am-
bushers, but seeking to demonstrate his prowess to his father, is instead surprised
by his intended victim, and is forced to flee to the far West. Returning years later
as a rich man, he stays at his parents' inn, but, as a practical joke, does not tell
them who he is. They, down on their luck but eager as always to improve what-
ever opportunities fate throws their way, murder Little Billie, only to discover
too late who their victim really was.

Interspersed with the narrative sections of the poem are sections of commen-
tary in a different style that develop the theme of a destructive access to absolute
knowledge, speculating that Little Billie's return to his parental home is a kind
of culmination of a destructive hunger for the truth and for the source of iden-
tity:

(The bee knows, and the eel's cold ganglia burn,
And the sad head lifting to the long return,
Through brumal deeps, in the great unsolsticed coil,
Carries its knowledge, navigator without star,
And under the stars, pure in its clamorous toil,
The goose hoots north where the starlit marshes are.
The salmon heaves at the fall, and, wanderer, you
Heave at the great fall of Time, and gorgeous, gleam
In the powerful arc, and anger and outrage like dew,
In your plunge, fling, and plunge to the thunderous stream:
Back to the silence, back to the pool, back
To the high pool, motionless, and the unmurmuring dream.
And you, wanderer, back,
Brother to pinion and the pious fin that cleave
The innocence of air and the disinfectant flood
And wing and welter and weave
The long compulsion and the circuit hope
Back,
And bear through that limitless and devouring fluidity

The itch and humble promise which is home.

And the father waits for the son.

The hour is late,
The scene familiar even in shadow,
The transaction brief,
And you, wanderer, back,
After the striving and the wind's word,
To kneel
Here in the evening empty of wind or bird,
To kneel in the sacramental silence of evening
At the feet of the old man
Who is evil and ignorant and old,
To kneel
With the little black mark under your heart,
Which is your name,
Which is shaped for luck,

Which is your luck.)

The publication of the 1943 *Selected Poems* began a ten-year period of poetic silence. It's odd to refer to that period in that way, because those ten years were also the period of Warren's greatest fame as a novelist; perhaps the fact that Warren himself described that period in that way is a measure of just how much more he thought of himself as a poet than as a novelist. When Warren's poetry began again, after the end of his troubled first marriage and his remarriage to the novelist and writer Eleanor Clark, his poetry had undergone a profound stylistic and political change.

Warren is one of the few writers of his time to move from right of center to left of center in middle age. The transformation of Warren's political views probably began somewhat earlier than the ten years of silence. Indeed, even the infamous defense of racial segregation in his 1929 essay "The Briar Patch" is half hearted, since the essay's main argument, that industrialization will not ease race relations because the factory owners will whip up racism to keep the unions out, is not an argument that a committed racist would ever make. (Indeed, even those genteel southerners who opposed naked race-hatred but not segregation — the young Warren is often grouped with them — might have balked at this argument.) The evolution of Warren's views was protracted, as all changes of a morally deep kind are, and can't really be described in the language of a sudden conversion. Throughout the civil rights era, Warren played an important role, arguing in such books as *Segregation: The Inner Conflict in the South* (1956), and *Who Speaks for the Negro?* (1965), that racial segregation had to end, and that ending it would not necessarily obliterate the South as a distinctive culture.

Certainly the civil rights era produced few more moving testaments to the white southerner's moral anguish over race and complicity in racism than *Brother to Dragons* (1953), the book-length "tale in verse and voices" that, in the year before the *Brown vs. Board of Education* decision, broke Warren's ten-year poetic silence. In *Brother to Dragons* the shade of Thomas Jefferson, disgusted with his own idealism, enraged with the failings of the country whose Declaration of Independence he authored, and revolted in general by human nature, argues with the figure of the poet himself about the meaning of the murder and dismemberment, in Smithland, Kentucky, in 1811, of a slave by Jefferson's two nephews, Lilburne and Isham Lewis. *Brother to Dragons* is not merely a book of the civil rights era, however, but also a book of the depths of the cold war, for in addition to its arguments about America's dark history of slavery and racism, the book also argues against America's sense of itself as a redeemer nation exempted from the histories of guilt and sorrow that entangle other nations. The book's argument against political idealism, so akin to contemporary arguments by Reinhold Niebuhr and Hannah Arendt, is intended as a warning to those who might destroy the world in order to save it. This gnarled and tangled poem, charged with so much political and personal urgency that it seems perpetually to be running away with its author, became a lifelong preoccupation: Warren published a complete revision of it in 1979, a play version in 1976, and worked on yet another version of the poem as late as 1987. The prophetic anger of the book is closer in feel to Allen Ginsberg's *Howl* than to Donald Davidson's *The Tall Men*, and it strikes the kind of personal note that some literary historians don't believe came into American poetry until Robert Lowell published *Life Studies* in 1960.

Warren's other breakthrough volume of the 1950s, *Promises* (1957), likewise fuses personal and political concerns in ways that seem more like the poetry of the next decade than like the poetry of the last one, and in the loosening of his style — the verse is still formal, but somehow feels less so — Warren anticipates the loosening of style common to many other poets of that decade, such as Adrienne Rich or Lowell. Uniquely among Warren's volumes, in *Promises* the poet, invigorated by the birth of his two children (the book divides into large sections devoted to each of them), seeks to assure himself that his earlier vision of human nature and human history, while not wrong, is at least capable of recognizing qualified exceptions. The dominant tone of the volume is struck early on, in the sonnet "The Child Next Door." The child next door to the ruined Italian fortress where the poet is staying with his wife and new baby is defective, because of some abortifacient pill its mother took. Contrasting the beauty of that child's sister, and the beauty of his own daughter, with the looks of the defective child, the poet is first tempted to rage against fate, then against beauty for its deceptiveness, but finally wins through to a very qualified form of acceptance of the world in the face of what that world is:

I think of your goldness, of joy, but how empires grind, stars are hurled.
I smile stiff, saying *ciao,* saying *ciao,* and think: *This is the world.*

Warren's two next volumes, *You, Emperors, and Others* (1960), *Tale of Time* (1966) — the latter being the section of new poems that opened *Selected Poems New and Old* — are widely considered to be low points, but even *You, Emperors, and Others* is graced by "Tiberius on Capri," in which even the emperor's debaucheries cannot free him from the sense that "all is nothing, nothing all," which he hears the sea singing to him; and by "Mortmain," Warren's powerful elegy for his father. *Tale of Time* includes Warren's caustic and ironic "Homage to Emerson, On Night Flight to New York" perhaps his definitive attack upon Emerson's style of idealism, but also one of the earliest examples of the hypnotic and associative kind of sequence that would come to characterize his poetry later.

Only Stevens and Hardy among recent poets have had a "late phase" like Warren's. It is a little misleading to consider the volumes from *Incarnations* (1968) onward a late phase, because although these poems begin in the poet's sixty-third year, they also represent somewhat more than half of his *oeuvre.* The main themes of *Incarnations* were not new to Warren — the predicament of bodily mortality, the demands of an intense but nonhuman spirit, the necessity of accounting for one's self to a power that brooks no accounting — but what is new in the volume is a stylistic boldness that lifts these poems from the realm of thought into the realm of the sublime. The poems of "Island of Summer," the sequence that makes up the first half of *Incarnations,* are perhaps equalled in intensity, but never surpassed, by any of Warren's other poetry. "Natural History" (a title that Warren would use again) considers the violent political past of one locale (the island of Port Cros, in the Mediterranean) against the background of the incessant violence of nature, a violence that continues into the recent past and projects itself into the future. The thought is daunting enough that the poet seeks to console himself with a sense that maybe that violence had meaning, only to reject that consolation with a rather curt irony:

Many have died here, but few
Have names, it is like the world, bodies
Have been eaten by dogs, gulls, rodents, ants,
And fish, and Messire Jean le Maingre,
He struck them, and they fled.
                    Et les Sarrasins
se retirèrent en une ile qui est devant

le dict chastel—
                          but little good that, for
The *Maréchal* was hot on them, and
                                      des leurs
y perdirent plus de quatre cent hommes,
que morts, que affolez,
                          and the root
Of the laurel has profited, the leaf
Of the live-oak achieves a new luster, the mouth
Of the mullet is agape, and my ten-year-old son,
In the island dump, finds a helmet, Nazi—from left
To right, entering at the temple, small and
Perfectly round at the point of entry, neat, but
At egress large, raw, exploding outward, desperate for
Light, air, and openness after
The hot enclosure and intense dark of
That brief transit: this
The track of the missile. Death
Came quick, for history,
Like nature, may have mercy,
Though only by accident. Neither
Has tears.
                  But at dusk
Le centre de recherche d'engins spéciaux, the rocket
Rises, the track of fume now feathers white—spins out, oh whiter—
Rises beyond the earth's shadow, in
Full light aspires. Then,
With no sound, the expected explosion. The glitters
Of flame fall, like shreds of bright foil, ice-bright, from
A Christmas tree, die in earth's shadow, but
The feathers of fume yet hang high, dissolve
White in that last light. The technicians
Now go to dinner.
                  Beauty
Is the fume-track of necessity. This thought
Is therapeutic.
                  If, after several
Applications, you do not find
Relief, consult your family physician.

At the end of "The Leaf," which concludes the sequence, the poet cries out in the dark, and his father's voice, from the dark of a far garden, calls out to him, yielding one of the most chilling moments of sublimity in Warren's poetry:

> The voice blesses me for the only
> Gift I have given: *teeth set on edge.*
>
> In the momentary silence of the cicada,
> I can hear the appalling speed,
> In space beyond stars, of
> Light. It is
>
> A sound like wind.

Incarnations began the most remarkable period of Warren's poetry, extending from *Audubon: A Vision* (1969), his book-length meditation on Audubon — who faced not so much death as the realization that death would never reveal to him its secret, and so discovered that he would have to walk in the world and learn to love its beauty — through the great sequence *Or Else* (1974), to the 1975 *Selected Poems* (*Can I See Arcturus From Where I Stand?*) and *Now and Then* (1979). These are poems of the most stern and most demanding ambition, poems that seek to survey the world of human destiny and folly from a more than human point of view. The keynote of this period is struck by Warren's most famous poem,"Evening Hawk":

> From plane of light to plane, wings dipping through
> Geometries and orchids that the sunset builds,
> Out of the peak's black angularity of shadow, riding
> The last tumultuous avalanche of
> Light above pines and the guttural gorge,
> The hawk comes.
> His wing
> Scythes down another day, his motion
> Is that of the honed steel-edge, we hear
> The crashless fall of stalks of Time.
>
> The head of each stalk is heavy with the gold of our error.
>
> Look! look! he is climbing the last light
> Who knows neither Time nor error, and under
> Whose eye, unforgiving, the world, unforgiven, swings
> Into shadow.
> Long now,
> The last thrush is still, the last bat

Now cruises in his sharp hieroglyphics. His wisdom
Is ancient, too, and immense. The star
Is steady, like Plato, over the mountain.

If there were no wind we might, we think, hear
The earth grind on its axis, or history
Drip in darkness like a leaking pipe in the cellar.

In the last five years of his publishing career, Warren continued to produce re-
markable poetry at a great rate. *Being Here* (1980) is a kind of shadow autobi-
ography in verse, with poems concerning most of the major incidents and
episodes of Warren's life, as well as the beautiful narratives "Sila," and "Part of
What Might Have Been a Short Story, Almost Forgotten." The poems of *Rumor
Verified* (1981), although contemporary with the poems included in *Being Here*,
differ strongly from them in tone, being marked throughout by a kind of poetic
and metaphysical self-doubt that sometimes edges toward despair. The book also
includes perhaps Warren's darkest meditation on American history, the poem
"Going West," in which the speaker, driving westward on the interstate and com-
paring the ease of his progress with what might be called the triumphal march of
American history, suddenly hits a pheasant, which explodes in blood on his wind-
shield. Warren develops some of the darker implications of this history in his
book-length *Chief Joseph of the Nez Perce* (1983), in which the title character,
beset by the ambition and treachery of the U.S. Army and the forces it repre-
sented, is nevertheless able to win through in the end at least to retain his per-
sonal dignity and his historic stature.

In *Altitudes and Extensions* (the new section of the 1985 *New and Selected
Poems*), Warren's last volume of poetry, the poet seeks a calmer and more re-
flective mode, surveying many of the incidents he had considered in earlier
autobiographical poems, such as those in *Promises* and in *Being Here*, with a
seasoned generosity rather different from the taut and tart assessments of the ear-
lier volumes. The volume also contains Warren's ambitious retelling and recon-
sideration of the atom-bombing of Hiroshima, the long sequence "New Dawn,"
originally written for a reissue of John Hersey's classic *Hiroshima*. In "Immor-
tality Over the Dakotas" Warren returns to a famous scene from his earlier poetry.
The speaker lolls, almost asleep, in his airplane seat high above the Dakotas, de-
tached from and superior to the human condition:

You feel as though you had just had a quick dip
In the Lamb's mystic blood. You laugh into manic darkness.
You laugh at the tiny glow that far, far down
Shines like a glowworm beside an unseeable stone.

It would be a little Dakota town where
Population has not been dipped in the mystic blood.

We find a similar state of abstraction in the speaker Warren ironizes in the first section of "Homage to Emerson, On Night Flight to New York." At 38,000 feet, Emerson is dead right, Warren had said. This distance delevation, above humankind, indifferent to mortality, indifferent even to specifics and particulars, is recognizably a parodic undoing of the metaphysical chill, the Pascalian nausea, that Warren describes in other poems, especially his hawk poems, such as "Evening Hawk," which likewise seek to survey mortality, with contempt, from above. In "Evening Hawk," that one might hear the crashless fall of the stalks of time was thought of as the hallmark of a visionary state, beyond ordinary consciousness but nevertheless a kind of consciousness. In "Immortality Over the Dakotas" the state of imaginative elevation seems more like intoxication than like visionary consciousness; instead of comprehending the entire history of time and error from the vantage of the Absolute, the speaker is merely dazed, having swallowed too much of the spirit, so that his reflections have a touch of unreal and self-ironizing hilarity. In "Homage to Emerson," the speaker had, with only equivocal success, attempted to call himself back to the imagined Earth by fixing his mind upon something specific — the wart that an old African American man had told him when he was a child was the product of too much masturbation, and the memory of how a drunk cripple had toppled over one evening in New Orleans, only to assuage the poet (after his second fall, the poet having propped him back up the first time):

Prithee, the voice
Expensively said, *do not trouble yourself*
Further. This is as good a position as any
From which to watch the stars. Then added:
Until, of course, the cops come.

In "Immortality Over the Dakotas," this attempt to return to the ground, to grasp the specific, to reach out and grab the limb of a tree, as Wordsworth did, to assure one's self that one still lives in a solid reality, has a different effect:

Now suddenly through glass, through dark fury, you see
Who must be down there, with collar up on the dirty sheepskin,
Snow on red hunter's cap, earflaps down.
Chores done. But he just can't bring himself to go in.
The doctor's just said he won't last till another winter.

She's sitting inside, white bun of hair neat as ever,
Squinting studiously down through bifocals at what she's knitting.
He knows her fire's getting low, but he can't go in.
He knows that if he did he might let something slip.
He couldn't stand that. So stares at the blackness of sky.
Stares at lights, green and red, that tread the dark of your immortality.

Now the poet here is by no means breaking through from an imagined ab-
solute into a concrete and particular reality, because the scene he depicts here is
of course an imagined one. But he is breaking through from one kind of imagi-
nation to another, from an inhumane one to a humane one, and because the poet's
attraction for the former is so strong, his adoption of the latter is not sentimental.
That is why the poem ends with an ironic parting shot at the speaker.

In July 1983, Warren worked on, but apparently did not bring to a state that
satisfied him, a poem variously called "A Version of Identity," or "Upon Reading
A Psalm." The cemetery it describes is probably the very one in which he was
buried a little more than six years later. But what is most remarkable about the
poem is its clear-sighted bravery about death:

Lisping in shadow of sound, stone-lipping in languor of darkness,
Bursting like bubbles into new syllables
Of what new tongue, the brook
Moves in the nighttide of cliff overhang—long later longs
To wander somewhere in tangled vastness of moonlight,
Then hide in the prickle-edged shadow where
No breath of air stirs sedge.

Or is it the brook that seems to flow through my sleep
As I lie in my dark dream of roof and being?
Perhaps the past makes a murmur like that,
An indecipherable sound as it flows from the point
Of its own lost origin to
This moment when it, in its shadow self,
Is the muted tune of my being. Is now. Is I.
And tomorrow will be. If tomorrow ever comes.

I have stood at sundown in a lost graveyard,
Where the forest impinges, year by year,
And the stones, those not fallen or lost,
Thrust up, crank, askew, from among
Butterflyweed now past bloom, ironweed
Twined with ivy leaves reddening fallward, and I read

What dates I could read — *Born 1783–Died 1826,*
1812–1860, 1841–1868— and on

And on to the last tear shed there a century back.
And the evening wind made, like tongues, the leaves of the forest vibrate
In that teasing language that led whence to whence,
And I wondered if those lying there, like me in my brookside sleep,
Were reliving the musical mystery of Time
That once had been the Self's deepest reality.
Deliver my soul from the sword: my darling from the power of the dog.

ABOUT THE TEXTS

Over a career of more than sixty years, Robert Penn Warren published volumes of selected poetry five times, from *Selected Poems 1923–1943*, through generous selections published in 1966, 1976, and 1985, to the limited-edition volume of Selected Poems brought out in Helsinki in 1986. For each of these volumes Warren revised his poems a great deal, although he did not as a rule seek to make his earlier poems sound like his later ones, nor did he seek to revise out political convictions with which he no longer agreed.

Because Warren often published his poems in long sequences of linked poems, and because I wished to represent those sequences in their entirety in *The Collected Poems of Robert Penn Warren*, I chose to use the first book appearances of his poems for my copy texts for that volume. In consequence I had to relegate all of the later revisions, sometimes fifty years' worth of rethinking in which something was changed in every line, to the endnotes of that book. Freed of that constraint for this volume, I have chosen to use here the latest texts for which I could make a persuasive case. The texts in this volume are therefore sometimes very different from those in *The Collected Poems of Robert Penn Warren*. To the extent that one can know such things, these texts represent Warren's final intentions for these poems.

For the most part I have followed the 1985 *New and Selected Poems (SP85)*. The publication of that book was, however, not the last occasion Warren had for revising his poems. All of the poems in the Helsinki limited edition, for instance, were extensively revised, and that edition was prepared from an entirely new typescript. And Warren provided Stuart Wright, who was preparing a Collected Poems in 1987, with marked-up copies of many of his books, copies that are now to be found in the Special Collections department of the Woodruff Library at Emory University. Both of these versions, however, are problematic, the Helsinki volume because Warren seems to have forgotten about it entirely when preparing his texts for Wright the next year (and because whether he saw that book as a final statement concerning his poems is not clear), and the Emory texts because Warren did not bring that project to completion, and it is not clear how settled his intentions were in the case of the revisions he offered. (For instance, Warren prepared the *Promises* section of that project from a copy of the early English edition of *Promises*, making small revisions to lines he had deleted when he republished those poems in 1966, 1976, and 1985.)

While I have used texts from *SP85* as my starting point, this volume is not simply a reissue of *SP85*. That volume, like those from 1966 and 1976, included a number of new poems, and, like those volumes, was arranged in reverse chronological order to showcase the new poems. All three necessarily slighted the early portions of Warren's career in favor of the most recent work. *SP85*, because it included eighty pages of new poems, and because it was also designed to feature the volumes that had appeared since the 1976 selection, treated the Warren's career up to 1976 with particular ruthlessness. A true Selected Poems should represent Warren's career more broadly, and should include selections from his book-length poems *Brother to Dragons* and *Chief Joseph of the Nez Perce*, as this volume does. I have also included five poems from very early in Warren's career (from before the publication of *Thirty-Six Poems* in 1935). I included "The Bird and Stone" because it has already attracted some scholarly commentary, and because it sheds interesting light upon similar early poems, such as the "Kentucky Mountain Farm" sequence. "Conquest" is an example of a kind of poem rare in Warren's work, although "Empire" and "History" resemble it somewhat. "Oxford City Wall" is the only poem that I know of that derives from Warren's time at Oxford as a Rhodes scholar, and "San Francisco Night Windows," which perhaps dates from Warren's period as a graduate student at Berkeley, makes an interesting contrast with his treatments of similar subjects and places in *Being Here*.

The 1985 texts required considerable emendation, since Warren did not proofread the galleys of that volume with care. For instance, the sections that represented Warren's volumes from before 1976 were prepared from cut-and-pasted sections of *Selected Poems 1923–1975*, but where the sections were not evenly pasted in, the typesetter often added or removed stanza breaks that Warren did not notice upon proofreading, and I have treated any difference between the galleys and the setting typescript of *SP85* for which I could find no note in Warren's hand on either text as uncorrected typesetter errors. (The *SP85* version of "The Ballad of Billie Potts" is an even more puzzling case than those of the other early poems in *SP85*, since it consists of cut-and-taped sections of a typeset [not typewritten] original, but that original corresponds to none of the other published forms of that poem. I have chosen to treat the places where that poem differs from the 1976 version — in almost every case the variants are only accidentals of punctuation — as unauthoritative, since, as is well known since W. W. Greg first laid out the rationale of a scholarly editor's choice of copy-text, authors who are proofreading new settings of old texts are likely to pay less attention to accidental than to substantive variants.) Even Warren's corrections on the galleys of the 1985 volume show signs of not having been made with care. I have generally adopted those revisions, except where they did not make grammatical sense, in which case I have fallen back upon earlier readings, or where I thought he had misread the punctuation in the poor photocopy he was using. I have relied upon

Warren's own corrected copy of the published *SP85* where I had evidence that what Warren wrote in that copy was genuinely a correction rather than yet another revision, and I have made cautious use of the Helsinki and Emory texts where they provided additional evidence for readings for which I had other grounds. For "Mortmain," I have followed Warren's very last version of that poem, in *Portrait of a Father,* since it reflects information about Warren's father's life that Warren discovered late in life, after *SP85.*

Acknowledgments

My first acknowledgment is to Mr. Warren himself, without whose help I could not have started this project, and to Eleanor Clark, who kept a keen and helpful eye on this project up to her death. Rosanna and Gabriel Warren have also given constant support to this project. Owen Laster, Mr. Warren's agent, helped this project along in uncountable ways. James A. Grimshaw's bibliography of Warren's works was of inestimable value, since Professor Grimshaw had already tracked down most of the variants. He graciously made available the drafts of his revised bibliography as they developed, keeping me apprised of new versions as they turned up. He also was a generous and thoughtful advisor to this project from the beginning, helping me to think out its many issues. Jon Eller, Susan Staves, Gary Taylor, William Flesch, Anthony Szczesiul, Randolph Runyon, James A. Perkins, Mark Miller, Lucy Ferriss, Robert Koppelman, Joseph Blotner, John Lavagnino, and George Franklin helped me think through many textual issues as well. I also have learned from conversations about Warren with the late Cleanth Brooks and with Joseph Blotner, R. W. B. Lewis, Harold Bloom, and John Hollander. During the preparation of *The Collected Poems of Robert Penn Warren* I had the help of many research assistants at Brandeis University who double-checked many of my collations. These included Stefan Gunther, Gary Roberts, Phil Chassler, Jonathan Kim, Leslee Thorne-Murphy, Michael Schwartz, Lisa Amber Phillips, Sharon Astyk, and Melissa Beauchesne. For this project, I also had the able assistance of Gretchen Holcombe.

Finally, I had the enthusiastic support of Leslie Phillabaum and John Easterly at Louisiana State University Press, without whose generosity and willingness to take a risk this book would never have seen print. And I have had excellent editorial and production support from Nicola Mason and Laura Gleason at the Press as well. Whatever mistakes there are in this edition are, of course, my own responsibility.

Research on this project was generously supported by the American Philosophical Society, whose grant enabled me to travel to Emory to examine the materials for Warren's 1987 projected edition of a Collected Poems, and by the Mazer fund of Brandeis University, whose grant enabled me to make countless trips to the Beinecke Library over the summers.

Last of all, but most important, too, I would like to thank Jo Anne Preston, whose encouragement and clear-sightedness and support helped me to bring this project into focus.

Note

The symbol * is used to indicate a space between sections of a poem wherever such spaces are lost in pagination.

Selected Poems of

ROBERT
PENN
WARREN

Early Unpublished Poems

The Bird and Stone

I.

You work injustice to the little streets
To bear your law which is of flesh alone
By theirs compacted of the lath and stone,
For some inviolable bird repeats
In them a song that no one understands
Who has forgot the shadowed rush
Of ultimate dark floods that wash
Nocturnally the lost and desolate lands.
But two or three have thought, perhaps, or read
10 Of a place where the slender foot might justly tread,
Where under enormous ridges, overgrown
With obscure cedar and the savage vine,
Lies basalt noble enough to bear the stain
Of centaur's blood or the spilled Grecian wine.

II.

Colder than figments on the wall of sleep,
Perfect and cold as the hard autumnal dawn
The mind resumes your image I have known,
Savage and subtle, engendered of the deep
Black lymbeck of the troubled head.
But once or twice in special I have heard,
When dimly the streetlight glimmered on the walls
Or lay in piteous fresco on the bed,
Your voice like some devout and final bird,
10 A strong and ultimate bird that calls,
Calling in the lost dark alone
Beside a bloody pool in a place of stone.

The Concert

That night, my dear, do you recall to mind
How above the aisles like ripe corn in the wind
The soul out from the body stood and bowed
Before the blast of sound, corrupt and loud,

From throaty horn and truculent thick drum?
Then violins ascended to resume
In silver fire the fabric of their pain,
And under them was fanned to glow again

Like dying coals the sullen tympanum.
10 The blood, commensurate to their diadrom,
Contrived its own inviolate refrain,
Stirring the heart and echoing to the brain;

Knowing your image there by me I knew
That then my blood's thick music might subdue
The *basso obstinato* of your own
To its intricate and savage tune.

Outside the motors throbbing in the rain
Bore us down streets where they have passed again,
Will pass, through morning, night, and afternoon,
20 Weaving their own remorseless monotone.

I would but remember, not regret,
The windy horns, and only would forget
The muted anguish of the dim bassoon,
While through the slanting autumn afternoon

A weary violin across the street
Insistently continues to repeat
Things we have thought but never said,
Things other men have thought who now are dead.

Conquest

Phoenician galley and the sweating slave
Over the flat Mediterranean,
Beating by Carthage in the sun.
Pillars of Hercules, gates that gave
On the deep's grey gardens and the Cornish coast.
Phoenician, Greek, men whom the summer lured
Past Carthage to the waters in the west ...
Black galleys beaked to westward like a bird.

*

Not the beginning, not the end.
10 They did not know that land and ocean bend
Downward to make the long, long circuit home.
This much great Caesar did not know
When shield to arm he leaped the prow
And over his feet there curled the strait's cold foam.
The mad tired eyes, fixed on the wild land
Under his eagles, saw not the long way home,
The world that closes like a tired closed hand.

Then others came who knew; the man
From Genoa knew on the high-pooped caraval.
20 Santa Maria ... O white and virginal
Incredible shore where morning breakers ran!
Bright fountain of the swollen Everglades,
De Leon's name. Magellan, Cortez, Drake,
Names down the track the bending oceans make,
Names hung along the westward, drumming trades.

Hendrick Hudson, icicles in his beard,
Northwest by west to the echo of a word.
India. By frozen coasts, the bitten spume;
Passage to India, passage home.

30 Many were hungry, many were cold.
By rocks, in withered grass, in the deep pinewood,
By rivers, they lay down. Their blood
To darkness spilled in westward vagrant gold.
Not the beginning, nor the ending now.
On obdurate headlands laced by foam,
Unquestioning eyes, the clear unbending brow
Puzzled a little here the long way come,
Still facing westward down the circuit home.

Oxford City Wall

More than to God or to the heart's last prayer
They trusted in the stone; stone after stone,
Parapet and port and bastion,
They raised their wall against the timeless air.
Three bowmen here might crouch within the deep
Embrasures and let fly the grey goose-feather;
In turrets all night long the sentinel
Kept watch and called the hours, though God might sleep.
Northward and stark against the autumn weather,
10 Under the sad vine strung along the wall,
Still bastion and parapet abide
While to the stone's wind-sheltered side
Gently the garden blooms into the fall.

*

Hard times there were. Strange horsemen in the land
Tramped down the corn; at dusk above a spot
Where some had ridden near, within bowshot,
The swollen rooks beat up against the wind.
And still the rooks beat up, when darkness comes,
Like memory from the fields; where men once fell
20 With mortal sudden coughing down the wall,
Barbed quarrel in the throat, the garden blooms.

Gently the garden blooms into the fall.
Red rose, white rose, late foxglove. In the wall
That faith abides by which the stone was set:
To hold off still the fatal season's issue,
Guarding the breath's faint bloom unto the last,
A little longer—a little longer yet—
From the proud heart, and the gentle blossoming tissue,
When rooks beat up, the importunate slow frost.

San Francisco Night Windows

So hangs the hour like fruit fullblown and sweet,
Our strict and desperate avatar,
Despite that antique westward gulls lament
Over enormous waters which retreat
Weary unto the white and sensual star.
Accept these images for what they are—
Out of the past a fragile element
Of substance into accident.
I would speak honestly and of a full heart;
10 I would speak surely for the tale is short,
And the soul's remorseless catalogue
Assumes its quick and piteous sum.
Think you, hungry is the city in the fog
Where now the darkened piles resume
Their framed and frozen prayer
Articulate and shafted in the stone
Against the void and absolute air.
If so the frantic breath could be forgiven,
And the deep blood subdued before it is gone
20 In a savage paternoster to the stone,
Then might we all be shriven.

Poems 1922–1943

The Fierce Horsemen

Pitiless, pitiless spoilers,
    Raiding the weeping land,
Wrenching the last frail leaf
    From the dying year's cold hand.

"Why do you ride your wild horses
    Shrieking over our roofs,
Ravage our fair, sweet silence
    With the thunder of their hoofs?"

"Why do we ride down the summer,
10   Under hoofs of the wind-hurled rain?
We needs must ride down the summer
    That a spring may come again."

Wild Oats

I am sowing wild oats
    On rocky hills and steep,
And when my harvest whitens
    I shall not be here to reap.

But the four wild winds shall winnow
    And the sun and rain shall reap;
And they shall glut my storehouse,
    But I shall be asleep.

Death Mask of a Young Man

I. The Mouse

Down the stair had creaked the doctor's feet
Shuffling. He heard them out thinking it queer
Tomorrow night at nine he would not hear
Feet shuffling out and down into the street
Past the one murky gas jet in the hall,
Past the discarded chair beside his door,
The Steinbach's entrance on the lower floor,
And the cracked patch of plaster on the wall.

Just how that crack came he could never think
10 To save his life, though he remembered yet
How once a mouse ran in, quick as a wink.
It must have said, "Why here's a hole in the wall!
I'll just whisk in, into the dark, and let
Heavy and terrible feet tramp down the hall."

II. The Moon

Remotely the moon across the window pane,
Was passing, as he had often watched it pass
When nights like this, too tired for sleep, he'd lain
Watching that moon beyond the dirty glass
Slide out of sight as if drawn by a string
Stretched through the stars; then he would count the tread
Of the deliberate clock that soon would bring
The moon past, and a shadow to his bed.

But now forgetful of slow pomp the clock
10 With slavering fangs and like the haggard dog
Harried the minutes in a desperate flock;
Dully the bell in the cathedral tower,
Mouthing the death of the expiring hour,
Bayed the white moon down to its lair of fog.

Portraits of Three Ladies

I.

He passed her only once in a crowded street,
A tangent flaring by her petty arc.
She did not hear black spurs clank on his feet
Or under his coat the black emblazoned sark;
For she, of course, knew no mythology
And could not thrill, as others might have done,
To pale and lunar murmurs of the sea
Or gilded savage clarions of the sun.

But often that lean smile his lean lips wore
10 Brutally gashed the drab peace of her mind;
If once at night she stretched upon the floor
Watching the wet moon glisten on the roofs,
It was not to catch on that strange April wind
The scent of damp fern crushed by satyr hoofs.

II.

"Since I can neither move you nor the fate
That parts us here, without recrimination
I beg, my dear, a niche in recollection,
That of your lover unregenerate."
She smiled and left him there to contemplate
His graceful posturings of adoration;
To think; "At least in this one situation
My rhetoric was deft and adequate."

She smiled but found no sudden blade of tears
10 To cut the strictured cruelty of that smile;
With eyes that were a broken desolation
She faced a shattered night, and all the while
Up to the taciturn and cynic stars
There streamed an immemorial lamentation.

III.

Strangely her heart yet clutched a strange twilight,
One that had lured with dream down a cypressed way
To glens where hairy-haunched and savage lay
The night. Could ever she forget that night
And one black pool, her image in the water,
Or how fat lily stalks were stirred and shifted
By terrible things beneath, and how there drifted
Through slimy trunks and fern a goatish laughter.

*

Sometimes at dusk before her looking glass
10 She thought how in that pool her limbs gleamed whitely;
She heard her husband watering the grass
Or his neat voice inquiring,"Supper dear?"
Across the table then she faced him nightly
With harried eyes in which he read no fear.

Alf Burt, Tenant Farmer

Despite that it is summer and the sun
Comes up at four and corn is rank with weed
Old Burt is abed and won't see the plowing done
Nor find a harvest where he laid the seed.

A fatter harvest than he's ever known
He will reap perhaps in field where he is gone—
Harvest of farmlands fairer than our own.
There will the plowshare never bite the stone,

Never will blight fall on the yellow pear,
10 Nor flood and wind defy the weary hand.
Never will work the plague and weevil there,
Nor yet descend the locust on the land.

Nor pestilence. It is a country where
No frost can come for Old Man Burt to fear.
Perpetual seedtime meets with summer there,
Harvest and spring together in the year.

And if not that at least for him will be
The steadfast earth of a narrow grave and deep
Beneath the fennel and the lean thorntree,
20 Whose haggard roots will quickly give a sleep.

Heavy as in the midnights of December.
And in that sleep where all things are the same
No dream can fall to stir him to remember
Thistle and drouth and the crops that never came.

The Wrestling Match

"Here in this corner, ladies and gentlemen,
I now presents 'Mug' Hill, weight two-hundred-ten,
Who will wrestle here tonight the 'Battling Pole,'
Boruff—" who, as insistently the stale

Loud voice behind asserts, is good as hell.
"Is good as hell, I says," and then the bell
Stabs up to life two engines of flesh and bone,
Each like a great and bronze automaton

That by black magic moves stupendously,
10 Moving with a machine's intensity,
To some obscure and terrible conclusion
Involving us as in an absurd vision

The truculent dull spirit is involved
There to contend above, while is dissolved
In sleep the twisted body on the bed.
The barker said—or was it this he said:

"Ladies and gentlemen, I now present—"
The voice here sank in some obscene intent—
"That which is body so you all may see
20 The bone and blood and sweat and agony

And thews that through the tortured years have striven
To breach the flesh so sure to spill when broken
The only breath, a cry, and the dark blood
That forever we would keep if we but could."

from Thirty-Six Poems

The Return: An Elegy

The east wind finds the gap bringing rain:
Rain in the pine wind shaking the stiff pine.
Beneath the wind the hollow gorges whine.
The pines decline.
Slow film of rain creeps down the loam again
Where the blind and nameless bones recline.

      all are conceded to the earth's absolute chemistry
      they burn like faggots in—of damp and dark—the monstrous bulging
            flame.
      calcium phosphate lust speculation faith treachery
10   it walked upright with habitation and a name

        tell me its name

The pines, black, like combers plunge with spray
Lick the wind's unceasing keel.
It is not long till day
The boughs like hairy swine in slaughter squeal.
They lurch beneath the thunder's livid heel.
The pines, black, snore *what does the wind say?*

        tell me its name

I have a name: I am not blind.
20 Eyes, not blind, press to the Pullman pane
Survey the driving dark and silver taunt of rain.
What will I find
What will I find beyond the snoring pine?
O eyes locked blind in death's immaculate design
Shall fix their last distrust in mine.

      give me the nickels off your eyes
      from your hands the violets
      let me bless your obsequies
      if you possessed conveniently enough three eyes
30   then I could buy a pack of cigarettes

*

In gorges where the dead fox lies the fern
Will rankest loop the battened frond and fall
Above the bare tushed jaws that turn
Their insolence unto the gracious catafalque and pall.
It will be the season when milkweed blossoms burn.

    the old bitch is dead
    what have I said!
    I have only said what the wind said
    wind shakes a bell the hollow head

40 By dawn, the wind, the blown rain
Will cease their antique concitation.
It is the hour when old ladies cough and wake,
The chair, the table, take their form again
And earth begins the matinal exhalation.

    does my mother wake

Pines drip without motion.
The hairy boughs no longer shake.
Shaggy mist, crookbacked, ascends.
Round hairy boughs the mist with shaggy fingers bends.
50 No wind: no rain:
Why do the steady pines complain?
Complain

    the old fox is dead
    what have I said

Locked in the roaring cubicle
Over the mountains through darkness hurled
I race the daylight's westward cycle
Across the groaning rooftree of the world.
The mist is furled.

60   a hundred years they took this road
    the lank hunters then men hard-eyed with hope:
    ox breath whitened the chill air: the goad
    fell: here on the western slope
    the hungry people the lost ones took their abode
    here they took their stand:
    alders bloomed on the road to the new land
    here is the house the broken door the shed
    the old fox is dead

The wheels hum hum
70 The wheels: I come I come.
Whirl out of space through time O wheels
Pursue down backward time the ghostly parallels
Pursue past culvert cut embankment semaphore

Pursue down gleaming hours that are no more.
The pines, black, snore

    turn backward turn backward O time in your flight
    and make me a child again just for tonight
    good lord he's wet the bed come bring a light

What grief has the mind distilled?
80 The heart is unfulfilled
The hoarse pine stilled.
I cannot pluck
Out of this land of pine and rock
Of red bud their season not yet gone
If I could pluck
(In drouth the lizard will blink on the hot limestone)

    the old fox is dead
    what is said is said
    heaven rest the hoary head
90   what have I said!
    ... I have only said what the wind said
    honor thy father and mother in the days of thy youth
    for time uncoils like the cottonmouth

If I could pluck
Out of the dark that whirled
Over the hoarse pine over the rock
Out of the mist that furled
Could I stretch forth like God the hand and gather
For you my mother
100 If I could pluck
Against the dry essential of tomorrow
To lay upon the breast that gave me suck
Out of the dark the dark and swollen orchid of this sorrow.

Kentucky Mountain Farm

I. Rebuke of the Rocks

Now on you is the hungry equinox,
O little stubborn people of the hill,
The season of the obscene moon whose pull
Disturbs the sod, the rabbit, the lank fox,
Moving the waters, the boar's dull blood,
And the acrid sap of the ironwood.

*

But breed no tender thing among the rocks.
Rocks are too old under the mad moon,
Renouncing passion by the strength that locks
10   The eternal agony of fire in stone.

Then quit yourselves as stone and cease
To break the weary stubble-field for seed;
Let not the naked cattle bear increase,
Let barley wither and the bright milkweed.
Instruct the heart, lean men, of a rocky place
That even the little flesh and fevered bone
May keep the sweet sterility of stone.

II. At the Hour of the Breaking of the Rocks

Beyond the wrack and eucharist of snow
The tortured and reluctant rock again
Receives the sunlight and the tarnished rain.
Such is the hour of sundering we know,
Who on the hills have seen stand and pass
Stubbornly the taciturn
Lean men that of all things alone
Were, not as water or the febrile grass,
Figured in kinship to the savage stone.

10   The hills are weary, the lean men have passed;
The rocks are stricken, and the frost has torn
Away their ridged fundaments at last,
So that the fractured atoms now are borne
Down shifting waters to the tall, profound
Shadow of the absolute deeps,
Wherein the spirit moves and never sleeps
That held the foot among the rocks, that bound
The tired hand upon the stubborn plow,
Knotted the flesh unto the hungry bone,
20   The redbud to the charred and broken bough,
And strung the bitter tendons of the stone.

III. History Among the Rocks

There are many ways to die
Here among the rocks in any weather:
Wind, down the eastern gap, will lie
Level along the snow, beating the cedar,
And lull the drowsy head that it blows over
To startle a cold and crystalline dream forever.

*

The hound's black paw will print the grass in May,
And sycamores rise down a dark ravine,
Where a creek in flood, sucking the rock and clay,
10   Will tumble the laurel, the sycamore away.
Think how a body, naked and lean
And white as the splintered sycamore, would go
Tumbling and turning, hushed in the end,
With hair afloat in waters that gently bend
To ocean where the blind tides flow.

Under the shadow of ripe wheat,
By flat limestone, will coil the copperhead,
Fanged as the sunlight, hearing the reaper's feet.
But there are other ways, the lean men said:
20   In these autumn orchards once young men lay dead—
Gray coats, blue coats. Young men on the mountainside
Clambered, fought. Heels muddied the rocky spring.
Their reason is hard to guess, remembering
Blood on their black mustaches in moonlight.
Their reason is hard to guess and a long time past:
The apple falls, falling in the quiet night.

IV. Watershed

From this high place all things flow.
Land of divided streams, of water spilled
Eastward, westward, without memento. . .
Land where the morning mist is furled
Like smoke above the ridgepole of the world.

The sunset hawk now rides
The tall light up the climbing deep of air.
Beneath him swings the rooftree that divides
The east and west. His gold eyes scan
10   The crumpled shade on gorge and crest
And streams that creep and disappear, appear,
Past fingered ridges and their shrivelling span.
Under the broken eaves men take their rest.

Forever, should they stir, their thought would keep
This place. Not love, happiness past, constrains,
But certitude. Enough, and it remains,
Though they who thread the flood and neap
Of earth itself have felt the earth creep;
In pastures hung against the rustling gorge
20   Have felt the shuddering and sweat of stone,
Knowing thereby no constant moon
Sustains the hill's lost granite surge.

V. The Return

Burly and clean, with bark in umber scrolled
About the sunlit bole's own living white,
The sycamore stood, drenched in the autumn light.
The same old tree. Again the timeless gold
Broad leaf released the tendoned bough, and slow,
Uncertain as a casual memory,
Wavered aslant the ripe unmoving air.
Up from the whiter bough, the bluer sky,
That glimmered in the water's depth below,
10 A richer leaf rose to the other there.
They touched; with the gentle clarity of dream,
Bosom to bosom, burned, one on, one in, the quiet stream.

But, backward heart, you have no voice to call
Your image back, the vagrant image again.
The tree, the leaf falling, the stream, and all
Familiar faithless things would yet remain
Voiceless. And he, who had loved as well as most,
Might have foretold it thus, for well he knew
How, glimmering, a buried world is lost
20 In the water's riffle or the wind's flaw;
How his own image, perfect and deep
And small within loved eyes, had been forgot,
Her face being turned, or when those eyes were shut
Past light in that fond accident of sleep.

Pondy Woods

The buzzards over Pondy Woods
Achieve the blue tense altitudes,
Black figments that the woods release,
Obscenity in form and grace,
Drifting high through the pure sunshine
Till the sun in gold decline.

Big Jim Todd was a slick black buck
Laying low in the mud and muck
Of Pondy Woods when the sun went down
10 In gold, and the buzzards tilted down
A windless vortex to the black-gum trees
To sit along the quiet boughs,
Devout and swollen, at their ease.

By the buzzard roost Big Jim Todd
Listened for hoofs on the corduroy road
Or for the foul and sucking sound

A man's foot makes on the marshy ground.
Past midnight, when the moccasin
Slipped from the log and, trailing in
20 Its obscured waters, broke
The dark algae, one lean bird spoke.

"Nigger, you went this afternoon
For your Saturday spree at the Blue Goose saloon,
So you've got on your Sunday clothes,
On your big splay feet got patent-leather shoes.
But a buzzard can smell the thing you've done;
The posse will get you—run, nigger, run—
There's a fellow behind you with a big shot-gun.
Nigger, nigger, you'll sweat cold sweat
30 In your patent-leather shoes and Sunday clothes
When down your track the steeljacket goes
Mean and whimpering over the wheat.

"Nigger, your breed ain't metaphysical."
The buzzard coughed. His words fell
In the darkness, mystic and ambrosial.
"But we maintain our ancient rite,
Eat the gods by day and prophesy by night.
We swing against the sky and wait;
You seize the hour, more passionate
40 Than strong, and strive with time to die—
With Time, the beaked tribe's astute ally.

"The Jew-boy died. The Syrian vulture swung
Remotely above the cross whereon he hung
From dinner-time to supper-time, and all
The people gathered there watched him until
The lean brown chest no longer stirred,
Then idly watched the slow majestic bird
That in the last sun above the twilit hill
Gleamed for a moment at the height and slid
50 Down the hot wind and in the darkness hid.
Nigger, regard the circumstance of breath:
Non omnis moriar, the poet saith."

Pedantic, the bird clacked its gray beak,
With a Tennessee accent to the classic phrase;
Jim understood, and was about to speak,
But the buzzard drooped one wing and filmed the eyes.

At dawn unto the Sabbath wheat he came,
That gave to the dew its faithless yellow flame
From kindly loam in recollection of
60 The fires that in the brutal rock once strove.
To the ripe wheat fields he came at dawn.
Northward the printed smoke stood quiet above

The distant cabins of Squiggtown.
A train's far whistle blew and drifted away
Coldly; lucid and thin the morning lay
Along the farms, and here no sound
Touched the sweet earth miraculously stilled.
Then down the damp and sudden wood there belled
The musical white-throated hound.

70   In Pondy Woods in the summer's drouth
Lurk fever and the cottonmouth.
And buzzards over Pondy Woods
Achieve the blue tense altitudes,
Drifting high in the pure sunshine
Till the sun in gold decline;
Then golden and hieratic through
The night their eyes burn two by two.

Eidolon

All night, in May, dogs barked in the hollow woods;
Hoarse, from secret huddles of no light,
By moonlit bole, hoarse, the dogs gave tongue.
In May, by moon, no moon, thus: I remember
Of their far clamor the throaty, infatuate timbre.

The boy, all night, lay in the black room,
Tick-straw, all night, harsh to the bare side.
Staring, he heard; the clotted dark swam slow.
Far off, by wind, no wind, unappeasable riot
10   Provoked, resurgent, the bosom's nocturnal disquiet.

What hungers kept the house? under the rooftree
The boy; the man, clod-heavy, hard hand uncurled;
The old man, eyes wide, spittle on his beard.
In dark was crushed the may-apple: plunging, the rangers
Of dark remotelier belled their unhoused angers.

Dogs quartered the black woods: blood black on
May-apple at dawn, old beech-husk. And trails are lost
By rock, in ferns lost, by pools unlit.
I heard the hunt. Who saw, in darkness, how fled
20   The white eidolon from the fangèd commotion rude?

History

Past crag and scarp,
At length way won:
And done
The chert's sharp
Incision,
The track-flint's bite.
Now done, the belly's lack,
Belt tight
—The shrunk sack,
10 Corn spent, meats foul,
The dry gut-growl.

Now we have known the last,
And can appraise
Pain past.
We came bad ways,
The watercourses
Dry,
No herb for horses.
(We slew them shamefastly,
20 Dodging their gaze.)
Sleet came some days,
At night no fuel.

And so, thin-wrapt,
We slept:
Forgot the frosty nostril,
Joints rotten and the ulcered knee,
The cold-kibed heel,
The cracked lip.
It was bad country of no tree,
30 Of abrupt landslip,
The glacier's snore.
Much man can bear.

How blind the passes were!

And now
We see, below,
The delicate landscape unfurled,
A world
Of ripeness blent, and green,
The fruited earth,
40 Fire on the good hearth,
The fireside scene.
(Those people have no name,
Who shall know dearth
And flame.)

It is a land of corn and kine,
Of milk
And wine,
And beds that are as silk:
The gentle thigh,
50 The unlit night-lamp nigh.
This much was prophesied:
We shall possess,
And abide
—Nothing less.
We may not be denied.
The inhabitant shall flee as the fox.
His foot shall be among the rocks.

In the new land
Our seed shall prosper, and
60 In those unsifted times
Our sons shall cultivate
Peculiar crimes,
Having not love, nor hate,
Nor memory.
Though some,
Of all most weary,
Most defective of desire,
Shall grope toward time's cold womb;
In dim pools peer
70 To see, of some grandsire,
The long and toothèd jawbone greening there.
(O Time, for them the aimless bitch
—Purblind, field-worn,
Slack dugs by the dry thorn torn—
Forever quartering the ground in which
The blank and fanged
Rough certainty lies hid.)

Now at our back
The night wind lifts,
80 Rain in the wind.
Downward the darkness shifts.
It is the hour for attack.
Wind fondles, far below, the leaves of the land,
Freshening the arbor.
Recall our honor,
And descend.
We seek what end?
The slow dynastic ease,
Travail's cease?
90 Not pleasure, sure:
Alloy of fact?
The act

Alone is pure.
What appetency knows the flood,
What thirst, the sword?
What name
Sustains the core of flame?
We are the blade,
But not the hand
100 By which the blade is swayed.
Time falls, but has no end.
Descend!

The gentle path suggests our feet;
The bride's surrender will be sweet.
We shall essay
The rugged ritual, but not of anger.
Let us go down before
Our thews are latched in the myth's languor,
Our hearts with fable gray.

Letter from a Coward to a Hero

What did the day bring?
The sharp fragment,
The shard,
The promise half-meant,
The impaired thing,
At dusk the hard word,
Good action by good will marred—
All
In the trampled stall:

10   I think you deserved better;
        Therefore I am writing you this letter.

The scenes of childhood were splendid,
And the light that there attended,
But is rescinded:
The cedar,
The lichened rocks,
The thicket where I saw the fox,
And where I swam, the river.
These things are hard
20 To reconstruct:
The word
Is memory's gelded usufruct.
But piety is simple,
And should be ample.

*

Though late at night we have talked,
I cannot see what ways your feet in childhood walked.
In what purlieus was courage early caulked?

Guns blaze in autumn and
The quail falls and
30 Empires collide with a bang
That shakes the pictures where they hang,
And democracy shows signs of dry rot
And Dives has and Lazarus not
And the time is out of joint,
But a good pointer holds the point
And is not gun-shy.
But I
Am gun-shy.

Though young, I do not like loud noise:
40 The sudden backfire,
The catcall of boys,
Drums beating for
The big war,
Or clocks that tick at night, and will not stop.
If you should lose your compass and map
Or a mouse get in the wall,
For sleep try love or veronal,
Though some prefer, I know, philology.
Does the airman scream in the flaming trajectory?

50 You have been strong in love and hate.
Disaster owns less speed than you have got,
But he will cut across the back lot
To lurk and lie in wait.
Admired of children, gathered for their games,
Disaster, like the dandelion, blooms,
And the delicate film is fanned
To seed the shaven lawn.
Rarely, you've been unmanned;
I have not seen your courage put to pawn.

60 At the blind hour of unaimed grief,
Of addition and subtraction,
Of compromise,
Of the smoky lecher, the thief,
Of regretted action,
At the hour to close the eyes,
At the hour when lights go out in the houses—
Then wind rouses
The kildees from their sodden ground.
Their commentary is part of the wind's sound.
70 What is that other sound,
Surf or distant cannonade?

*

You are what you are without our aid.
No doubt, when corridors are dumb
And the bed is made,
It is your custom to recline,
Clutching between the forefinger and thumb
Honor, for death shy valentine.

Late Subterfuge

The year dulls toward its eaves-dripping end.
We have kept honor yet, or lost a friend;
Observed at length the inherited defect;
Known error's pang—but then, what man is perfect?
The grackles, yellow-beaked, beak-southward, fly
To the ruined ricelands south, leaving empty our sky.

This year was time for decision to be made.
No time to waste, we said, and so we said:
This year is time. Our grief can be endured,
10 For we, at least, are men, being inured
To wrath, to the unjust act, if need, to blood;
And we have faith that from evil may bloom good.

Our feet in the sopping woods will make no sound,
The winter's rot begun, the fox in ground,
The snake cold-coiled, secret in cane the weasel.
In pairs we walk, heads bowed to the long drizzle—
With women some, and take their rain-cold kiss;
We say to ourselves we learn some strength from this.

Ransom

Old houses, and new-fangled violence;
Old bottles but new wine, and newly spilled.
Doom has, we know, no shape but the shape of air.
That much for us the red-armed augurs spelled,
Or flights of fowl lost early in the long air.

The mentioned act: barbarous, bloody, extreme,
And fraught with bane. The actors: nameless and
With faces turned (I cannot make them out).
Christ bled, indeed, but after fasting and
10 Bad diet of the poor; wherefore thin blood came out.

*

What wars and lecheries! and the old zeal
Yet unfulfilled, unrarefied, unlaced.
At night the old man coughs: thus history
Strikes sum, ere dawn in rosy buskins laced
Delivers cool with dew the recent news-story.

Defeat is possible, and the stars rise.
Our courage needs, perhaps, new definition.
By night, my love, and noon, infirm of will
And young, we may endeavor definition;
20   Though frail as the claspèd dream beneath the blanket's wool.

To a Friend Parting

Endure friend-parting yet, old soldier,
Scarred the heart, and wry: the wild plum,
Rock-rent axe-bit, has known with the year bloom,
And tides, the neap and spring, bear faithfully.
Much you have done in honor, though wrathfully.
That, we supposed, was your doom.

O you who by the grove and shore walked
With us, your heart unbraced yet unbetrayed,
Recall: the said, the unsaid, though chaff the said
10   And backward blown. We saw above the lake
The hawk tower, his wings the light take.
What can be foresaid?

Follow the defiles down. Forget not,
When journey-bated the nag, rusty the steel,
The horny clasp of hands your hands now seal;
And prayers of friends, ere this, kept powder dry.
Rough country of no birds, the tracks sly:
Thus faith has lived, we feel.

So Frost Astounds

I have thought: it will be so
Nothing less

You sat by the window in a dull blue dress;
it was the season when blackbirds go.

Shut to light—too much of light—the classic lids

*

You were sustained in the green translucence that resides
all afternoon under the maple trees.
I observed your hands which lay, on the lap, supine.

So frost astounds the summer calyxes

10 And so was locked their frail articulation
by will beneath the pensive skin:
as though composed by the will of an artist on dull blue cloth,
forever beyond the accident of flesh and bone,
or principle of thief and rat and moth,
or beyond the stately perturbation of the mind.

I have thought: this will I find.

Cold Colloquy

She loitered to heed his heart's pouring-out,
Her heart sick within her, she sickening with doubt
That again it might stir, as it once had stirred,
At another's pain snared in gesture or throaty word.
She hearkened, eyeless and sunk like the uncarved stone,
Till the light in his face, an empty candle, was blown:
She hearkened, and all was something once read about,
Or a tale worn glossless in time and bandied about.

She turned, a puzzlement on fair features wrought
10 That of words so freighted with woe so little she caught.
She turned; with fair face troubled thus would go,
In season of sun when all the green things grow
Or of dry aster and the prattling leaves,
To stand apart, pondering, as one who grieves
Or seeks a thing long lost among the fallen leaves.

The Garden

On prospect of a fine day in early autumn

How kind, how secret, now the sun
Will bless this garden frost has won,
And touch once more, as once it used,
The furled boughs by cold bemused.
Though summered brilliance had but room
In blossom, now the leaves will bloom
Their time, and take from milder sun
An unreviving benison.

*

      No marbles whitely gaze among
10 These paths where gilt the late pear hung:
    But branches interlace to frame
    The avenue of stately flame
    Where yonder, far more bold and pure
    Than marble, gleams the sycamore,
    Of argent torse and cunning shaft
    Propped nobler than the sculptor's craft.

      The hand that crooked upon the spade
    Here plucked the peach, and thirst allayed;
    Here lovers paused before the kiss,
20 Instructed of what ripeness is:
    Where all who came might stand to prove
    The grace of this imperial grove,
    Now jay and cardinal debate,
    Like twin usurpers, the ruined state.

      But he who sought, not love, but peace
    In such rank plot could take no ease:
    Now poised between the two alarms
    Of summer's lusts and winter's harms,
    Only for him these precincts wait
30 In sacrament that can translate
    All things that fed luxurious sense
    From appetite to innocence.

To a Face in a Crowd

Brother, my brother, whither do you pass?
Unto what hill at dawn, unto what glen,
Where among the rocks the faint lascivious grass
Fingers in lust the arrogant bones of men?

Beside what bitter waters will you go
Where the lean gulls of your heart along the shore
Rehearse to the cliffs the rhetoric of their woe?
In dream, perhaps, I have seen your face before.

A certain night has borne both you and me;
10 We are the children of an ancient band
Broken between the mountains and the sea.
A cromlech marks for you that utmost strand

And you must find the dolorous place they stood.
Of old I know that shore, that dim terrain,
And know how black and turbulent the blood
Will beat through iron chambers of the brain

*

When at your back the taciturn tall stone,
Which is your fathers' monument and mark,
Repeats the waves' implacable monotone,
20 Ascends the night and propagates the dark.

Men there have lived who wrestled with the ocean;
I was afraid—the polyp was their shroud.
I was afraid. That shore of your decision
Awaits beyond this street where in the crowd

Your face is blown, an apparition, past.
Renounce the night as I, and we must meet
As weary nomads in this desert at last,
Borne in the lost procession of these feet.

from Eleven Poems on the Same Theme

Bearded Oaks

The oaks, how subtle and marine,
Bearded, and all the layered light
Above them swims; and thus the scene,
Recessed, awaits the positive night.

So, waiting, we in the grass now lie
Beneath the languorous tread of light:
The grasses, kelp-like, satisfy
The nameless motions of the air.

Upon the floor of light, and time,
10 Unmurmuring, of polyp made,
We rest; we are, as light withdraws,
Twin atolls on a shelf of shade.

Ages to our construction went,
Dim architecture, hour by hour:
And violence, forgot now, lent
The present stillness all its power.

The storm of noon above us rolled,
Of light the fury, furious gold,
The long drag troubling us, the depth:
20 Dark is unrocking, unrippling, still.

Passion and slaughter, ruth, decay
Descend, minutely whispering down,
Silted down swaying streams, to lay
Foundation for our voicelessness.

All our debate is voiceless here,
As all our rage, the rage of stone;
If hope is hopeless, then fearless is fear,
And history is thus undone.

Our feet once wrought the hollow street
30 With echo when the lamps were dead
At windows, once our headlight glare
Disturbed the doe that, leaping, fled.

*

I do not love you less that now
The caged heart makes iron stroke,
Or less that all that light once gave
The graduate dark should now revoke.

We live in time so little time
And we learn all so painfully,
That we may spare this hour's term
40   To practice for eternity.

Picnic Remembered

That day, so innocent appeared
The leaf, the hill, the sky, to us,
Their structures so harmonious
And pure, that all we had endured
Seemed the quaint disaster of a child,
Now cupboarded, and all the wild
Grief canceled; so with what we feared.

We stood among the painted trees:
The amber light laved them, and us;
10   Or light then so untremulous,
So steady, that our substances,
Twin flies, were as in amber tamed
With our perfections stilled and framed
To mock Time's marveling after-spies.

Joy, strongest medium, then buoyed
Us when we moved, as swimmers, who,
Relaxed, resign them to the flow
And pause of their unstained flood.
Thus wrapped, sustained, we did not know
20   How darkness darker staired below;
Or knowing, but half understood.

The bright deception of that day!
When we so readily could gloze
All pages opened to expose
The trust we never would betray;
But darkness on the landscape grew
As in our bosoms darkness, too;
And that was what we took away.

And it abides, and may abide:
30   Though ebbed from the region happier mapped,
Our hearts, like hollow stones, have trapped
A corner of that brackish tide.

The jaguar breath, the secret wrong,
The curse that curls the sudden tongue,
We know; for fears have fructified.

Or are we dead, that we, unmanned,
Are vacant, and our clearest souls
Are sped where each with each patrols,
In still society, hand in hand,
40　That scene where we, too, wandered once
Who now inherit a new province:
Love's limbo, this lost under-land?

The *then*, the *now*: each cenotaph
Of the other, and proclaims it dead.
Or is the soul a hawk that, fled
On glimmering wings past vision's path,
Reflects the last gleam to us here
Though sun is sunk and darkness near
—Uncharted Truth's high heliograph?

Crime

Envy the mad killer who lies in the ditch and grieves,
Hearing the horns on the highway, and the tires scream;
He tries to remember, and tries, but he cannot seem
To remember what it was he buried under the leaves.

By the steamed lagoon, near the carnivorous orchid,
Pirates hide treasure and mark the place with a skull,
Then lose the map, and roar in pubs with a skinful,
In Devon or Barbados; but remember what they hid.

But what was the treasure he buried? He's too tired to ask it.
10　An old woman mumbling her gums like incertitude?
The proud stranger who asked the match by the park wood?
Or the child who crossed the park every day with the lunch-basket?

He cannot say, nor formulate the delicious
And smooth convolution of terror, like whipped cream,
Nor the mouth, rounded and white for the lyric scream
Which he never heard, though he still tries, nodding and serious.

His treasure: for years down streets of contempt and trouble,
Hugged under his coat, among sharp elbows and rows
Of eyes hieratic like foetuses in jars.
20　Or he nursed it unwitting, like a child asleep with a bauble.

*

Happiness: what the heart wants. That is its fond
Definition, and wants only the peace in God's eye.
Our flame bends in that draft, and that is why
He clutched at the object bright on the bottom of the murky pond.

All he asked was peace. Past despair and past the uncouth
Violation, he snatched at the fleeting hem, though in error;
Nor gestured before the mind's sycophant mirror,
Nor made the refusal and spat from the secret side of his mouth.

Though a tree for you is a tree, and in the long
30   Dark, no sibilant tumor inside your enormous
Head, though no walls confer in the silent house,
Nor the eyes of pictures protrude, like a snail's, each on its prong,

Yet envy him, for what he buried is buried
By the culvert there, till the boy with the air-gun
In spring, at the violet, comes; nor is ever known
To go on any vacations with him, lend money, break bread.

And envy him, for though the seasons stammer
Past pulse in the yellow throat of the field-lark,
Still memory drips, a pipe in the cellar-dark,
40   And in its hutch and hole, as when the earth gets warmer,

The cold heart heaves like a toad, and lifts its brow
With that bright jewel you have no use for now;
While puzzled yet, despised with the attic junk, the letter
Names over your name, and mourns under the dry rafter.

Original Sin: A Short Story

Nodding, its great head rattling like a gourd,
And locks like seaweed strung on the stinking stone,
The nightmare stumbles past, and you have heard
It fumble your door before it whimpers and is gone:
It acts like the old hound that used to snuffle your door and moan.

You thought you had lost it when you left Omaha,
For it seemed connected then with your grandpa, who
Had a wen on his forehead and sat on the veranda
To finger the precious protuberance, as was his habit to do,
10   Which glinted in sun like rough garnet or the rich old brain bulging through.

But you met it in Harvard Yard as the historic steeple
Was confirming the midnight with its hideous racket,
And you wondered how it had come, for it stood so imbecile,
With empty hands, humble, and surely nothing in pocket:
Riding the rods, perhaps—or Grandpa's will paid the ticket.

*

You were almost kindly then, in your first homesickness,
As it tortured its stiff face to speak, but scarcely mewed.
Since then you have outlived all your homesickness,
But have met it in many another distempered latitude:
20 Oh, nothing is lost, ever lost! at last you understood.

It never came in the quantum glare of sun
To shame you before your friends, and had nothing to do
With your public experience or private reformation:
But it thought no bed too narrow—it stood with lips askew
And shook its great head sadly like the abstract Jew.

Never met you in the lyric arsenical meadow
When children call and your heart goes stone in the bosom—
At the orchard anguish never, nor ovoid horror,
Which is furred like a peach or avid like the delicious plum.
30 It takes no part in your classic prudence or fondled axiom.

Not there when you exclaimed: "Hope is betrayed by
Disastrous glory of sea-capes, sun-torment of whitecaps
—There must be a new innocence for us to be stayed by."
But there it stood, after all the timetables, all the maps,
In the crepuscular clutter of *always, always,* or *perhaps.*

You have moved often and rarely left an address,
And hear of the deaths of friends with a sly pleasure,
A sense of cleansing and hope which blooms from distress;
But it has not died, it comes, its hand childish, unsure,
40 Clutching the bribe of chocolate or a toy you used to treasure.

It tries the lock. You hear, but simply drowse:
There is nothing remarkable in that sound at the door.
Later you may hear it wander the dark house
Like a mother who rises at night to seek a childhood picture;
Or it goes to the backyard and stands like an old horse cold in the pasture.

End of Season

Leave now the beach, and even that perfect friendship
—Hair frosting, careful teeth—that came, oh! late,
Late, late, almost too late: that thought like a landslip;
Or only the swimmer's shape for which you would wait,
Bemused and pure among the bright umbrellas, while
Blue mountains breathed and the dark boys cried their bird-throated syllable.

Leave beach, *spiagga, playa, plage,* or *spa,*
Where beginnings are always easy; or leave, even,
The Springs where your grandpa went in Arkansas
10 To purge the rheumatic guilt of beef and bourbon,
And slept like a child, nor called out with the accustomed nightmare,
But lolled his old hams, stained hands, in that Lethe, as others, others, before.

*

For waters wash our guilt and dance in the sun—
And the prophet, hairy and grim in the leonine landscape,
Came down to Jordan; toward moon-set de Leon
Woke while, squat, Time clucked like the darkling ape;
And Dante's *duca,* smiling in the blessèd clime,
With rushes, sea-wet, wiped from that sad brow the infernal grime.

You'll come, you'll come! and with the tongue gone wintry
20   You'll greet in town the essential face, which now wears
The mask of travel, smudge of history.
Then wordless, each one clasps, and stammering, stares:
You will have to learn a new language to say what is to say,
But it will never be useful in schoolroom, customs, or café.

For purity was wordless, and perfection
But the bridegroom's sleep or the athlete's marble dream,
And the annual sacrament of sea and sun,
Which browns the face and heals the heart, will seem
Silence, expectant to the answer, which is Time:
30   For all our conversation is index to our common crime.

On the last day swim far out, should the doctor permit
—Crawl, trudgeon, breast—or deep and wide-eyed, dive
Down the glaucous glimmer where no voice can visit.
But the mail lurks in the box at the house where you live:
Summer's wishes, winter's wisdom—you must think
On the true nature of Hope, whose eye is round and does not wink.

Revelation

Because he had spoken harshly to his mother,
The day became astonishingly bright,
The enormity of distance crept to him like a dog now,
And earth's own luminescence seemed to repel the night.

Rent was the roof like loud paper to admit
Sun-sulphurous splendor where had been before
But a submarine glimmer by kindly countenances lit,
As slow, phosphorescent dignities light the ocean floor.

By walls, by walks, chrysanthemum and aster,
10   All hairy, fat-petaled species, lean, confer,
And his ears, and heart, should burn at that insidious whisper
Which concerns him so, he knows; but he cannot make out the words.

The peacock screamed, and his feathered fury made
Legend shake, all day, while the sky ran pale as milk;
That night, all night, the buck rabbit stamped in the moonlit glade,
And the owl's brain glowed like a coal in the grove's combustible dark.

*

When Sulla smote and Rome was racked, Augustine
Recalled how Nature, shuddering, tore her gown,
And kind changed kind, and the blunt herbivorous tooth dripped blood;
20 At Inverness, at Duncan's death, chimneys blew down.

But, oh! his mother was kinder than ever Rome,
Dearer than Duncan—no wonder, then, Nature's frame
Thrilled in voluptuous hemispheres far off from his home;
But not in terror: only as the bride, as the bride.

In separateness only does love learn definition,
Though Brahma smiles beneath the dappled shade,
Though tears, that night, wet the pillow where the boy's head was laid,
Dreamless of splendid antipodal agitation;

And though across what tide and tooth Time is,
30 He was to lean back toward that irredeemable face,
He would think, than Sulla more fortunate, how once he had learned
Something important above love, and about love's grace.

Pursuit

The hunchback on the corner, with gum and shoelaces,
Has his own wisdom and pleasures, and may not be lured
To divulge them to you, for he has merely endured
Your appeal for his sympathy and your kind purchases;
And wears infirmity but as the general who turns
Apart, in his famous old greatcoat there on the hill
At dusk when the rapture and cannonade are still,
To muse withdrawn from the dead, from his gorgeous subalterns;
Or stares from the thicket of his familiar pain, like a fawn
10 That meets you a moment, wheels, in imperious innocence is gone.

Go to the clinic. Wait in the outer room
Where like an old possum the snag-nailed hand will hump
On its knee in murderous patience, and the pomp
Of pain swells like the Indies, or a plum.
And there you will stand, as on the Roman hill,
Stunned by each withdrawn gaze and severe shape,
The first barbarian victor stood to gape
At the sacrificial fathers, white-robed, still;
And even the feverish old Jew stares stern with authority
Till you feel like one who has come too late, or improperly clothed, to a
20   party.

The doctor will take you now. He is burly and clean;
Listening, like lover or worshiper, bends at your heart.
He cannot make out just what it tries to impart,

So smiles; says you simply need a change of scene.
Of scene, of solace: therefore Florida,
Where Ponce de Leon clanked among the lilies,
Where white sails skit on blue and cavort like fillies,
And the shoulder gleams white in the moonlit corridor.
A change of love: if love is a groping Godward, though blind,
30 No matter what crevice, cranny, chink, bright in dark, the pale tentacle find.

In Florida consider the flamingo,
Its color passion but its neck a question.
Consider even that girl the other guests shun
On beach, at bar, in bed, for she may know
The secret you are seeking, after all;
Or the child you humbly sit by, excited and curly,
That screams on the shore at the sea's sunlit hurlyburly,
Till the mother calls its name, toward nightfall.
Till you sit alone: in the dire meridians, off Ireland, in fury
Of spume-tooth and dawnless sea-heave, salt rimes the lookout's devout
40   eye.

Till you sit alone—which is the beginning of error—
Behind you the music and lights of the great hotel:
Solution, perhaps, is public, despair personal,
But history held to your breath clouds like a mirror.
There are many states, and towns in them, and faces,
But meanwhile, the little old lady in black, by the wall,
Admires all the dancers, and tells you how just last fall
Her husband died in Ohio, and damp mists her glasses;
She blinks and croaks, like a toad or a Norn, in the horrible light,
50 And rattles her crutch, which may put forth a small bloom, perhaps white.

Love's Parable

As kingdoms after civil broil,
Long faction-bit and sore unmanned,
Unlaced, unthewed by lawless toil,
Will welcome to the cheering strand
A prince whose tongue, not understood,
Yet frames a new felicity,
And alien, seals domestic good:
Once, each to each, such aliens, we.

That time, each was the other's sun,
10 Ecliptic's charter, system's core;
Locked in its span, the wandering one,
Though colder grown, might yet endure
Ages unnumbered, for it fed
On light and heat flung from the source
Of light that lit dark as it fled:
Wonder of dull astronomers.
*

No wonder then to us it was!
For miracle was daily food—
That darkness fled through darklessness
20 And endless light the dark pursued:
No wonder then, for we had found
Love's mystery, then still unspent,
That substance long in grossness bound
Might bud into love's accident.

Then miracle was corner-cheap;
And we, like ignorant quarriers,
Ransacked the careless earth to heap
For highways our most precious ores;
Or like the blockhead masons who
30 Burnt Rome's best grandeur for its lime,
And for their slattern hovels threw
Down monuments of nobler time.

We did not know what worth we owned,
Or know what ambient atmosphere
We breathed, who daily then postponed
A knowledge that, now bought too dear,
Is but ironic residue:
As gouty pang and tarnished vest
Remind the wastrel bankrupt who,
40 For gut and back, let substance waste.

That all the world proportionate
And joyful seemed, did but consent
That all unto our garden state
Of innocence was innocent;
And all on easy axle roved
That now, ungeared, perturbed turns,
For joy sought joy then when we loved,
As iron to the magnet yearns.

But we have seen the fungus eyes
50 Of misery spore in the night,
And marked, of friends, the malices
That stain, like smoke, the day's fond light,
And marked how ripe injustice flows,
How ulcerous, how acid, then
How proud flesh on the sounder grows
Till rot engross the estate of men;

And marked, within, the inward sore
Of self that cankers at the bone,
Contempt of the very love we bore
60 And hatred of the good once known
—So weakness has become our strength,
And strength, confused, can but reject

Its object, so that we at length,
Itching and slumwise, each other infect.

Are we but mirror to the world?
Or does the world our ruin reflect,
Or is our gazing beauty spoiled
But by the glass' flawed defect?
What fault? What cause? What matter for
70 The hurled leaf where the wind was brewed,
Or matter for the pest-bit whore
What coin her virtue first beshrewed?

O falling-off! O peace composed
Within my kingdom when your reign
Was fulgent-full! and nought opposed
Your power, that slack is, but again
May sway my sullen elements,
And bend ambition to his place.
That hope: for there are testaments
80 That men, by prayer, have mastered grace.

Terror

> "*I Volontari Americani Presso Eserciti Stranieri Non Perdono La Cittadinanza.*"
>
> Il Messaggero, *Roma, Sabato, 27 Gennaio, 1940.*

Not picnics or pageants or the improbable
Powers of air whose tongues exclaim dominion
And gull the great man to follow his terrible
Star, suffice; not the window-box, or the bird on
The ledge, which means so much to the invalid,
Nor the joy you leaned after, as by the tracks the grass
In the emptiness after the lighted Pullmans fled,
Suffices; nor faces, which, like distraction, pass
Under the street-lamps, teasing to faith or pleasure,
10 Suffice you, born to no adequate definition of terror.

For yours, like a puppy, is darling and inept,
Though his cold nose brush your hand while you laugh at his clowning;
Or the kitten you sleep with, though once or twice while you slept
It tried to suck your breath, and you dreamed of drowning,
Perjured like Clarence, sluiced from the perilous hatches;
But never of lunar wolf-waste or the arboreal
Malignancy, with the privy breath, which watches
And humps in the dark; but only a dream, after all.
At the worst, you think, with a little twinge of distress,
20 That contagion may nook in the comforting fur you love to caress.

*

Though some, unsatisfied and sick, have sought
That immitigable face whose smile is ice,
And fired their hearts like pitch-pine, for they thought
Better flame than the damp worm-tooth of compromise:
So Harry L., my friend, whose whores and gin
Would have dwindled to a slick smile in the drug store
But for the absurd contraption of the plane
Which flung on air the unformulable endeavor
While his heart bled speed to lave the applauded name.
30 The crash was in an old cornfield— not even flame.

So some, whose passionate emptiness and tidal
Lust swayed toward the debris of Madrid,
And left New York to loll in their fierce idyll
Among the olives, where the snipers hid.
And now the North— to seek that visioned face
And polarize their iron of despair,
Who praise no beauty like the boreal grace
Which greens the dead eye under the rocket's flare.
They fight old friends, for their obsession knows
40 Only the immaculate itch, not human friends or foes.

They sought a secret which fat Franco's Moor,
Hieratic, white-robed, pitiless, might teach,
Who duped and dying but for pride, therefore
Hugged truth which cause or conscience scarcely reach.
As Jacob all night with the angelic foe,
They wrestled him who did not speak, but died,
And wrestle now, by frozen fen and floe,
New Courier, in fury sanctified;
And seek that face which, greasy, frost-breathed, in furs,
50 Bends to the bomb-sight over bitter Helsingfors.

Blood splashed on the terrorless intellect creates
Corrosive fizzle like the spattered lime,
And its enseamed stew but satiates
Itself, in that lewd and faceless pantomime.
You know, by radio, how hotly the world repeats,
When the brute crowd roars or the blunt boot-heels resound
In the Piazza or the Wilhelmplatz,
The crime of Onan, spilled upon the ground;
You know, whose dear hope Alexis Carrel kept
60 Alive in a test tube, where it monstrously grew, and slept.

But it is dead, and you now, guiltless, sink
To rest in lobbies, or pace gardens where
The slow god crumbles and the fountains prink,
Nor heed the criminal king, who paints the air
With discoursed madness and protruding eye—
Nor give the alarm, nor ask tonight where sleeps
That head which hooped the jewel Fidelity,

But like an old melon now, in the dank ditch, seeps;
For you crack nuts, while the conscience-stricken stare
70 Kisses the terror; for you see an empty chair.

from Selected Poems 1923–1943

The Ballad of Billie Potts

*(When I was a child I heard this story from an old lady who was a relative
of mine. The scene, according to her version, was in the section of West-
ern Kentucky known as "Between the Rivers," the region between the
Cumberland and the Tennessee. The name of Bardstown in the present
account refers to Bardstown, Kentucky, where the first race track west of
the mountains was laid out late in the eighteenth century.)*

Big Billie Potts was big and stout
In the land between the rivers.
His shoulders were wide and his gut stuck out
Like a croker of nubbins and his holler and shout
Made the bob-cat shiver and the black-jack leaves shake
In the section between the rivers.
He would slap you on your back and laugh.

Big Billie had a wife, she was dark and little
In the land between the rivers,
10 And clever with her wheel and clever with her kettle,
But she never said a word and when she sat
By the fire her eyes worked slow and narrow like a cat.
Nobody knew what was in her head.

They had a big boy with fuzz on his chin
So tall he ducked the door when he came in,
A clabber-headed bastard with snot in his nose
And big red wrists hanging out of his clothes
And a whicker when he laughed where his father had a bellow
In the section between the rivers.
20 They called him Little Billie.
He was their darling.

(It is not hard to see the land, what it was.
Low hills and oak. The fetid bottoms where
The slough uncoils, and in the tangled cane,
Where no sun comes, the muskrat's astute face
Is lifted to the yammering jay; then dropped.
A cabin where the shagbark stood and the
Magnificent tulip-tree; both now are gone.

But the land is there, and as you top a rise,
30 Beyond you all the landscape steams and simmers
—The hills, now gutted, red, cane-brake and black-jack yet.
The oak leaf steams under the powerful sun.
"Mister, is this the right road to Paducah?"
The red face, seamed and gutted like the hill,
Slow under time, and with the innocent savagery
Of Time, the bleared eyes rolling, answers from
Your dream: "They names hit so, but I ain't bin.")

Big Billie was the kind who laughed but could spy
The place for a ferry where folks would come by.
40 He built an inn and folks bound West
Hitched their horses there to take their rest
And grease the gall and grease the belly
And jaw and spit under the trees
In the section between the rivers.
Big Billie said: "Git down, friend, and take yore ease!"
He would slap you on your back and set you at his table.

(Leaning and slow, you see them move
In massive passion colder than any love:
Their lips move but you do not hear the words,
50 Nor trodden twig nor fluted irony of birds,
Nor hear the rustle of the heart
That, heave and settle, gasp and start,
Heaves like a fish in the ribs' dark basket borne
West from the great water's depth whence it was torn.

Their names are like the leaves, but are forgot
—The slush and swill of the world's great pot
That foamed at the Appalachian lip, and spilled
Like quicksilver across green baize, the unfulfilled
Disparate glitter, gleam, wild symptom, seed
60 Flung in the long wind: silent, they proceed
Past meadow, salt-lick, and the lyric swale;
Enter the arbor, shadow of trees, fade, fail.)

Big Billie was sharp at swap and trade
And could smell the nest where the egg was laid.
He could read and cipher and they called him squire,
And he added up his money while he sat by the fire,
And sat in the shade while folks sweated and strove,
For he was the one who fatted and throve
In the section between the rivers.
70 "Thank you kindly, sir," Big Billie would say
When the man in the black coat paid him at streak of day
And swung to the saddle, was ready to go,
And rode away and didn't know
That he was already as good as dead,

For at midnight the message had been sent ahead:
"Man in black coat, riding bay mare with star."

(There was a beginning but you cannot see it.
There will be an end but you cannot see it.
They will not turn their faces to you though you call,
80 Who pace a logic merciless as light,
Whose law is their long shadow on the grass,
Sun at the back; who pace, pass,
And passing nod in that glacial delirium
While the tight sky shudders like a drum
And speculation rasps its idiot nails
Across the dry slate where you did the sum.

The answer is in the back of the book but the page is gone.
And Grandma told you to tell the truth but she is dead.
And heedless, their hairy faces fixed
90 Beyond your call or question now, they move
Under the infatuate weight of their wisdom,
Precious but for the preciousness of their burden,
Sainted and sad and sage as the hairy ass, these who bear
History like bound faggots, with stiff knees;
And breathe the immaculate climate where
The lucent leaf is lifted, lank beard fingered, by no breeze,
Rapt in the fabulous complacency of fresco, vase, or frieze:

And the testicles of the fathers hang down like old lace.)

Little Billie was full of vinegar
100 And full of sap as a maple tree
And full of tricks as a lop-eared pup,
So one night when the runner didn't show up,
Big Billie called Little and said, "Saddle up,"
And nodded toward the man who was taking his sup
With his belt unlatched and his feet to the fire.
Big Billie said, "Give Amos a try,
Fer this feller takes the South Fork and Amos'll be nigher
Than Baldy or Buster, and Amos is sly
And slick as a varmint, and I don't deny
110 I lak business with Amos fer he's one you kin trust
In the section between the rivers,
And it looks lak they's mighty few.
Amos will split up fair and square."

Little Billie had something in his clabber-head
By way of brains, and he reckoned he knew
How to skin a cat or add two and two.
So long before the sky got red
Over the land between the rivers,
He hobbled his horse back in the swamp

120 And squatted on his hams in the morning dew and damp
     And scratched his stomach and grinned to think
     How Pap would be proud and Mammy glad
     To know what a thriving boy they had.
     He always was a good boy to his darling Mammy.

     (Think of yourself riding away from the dawn,
     Think of yourself and the unnamed ones who had gone
     Before, riding, who rode away from *goodbye, goodbye,*
     And toward *hello,* toward Time's unwinking eye;
     And like the cicada had left, at cross-roads or square,
130 The old shell of self, thin, ghostly, translucent, light as air;
     At dawn riding into the curtain of unwhispering green,
     Away from the vigils and voices into the green
     World, land of the innocent bough, land of the leaf.
     Think of your own face green in the submarine light of the leaf.

     Or think of yourself crouched at the swamp-edge:
     Dawn-silence past last owl-hoot and not yet at day-verge
     First bird-stir, titmouse or drowsy warbler not yet.
     You touch the grass in the dark and your hand is wet.
     Then light: and you wait for the stranger's hoofs on the soft trace,
140 And under the green leaf's translucence the light bathes your face.

     Think of yourself at dawn: Which one are you? What?)

     Little Billie heard hoofs on the soft grass,
     But squatted and let the rider pass,
     For he wouldn't waste good lead and powder
     Just to make the slough-fish and swamp-buzzards prouder
     In the land between the rivers.
     But he saw the feller's face and thanked his luck
     It's the one Pap said was fit to pluck.
     So he got on his horse and cantered up the trace.
150 Called, "Hi thar!" and the stranger watched him coming,
     And sat his mare with a smile on his face,
     Just watching Little Billie and smiling and humming.
     Little Billie rode up and the stranger said,
     "Why, bless my heart, if it ain't Little Billie!"

     "Good mornen," said Billie, and said, "My Pap
     Found somethen you left and knowed you'd be missen,
     And Pap don't want nuthen not proper his'n."
     But the stranger didn't do a thing but smile and listen
     Polite as could be to what Billie said.
160 But he must have had eyes in the side of his head
     As they rode along beside the slough
     In the land between the rivers,
     Or guessed what Billie was out to do,
     For when Billie said, "Mister, I've brung it to you,"

And reached his hand for it down in his britches,
The stranger just reached his own hand, too.

"Boom!" Billie's gun said, and the derringer, "Bang!"
"Oh, I'm shot!" Billie howled and grabbed his shoulder.
"Not bad," said the stranger, "for you're born to hang,
170   But I'll save some rope 'fore you're a minute older
If you don't high-tail to your honest Pap
In the section between the rivers."
Oh, Billie didn't tarry and Billie didn't linger,
For Billie didn't trust the stranger's finger
And didn't admire the stranger's face
And didn't like the climate of the place,
So he turned and high-tailed up the trace,
With blood on his shirt and snot in his nose
And pee in his pants, for he'd wet his clothes,
180   And the stranger just sits and admires how he goes,
And says, "Why, that boy would do right well back on the Bardstown track!"

"You fool!" said his Pap, but his Mammy cried
To see the place where the gore-blood dried
Round the little hole in her darling's hide.
She wiped his nose and patted his head,
But Pappy barred the door and Pappy said,
"Two hundred in gold's in my money belt,
And take the roan and the brand-new saddle
And stop yore blubberen and skeedaddle,
190   And next time you try and pull a trick
Fer God's sake don't talk but do it quick."

So Little Billie took his leave
And left his Mammy there to grieve
And left his Pappy in Old Kaintuck
And headed West to try his luck,
For it was Roll, Missouri,
It was Roll, roll, Missouri.
And he was gone nigh ten long year
And never sent word to give his Pappy cheer
200   Nor wet pen in ink for his Mammy dear.
For Little Billie never was much of a hand with a pen-staff.

(There is always another country and always another place.
There is always another name and another face.
And the name and the face are you, and you
The name and the face, and the stream you gaze into
Will show the adoring face, show the lips that lift to you
As you lean with the implacable thirst of self,
As you lean to the image which is yourself,
To set lip to lip, fix eye on bulging eye,
210   To drink not of the stream but of your deep identity,
But water is water and it flows,

Under the image on the water the water coils and goes
And its own beginning and its end only the water knows.

There are many countries and the rivers in them
—Cumberland, Tennessee, Ohio, Colorado, Pecos, Little Big Horn,
And Roll, Missouri, roll.
But there is only water in them.

And in the new country and in the new place
The eyes of the new friend will reflect the new face
220   And his mouth will speak to frame
The syllables of the new name
And the name is you and is the agitation of the air
And is the wind and the wind runs and the wind is everywhere.

The name and the face are you.
The name and the face are always new,
And they are you.
And new.

For they have been dipped in the healing flood.
For they have been dipped in the redeeming blood.
230   For they have been dipped in Time.
For Time is always the new place,
And no-place.
For Time is always the new name and the new face,
And no-name and no-face.

For Time is motion
For Time is innocence
For Time is West.)

Oh, who is coming along the trace,
Whistling along in the late sunshine,
240   With a big black hat above his big red face
And a long black coat that swings so fine?
Oh, who is riding along the trace
Back to the land between the rivers,
With a big black beard growing down to his guts
And silver mountings on his pistol-butts
And a belt as broad as a saddle-girth
And a look in his eyes like he owned the earth?
And meets a man riding up the trace
And squints right sharp and scans his face
250   And says, "Durn if it ain't Joe Drew!"
"I reckin it's me," says Joe and gives a spit,
"But whupped if I figger how you knows it,
Fer if I'm Joe, then who air you?"
And the man with the black beard says: "Why, I'm Little Billie!"
And Joe Drew says: "Wal, I'll be whupped."

*

"Be whupped," Joe said, "and whar you goen?"
"Oh, just visiten back whar I done my growen
In the section between the rivers,
Fer I bin out West and taken my share
260 And I reckin my luck helt out fer fair,
So I done come home," Little Billie said,
"To see my folks if they ain't dead."
"Ain't dead," Joe answered, and shook his head,
"But that's the best a man kin say,
Fer it looked lak when you went away
You taken West yore Pappy's luck."
Little Billie jingled his pockets and said: "Ain't nuthen wrong with my luck."

And said: "Wal, I'll be gitten on home,
But after yore supper why don't you come
270 And we'll open a jug and you tell me the news
In the section between the rivers.
But not too early, fer it's my aim
To git me some fun 'fore they know my name,
And tease 'em and fun 'em, fer you never guessed
I was Little Billie what went out West."
And Joe Drew said: "Durn if you always wasn't a hand to git yore fun."

(Over the plain, over mountain and river, drawn,
Wanderer with slit-eyes adjusted to distance,
Drawn out of distance, drawn from the great plateau
280 Where the sky heeled in the unsagging wind and the cheek burned,
Who stood beneath the white peak that glimmered like a dream,
And spat, and it was morning and it was morning.
You lay among the wild plums and the kildees cried.
You lay in the thicket under the new leaves and the kildees cried,
For all your luck, for all the astuteness of your heart,
And would not stop and would not stop
And the clock ticked all night long in the furnished room
And would not stop
And the *El*-train passed on the quarters with a whish like a terrible broom
290 And would not stop
And there is always the sound of breathing in the next room
And it will not stop
And the waitress says, "Will that be all, sir, will that be all?"
And will not stop
For nothing is ever all and nothing is ever all,
For all your experience and your expertness of human vices and of valor
At the hour when the ways are darkened.

Though your luck held and the market was always satisfactory,
Though the letter always came and your lovers were always true,
300 Though you always received the respect due to your position,
Though your hand never failed of its cunning and your glands always
                    thoroughly knew their business,
Though your conscience was easy and you were assured of your innocence,

You became gradually aware that something was missing from the picture,
And upon closer inspection exclaimed: "Why, I'm not in it at all!"
Which was perfectly true.

Therefore you tried to remember when you had last had
Whatever it was you had lost,
And you decided to retrace your steps from that point,
But it was a long way back.
310   It was, nevertheless, absolutely essential to make the effort,
And since you had never been a man to be deterred by difficult circumstances,
You came back.
For there is no place like home.)

He joked them and teased them and he had his fun
And they never guessed that he was the one
Had been Mammy's darling and Pappy's joy
When he was a great big whickering boy
In the land between the rivers.
He jingled his pockets and took his sop
320   And patted his belly which was full nigh to pop
And wiped the buttermilk out of his beard
And took his belch and up and reared
Back from the table and cocked his chair
And said: "Old man, ain't you got any fresh drinken water, this here ain't
                    fresher'n a hoss puddle?"
And the old woman said: "Pappy, take the young gentleman down to the spring
                    so he kin git it good and fresh?"
The old woman gave the old man a straight look.
She gave him the bucket but it was not empty but it was not water.

The stars are shining and the meadow is bright
But under the trees is dark and night
330   In the land between the rivers.
The leaves hang down in the dark of the trees,
And there is the spring in the dark of the trees,
And there is the spring as black as ink,
And one star in it caught through a chink
Of the leaves that hang down in the dark of the trees.
The star is there but it does not wink.
Little Billie gets down on his knees
And props his hands in the same old place
To sup the water at his ease;
340   And the star is gone but there is his face.
"Just help yoreself," Big Billie said;
Then set the hatchet in his head.

They went through his pockets and they buried him in the dark of the trees.
"I figgered he was a ripe 'un," the old man said.
"Yeah, but you wouldn't done nuthen hadn't bin fer me," the old woman said.

*

(The reflection is shadowy and the form not clear,
For the hour is late, and scarcely a glimmer comes here
Under the leaf, the bough, in innocence dark;
And under your straining face you can scarcely mark
350 The darkling gleam of your face little less than the water dark.

But perhaps what you lost was lost in the pool long ago
When childlike you lost it and then in your innocence rose to go
After kneeling, as now, with your thirst beneath the leaves:
And years it lies here and dreams in the depth and grieves,
More faithful than mother or father in the light or dark of the leaves.

So, weary of greetings now and the new friend's smile,
Weary in art of the stranger, worn with your wanderer's wile,
Weary of innocence and the husks of Time,
You come, back to the homeland of no-Time,
360 To ask forgiveness and the patrimony of your crime;

And kneel in the untutored night as to demand
What gift—oh, father, father—from that dissevering hand?)

"And whar's Little Billie?" Joe Drew said.
"Air you crazy," said Big, "and plum outa yore head,
Fer you knows he went West nigh ten long year?"
"Went West," Joe said, "but I seen him here
In the section between the rivers,
Riden up the trace as big as you please
With a long black coat comen down to his knees
370 And a big black beard comen down to his guts
And silver mountens on his pistol-butts,
And he said out West how he done struck
It rich and wuz bringen you back your luck."
"I shore-God could use some luck," Big Billie said,
But his woman wet her lips and craned her head,
And said: "Come riden with a big black beard, you say?"
And Joe: "Oh, hit wuz Billie as big as day."
And the old man's eyes bugged out of a sudden and he croaked like a sick
                    bull-frog and said: "Come riden with a long black coat?"

The night is still and the grease-lamp low
380 And the old man's breath comes wheeze and slow.
Oh, the blue flame sucks on the old rag wick
And the old woman's breath comes sharp and quick,
And there isn't a sound under the roof
But her breath's hiss and his breath's puff,
And there isn't a sound outside the door
As they hearken but cannot hear any more
The creak of saddle or the plop of hoof,
For a long time now Joe Drew's been gone
And left them sitting there alone

390 In the land between the rivers.
And so they sit and breathe and wait
And breathe while the night gets big and late,
And neither of them gives move or stir.
She won't look at him and he won't look at her.
He doesn't look at her but he says: "Git me the spade."

She grabbled with her hands and he dug with the spade
Where leaves let down the dark and shade
In the land between the rivers.
She grabbled like a dog in the hole they made,
400 But stopped of a sudden and then she said,
"My hand's on his face."
They light up a pine-knot and lean at the place
Where the man in the black coat slumbers and lies
With trash in his beard and dirt on his face;
And the torch-flame shines in his wide-open eyes.
Down the old man leans with the flickering flame
And moves his lips, says: "Tell me his name."

"Ain't Billie, ain't Billie," the old woman cries,
"Oh, it ain't my Billie, fer he wuz little
410 And helt to my skirt while I stirred the kittle
And called me Mammy and hugged me tight
And come in the house when it fell night."
But the old man leans down with the flickering flame
And croaks: "But tell me his name."

"Oh, he ain't got none, he jist come riden
From some fer place whar he'd bin biden.
Ain't got a name and never had none—
But Billie, my Billie, he had one,
And hit was Billie, it was his name."
420 But the old man croaked: "Tell me his name."
"Oh, he ain't got none and it's all the same,
But Billie had one, and he was little
And offen his chin I would wipe the spittle
And wiped the drool and kissed him thar
And counted his toes and kissed him whar
The little black mark was under his tit,
Shaped lak a clover under his left tit,
With a shape fer luck, and I'd kiss hit—"

The old man blinks in the pine-knot flare
430 And his mouth comes open like a fish for air,
Then he says right low, "I had nigh fergot."
"Oh, I kissed him on his little luck-spot
And I kissed and he'd laugh as lak as not—"
The old man said: "Git his shirt open."
The old woman opened the shirt and there was the birthmark under the left tit.
It was shaped for luck.

    *

(The bee knows, and the eel's cold ganglia burn,
And the sad head lifting to the long return,
Through brumal deeps, in the great unsolsticed coil,
440 Carries its knowledge, navigator without star,
And under the stars, pure in its clamorous toil,
The goose hoots north where the starlit marshes are.
The salmon heaves at the fall, and, wanderer, you
Heave at the great fall of Time, and gorgeous, gleam
In the powerful arc, and anger and outrage like dew,
In your plunge, fling, and plunge to the thunderous stream:
Back to the silence, back to the pool, back
To the high pool, motionless, and the unmurmuring dream.
And you, wanderer, back,
450 Brother to pinion and the pious fin that cleave
The innocence of air and the disinfectant flood
And wing and welter and weave
The long compulsion and the circuit hope
Back,
And bear through that limitless and devouring fluidity
The itch and humble promise which is home.

And the father waits for the son.

The hour is late,
The scene familiar even in shadow,
460 The transaction brief,
And you, wanderer, back,
After the striving and the wind's word,
To kneel
Here in the evening empty of wind or bird,
To kneel in the sacramental silence of evening
At the feet of the old man
Who is evil and ignorant and old,
To kneel
With the little black mark under your heart,
470 Which is your name,
Which is shaped for luck,

Which is your luck.)

Mexico is a Foreign Country:
Four Studies in Naturalism

I. Butterflies Over the Map

Butterflies, over the map of Mexico,
Over jungle and somnolent, sonorous mountains, flitter,
Over the death-gaudy dog whose spangles the sun makes glitter,
And over the red lines which are the highways where you will go.

The highways are scenic, like destiny marked in red,
And the faithful heart inside you purrs like a cat;
While distance drowses and blinks and broods its enormous fiat,
Butterflies dream gyres round the precious flower which is your head.

Their colors are astonishing, and so
10 Like Brutus, you wrathless rose and, robed in the pure
Idea, smote and fled, while benches burned, the clamor:
The black limousine was not detected at Laredo.

Tragedy is a dance, as Brutus knew;
But when a little child dies in Jalisco,
They lay the corpse, pink cloth on its face, in the patio,
And bank it with blossoms, yellow, red, and the Virgin's blue.

The pink cloth is useful to foil the flies, which are not few.

II. The World Comes Galloping: A True Story

By the ruined arch, where the bougainvillea bled,
And pigeons simmered and shat in the barbaric vine
And made a noise like Plato in the barbaric vine,
He stood: old.
Old, bare feet on stone, and the serape's rose
Unfolded in the garden of his rags;
Old, and all his history hung from his severe face
As from his frame the dignity of rags.

We could not see his history, we saw
10 Him.
And he saw us, but could not see we stood
Huddled in our history and stuck out hand for alms.

But he could give us nothing, and asked for nothing,
Whose figure, sharp against the blue lake and violet mountains,
Was under the arch, the vine, the violent blue vulgarity of sky.
He ate a peach and wiped the pulp across his gums;
His mouth was no less ruinous than the arch.

*

Then at the foot of that long street,
Between the pastel stucco and the feathery pepper trees,
20 Horse and horseman, sudden as light, and loud,
Appeared,
And up the rise, banging the cobbles like castanets,
Lashed in their fury and fever,
Plunged:
Wall-eyed and wheezing, the lurching hammer-head,
The swaying youth, and flapping from bare heels,
The great wheel-spurs of the Conquistador.
Plunged past us, and were gone:
The crow-bait mount, the fly-bit man.

30 So the old one, dropping his peach-pit, spat;
Regarding the street's astonishing vacancy, said:
"Viene galopando"—and spat again—"el mundo."

III. Small Soldiers with Drum in Large Landscape

The little soldiers thread the hills.
Remote, the white Sierra nods
Like somnolent ice cream piled up
To tempt a tourist's taste, or God's.

I saw them in the Plaza when
They huddled there like hens, at dawn,
And forming ranks, took time to gouge
Sleep from their eyes, and spit, and yawn.

Their bearing lacked ferocity.
10 Their eyes were soft, their feet were splayed,
And dirt, no doubt, behind the ears
Did them no credit on parade.

They did not tell me why they march—
To give some cattle-thief a scare
Or make their captain happy or
Simply take the mountain air.

But now two hours off, they move
Across the scene, and to the eye
Give interest, and focus for
20 The composition's majesty.

The little drum goes rum-tum-tum,
The little hearts go rat-tat-tat,
And I am I, and they are they,
And *this* is *this,* and *that* is *that,*

*

And the single pine is black upon
The crag; and the buzzard, absolute
In the sun's great gold eye, hangs;
And leaf is leaf, and root is root;

And the wind has neither home nor hope;
30 And cause is cause, effect, effect;
And all Nature's jocund atoms bounce
In tune to keep the world intact.

And shrouded in the coats and buttons,
The atoms bounce, and under the sky,
Under the mountain's gaze, maintain
The gallant little formulae

Which sweat and march, and marching, go
On errands which I have not guessed,
Though here I stand and watch them go
40 From dawn to dark, from East to West,

From *what* to *what,* from *if* to *when,*
From ridge to ridge, and cross the wide
Landscape of probability.
They cross the last ridge now, and hide

In valleys where the unprinted dust
Yearns for the foot it does not know;
They march under the same sun,
Appear once more, are gone, but go

Across the high waste of the mind,
50 Across the distance in the breast,
And climbing hazier heights, proceed
To a bivouac in a farther West.

IV. The Mango on the Mango Tree

The mango on the mango tree—
I look at it, it looks at me,
And thus we share our guilt in decent secrecy

(As once in the crowd I met a face
Whose lineaments were my disgrace
And whose own shame my forehead bore from place to place).

The mango is a great gold eye,
Like God's, set in the leafy sky
To harry heart, block blood, freeze feet, if I would fly.

*

10 For God has set it there to spy
And make report, and here am I,
A cosmic Hawkshaw to track down its villainy.

Gumshoe, *agent provocateur,*
Stool, informer, whisperer
—Each pours his tale into the Great Schismatic's ear.

For God well works the Roman plan,
Divide and rule, mango and man,
And on hate's axis the great globe grinds in its span.

I do not know the mango's crime
20 In its far place and different time,
Nor does it know mine committed in a frostier clime.

But what to God's were ours, who pay,
Drop by slow drop, day after day,
Until His monstrous, primal guilt be washed away,

Who till that time must thus atone
In pulp and pit, in flesh and bone,
By our vicarious sacrifice fault not our own?

For, ah, I do not know what word
The mango might hear, or if I've heard
30 A breath like *pardon, pardon,* when its stiff lips stirred.

If there were a word that it could give,
Or if I could only say *forgive,*
Then we might lift the Babel curse by which we live,

And I could leap and laugh and sing
And it could leap, and everything
Take hands with us and pace the music in a ring,

And sway like the multitudinous wheat
In a blessedness so long forfeit—
Blest in that blasphemy of love we cannot now repeat.

from Brother to Dragons

[Jefferson's Opening Monologue]

My name is Jefferson. Thomas. I
Lived. Died. But
Dead, cannot lie down in the
Dark. Cannot, though dead, set
My mouth to the dark stream that I may unknow
All my knowing. Cannot, for if,
Kneeling in that final thirst, I thrust
Down my face, I see come glimmering upward,
White, white out of the absolute dark of depth,
10 My face. And it is only human.

Have you ever tried to kiss that face in the mirror?
Or—ha, ha—has it ever tried to kiss you? Well,
You are only human. Is that a boast?

R.P.W.: Well, I've read your boast
Cut in stone, on the mountain, off in Virginia.

JEFFERSON: What else had I in age to cling to,
Even in the face of knowledge?
I tried to bring myself to say:
Knowledge is only incidental, hope is all—
20 Hope, a dry acorn, but some green germ
May split it yet, then joy and the summer shade.
Even after age and the tangle of experience
I still might—
Oh, grandeur green and murmuring instancy of leaf,
Beneath that shade we'll shelter. So, in senility
And moments of indulgent fiction I might try
To defend my old definition of man.

In Philadelphia first it came, my heart
Shook, shamefast in glory, and I saw, I saw—
30 But I'll tell you quietly, in system, what I saw.
In Philadelphia—delegates by accident, in essence men,
Marmosets in mantles, beasts in boots, parrots in pantaloons,
That is to say, men. Only ourselves, in the end,

Offal of history, tangents of our father's pitiful lust
At midnight heat or dawn-bed ease of a Sunday.
Why should that fuddling glory,
The gasp and twitch of our begetting, seem
Pitiful? Is it not worthy of us?
Or we of it? Too much crowds in
40 To break the thread of discourse and make me forget
That irony is always, and only, a trick of light on the late landscape.

But what I had meant to say, we were only ourselves,
Packed with our personal lusts and languors, lost,
Every man-jack of us, in some blind alley, enclave,
Crank cul-de-sac, couloir, or corridor
Of Time. Or Self.
And in that dark, no thread,
Airy as breath by an Ariadne's fingers forged—
No thread, and beyond some groped-at corner, hulked
50 In the dark, hock-deep in ordure, its beard
And shag foul-scabbed, and when the hoof heaves—
Listen!—the foulness sucks like mire.

He waits. He is the infamy of Crete.
He is the midnight's enormity. And is
Our brother, our darling brother. And Pasiphaë!
Dear mother, mother of all, poor Pasiphaë—
Huddled and hutched in the cow's hide,
Laced, latched, thonged up, and breathlessly ass-humped
For the ecstatic stroke.

60 What was your silence then?

Before the scream?

And through the pain, like a curtain split,
In your mind did you see some meadow green,
Some childhood haven, water and birdsong, and you a child?

The bull plunged. You screamed like a girl, and strove.
But the infatuate machine of your invention held.
Later they lifted you out and wiped
Foam from your lips in the dark palace.

We have not loved you less, poor Pasiphaë.

70 Even if, after all, it was your own invention.

But no, God no!—I tell you my mother's name was Jane.
She was Jane Randolph, born in England,
Baptized in the Parish of Shadwell, London.

*

Yes, what was I saying? Language betrays.
There are no words to tell Truth.

To begin again. When I to Philadelphia came
I knew what the world was. Oh, I wasn't
That ilk of a fool! Then when I saw individual evil,
I rationally said, it is only provisional paradox
80 To resolve itself in Time. Oh, easy,
Plump-bellied comfort!

Philadelphia, yes. I knew we were only men,
Defined in our errors and interests. But I, a man too—
Yes, laugh if you will—stumbled into
The breathless awe of vision, saw sudden
On every face, face after face,
Bleared, puffed, lank, lean red-fleshed or sallow, all—
On all saw the brightness blaze,
And knew my own days,
90 Times, hopes, horsemanship, respect of peers,
Delight, desire, and even my love, but straw
Fit for the flame, and in that fierce combustion, I—
Why, I was nothing, nothing but joy,
And my heart cried out:
"Oh, this is Man!"

And thus my minotaur. There at the blind
Labyrinthine turn of my personal time—
What do they call it? Yes,
Nel mezzo del cammin—yes, then met
100 The beast, in beauty masked. And the time
I met it was—at least, it seems so now—
That moment when the first alacrity
Of blood stumbles, and all natural joy
Sees Nature but as a mirror for its natural doom.
And so to hold joy you must deny mere Nature, and leap
Beyond man's natural bourne and constriction
To find justification in a goal
Hypothesized in Nature.

Well, thus the infatuate encounter. But
110 No beast then, the towering
Definition, angelic, arrogant, abstract,
Greaved in glory, thewed with light, the bright
Brow tall as dawn.

I could not see the eyes.

So seized the pen, and in the upper room,
With the excited consciousness that I was somehow
Rectified, annealed, my past annulled

And fate confirmed, wrote. And far off,
In darkness, the watch called out.

120 Time came, we signed the document, went home.
I had not seen the eyes of that bright apparition.
I had been blind with light.

I did not know its eyes were blind.

[The *annus mirabilis*]

R.P.W.: And the year drives on.
Now is the hour of iron: accept the obligation,
And the sap of compassion withdraws uttermost inward
To sleep in the secret chamber of Being.
Where is that chamber? And the year drives on.

And now is a new year: 1811.
This is the *annus mirabilis*. Signs will be seen.
The gates of the earth shall shake, the locked gate
Of the heart be struck in might by the spear-butt.
10 Men shall speak in sleep, and the darkling utterance
Shall wither the bride's love, and her passion become
But itch like a disease: scab of desire.
Hoarfrost lies thick in bright sun, past season,
And twitches like wolf fur.

The call of the owl discovers a new register.
When ice breaks, the rivers flood effortlessly,
And the dog-fox, stranded on the lost hillock,
Barks in hysteria among the hazel stems.
Then the bark assumes a metronomic precision.
20 The first water coldly fingers
The beast's belly. Then silence. He shudders, lets
The hind quarters droop beneath the icy encroachment.
But the head holds high. The rigid
Muzzle triangulates the imperial moon.
Until the spasm, the creature stares at the moon
With the aggrieved perplexity of a philosopher.

Sullen, the waters withdraw. Mud crusts the high
White boughs of the sycamore. Slime
Crusts the creek-flats.
30 It is green like velvet. Sickness begins in June.
Strong men die willingly.
Breath shakes the pole-shanty.
Dog-days, and stars fall, and prayers have ceased.
Men had come West in hope. This is the West.

*

Therefore, what more is there to hope for?

The arrogant comet shoulders the old constellations.
It comes too late, men now past fear or wonder:
From clearing or keelboat only a dull eye observes.
Night after night and it sheds a twilight of shuddering green
40 Over the immensity of forest. The beasts
Of the forest participate in the peculiar dislocation.
Habit and courage of kind change, and lust
Out of season, and lust for strange foods, as when
Rome shook with civil discord, and therefore beasts,
Augustine says, kept not their order, for the wild
Clang of that untunement echoed in all things.
Squirrels flee South, but cannot cross the Ohio.
They drown there, by thousands. Their bodies bloat on the sand bars.
The wild pigeon migrates early this year.
50 Their droppings have a strange odor, and men
With nausea reject this once-esteemed fowl.
The worst is to come yet, when the earth shall shake.

[The Murder of John]

ISHAM: I roused our people out, all but Aunt Cat,
She's up at the big house, case of Tishie calling.
They built the fire, and got the meat-house ready.

R.P.W.: Ready for what?

ISHAM: For what? — If I'd just known—
And that's so God-durn queer,
How knowing and not knowing are the same,
And if what's going to happen
Will happen anyway, then what's the use—
10 But if I'd known—

R.P.W.: Well, there you go again,
Back on the old track, the desperate circle:
"If I'd known"—and the great Machine of History
Will mesh its gears sweetly in that lubrication
Of human regret, and the irreversible
Dialectic will proceed. That is, unless—
"If I had known!"—that is, unless we get
Some new and better definition of *knowing*.

ISHAM: Well, knowing—hell, it's just to know a thing,
20 Like anything you know—

*

R.P.W.: No, knowing can be,
Maybe, a kind of being, and if you know,
Can really know, a thing in all its fullness,
Then you are different, and maybe everything
Is different, somehow, too.

Oh, well, this won't help now,
For fire cracked high and made the chimney hum,
And light and shadow danced and swung together,
And your hands are sweating on the pistol butts,
30 And the people scrouge and hunker by the wall,
And you feel your own mouth moving, but can't hear
The words. And then—the door—

ISHAM: 'Twas John fell in.
Fell on his knees and elbows, like you'd shoved him.
But nobody shoved him, him just falling in,
Like somebody running and barely makes it.
Or somebody swimming out too far,
And suck or chute nigh gets him, and the sky
Swings high and the sun looks black and eyeballs bulging,
40 But he makes it in. He falls down on the ground.
So that nigger just fell in.

The pitcher-handle, he held it in his hand.

But the pitcher was gone. The pitcher wasn't there.

R.P.W.: Did that surprise you?

ISHAM: No, 'twas natural-like, and no surprise,
Like happened long ago.

R.P.W.: And John himself, no doubt, felt it as some
Peculiar fulfillment he had long lived with.

ISHAM: And the voice came from the dark outside.
50 'Twas like a voice that came from dark and air,
But it was Lilburne's face. It said: "Get in!"

So John crawled in. Lil shut the door.
"Now tie him up." Yeah, that was Lil.
Nobody moved. Not me, and not a nigger.
Lil said: "I give you niggers exactly one minute
To get that bastard tied." Two came and tied him.
John squinched eyes tight, lay nigger-mum.

Lil stepped across him, like he wasn't there.
And there was the meat-block there,
60 Nice tulip-wood, come from a whopping tree,
A section cross, and smooth to lay your hand.

Lil slapped his hand down. "Lay the bastard here."
And that fool nigger, he curled up little
To lie on that tulip-wood, his eyes squinched shut.

I reckon that fool nigger sort of figured
That what you never saw just couldn't be real,
So squinched his eyes. And Lilburne saying:
"Hand me that meat-axe, Ishey."

And me, I did.

70 The people moaned and hunkered to the wall.
And maybe that fool nigger never heard
What Lil was saying about spoons and sheets,
Nor heard him say: "But now's the last
Black son-of-a-bitching hand that ever,
So help me God, will make my mother grieve!"

The axe came down, Lil flung the hands in the fire.

JEFFERSON: Enough! We know the rest.

ISHAM: And the axe
Came down, and whacked his feet that ran away.
80 Lil flung 'em into the fire,
And the axe—

R.P.W.: All right, we know the whole preposterous
Butchery. But one thing more:
Did John cry out at the last?

ISHAM: Yeah, that fool nigger spread his mouth to yell.
You got to yell if ever they start chopping.
But me, I ne'er heard—
Like all that nigger could yell was just a hunk
Of silence—you don't even hear it when the meat-axe
90 Gets in, gets through, goes *chunk*, chunks on the wood.
It's funny how that *chunk* just won't come clear.
Yeah, the axe comes down,
But not a sound, and that nigger spreads his mouth,
And I strain and strive
To hear—oh, Lord, if only—
Then maybe something gets finished.

Or maybe it's not real, since I can't hear—
But I know—

JEFFERSON: Oh, it is the only real thing.
100 We are born to joy that joy may become pain.
We are born to hope that hope may become pain.
We are born to love that love may become pain.
We are born to pain that from that inexhaustible superflux
We may give others pain—

*

MERIWETHER: Yes, we are born to—

ISHAM: And when that nigger spreads his mouth so wide—

JEFFERSON: Oh, what's one nigger more
In the economy of pain?
And Lilburne—what's one more
110 Bloody and sentimental maniac?
Or you, Isham, trapped and stupid—
What's one more corruptible simpleton?
Or those people hunched by the wall—
Oh, yes, they moaned, but don't forget they tied him.

I am talking about the texture in which
One episode of anguish evokes all anguish
And sets nerves screaming and white tendrils curl
In black peripheries beyond the last stars, and—

R.P.W.: If I am informed on the facts,
120 Though you could not, apparently, bring yourself to speak
Of the family scandal, you continued to declare,
In general terms of course, your old faith
In man and made the boast
Cut in the stone, on your mountain in Albemarle.

[Jefferson on the Aftermath]

JEFFERSON: But there were my sister's sons, the sister who
Had lived, somehow, all the years in my imagination—
Gentle by cradle and hearthside,
And I felt a pang of sweetness at what had been long denied me.
I controlled the pang. There was always contrivance
And the larger hope.
She left her sons, and I said that they, far away,
By swale or inimical forest,
Would fulfill her, and my heart.
10 You know the rest.

But I could not accept it. I tried
To buckle the heart past fondness or failure.
But the pain persisted, and the encroachment of horror.
I saw the smile of friendship as a grimace of calculation.
I saw the victuals on my plate in their undeclared context,
Mucous of oyster, beard of mussel, harslet of hog,
And even the choice viand as a shadow of ordure.
My eyes would wander from the instructive page,
And my heart crunched like a chick in the sow's jaw.

*

20 I said, I must cling more sternly to the rational hope.

Well, when in privacy of pain I died, I let
The old epitaph be put on stone. But only
Because I had no right to rob
Man of what hope he had. And what's
One more lie in the tissue of lies we live by?
But long since
The axe had been set at the root of hope,
And as history divulged itself,
I saw how the episode in the meat-house
30 Would bloom in Time, and bloom in the lash-bite
And the child's last cry, down in the quarters when
The mother's sold. And for another joke,
Ask the Christian Cherokee
How the heart bled westward on the Trail of Tears.

R.P.W..: Well, speaking of Indians, the Smithland courthouse
Has one nice record, how on Saturday night
In Eddyville, down in the tavern there,
Some heroes of our national destiny
Kicked an old Chickasaw to death, for sport.
40 And a slave—

JEFFERSON: And for another joke, I've seen
How vanity, greed, and blood-lust may obscenely
Twine in the excuse of moral ardor and crusade.
Yes, that's your funniest!
Oh, it's always the same,
And the dust drinks blood—
And Bloody Angle and the Bloody Pond—
Or listen, flames crackle through the Wilderness
And the green briar burning smells like myrrh, but that other
50 More pungent odor is not myrrh, the odor
That so reminds you of the odor in the meat-house.
The wounded scream. Then cease. The flame has found them.

Well, let them scream. All's one in the common collusion.

But a few more items from the ample documentation—
Pittsburgh and Pinkerton and the Polack bleeding
In some blind alley, while the snow falls slow,
And Haymarket, Detroit and Henry's goons—
Oh, that's enough—and how much since!
And Boston sleeps and Philadelphia, too,
60 And sleep is easy over the starlit continent I once loved,
For all is safe now, and the stars hold their
Accustomed formations. Take your screw. And sleep.
If you can sleep. If you
Can no longer hear the scream from the meat-house.

[John's Lament]

JOHN: I was lost in the world, and the trees were tall.
I was lost in the world and the dark swale heaved.
I was lost in my anguish and did not know the reason.

[The Recognition of Complicity]

(from the 1953 edition)

The recognition of complicity is the beginning of innocence.
The recognition of necessity is the beginning of freedom.
The recognition of the direction of fulfillment is the death of the self,
And the death of the self is the beginning of selfhood.
All else is surrogate of hope and destitution of spirit.

from Promises

To a Little Girl, One Year Old, in a Ruined Fortress

To Rosanna

I. Sirocco

To a place of ruined stone we brought you, and sea-reaches.
Rocca: fortress, hawk-heel, lion-paw, clamped on a hill.
A hill, no. On a sea cliff, and crag-cocked, the embrasures commanding the
        beaches,
Range easy, with most fastidious mathematic and skill.

Philipus me fecit: he of Spain, the black-browed, the anguished,
For whom nothing prospered, though he loved God.
His arms, a great scutcheon of stone, once over the drawbridge, have
        languished
Now long in the moat, under garbage; at moat-brink, rosemary with blue,
        thistle with gold bloom, nod.

Sun blaze and cloud tatter, now the sirocco, the dust swirl is swirled
Over the bay face, mounts air like gold gauze whirled; it traverses the
10   blaze-blue of water.
We have brought you where geometry of a military rigor survives its own
        ruined world,
And sun regilds your gilt hair, in the midst of your laughter.

Rosemary, thistle, clutch stone. Far hangs Giannutri in blue air. Far to that
        blueness the heart aches,
And on the exposed approaches the last gold of gorse bloom, in the sirocco,
        shakes.

II. Gull's Cry

White goose by palm tree, palm ragged, among stones the white oleander,
And the she-goat, brown, under pink oleanders, waits.
I do not think that anything in the world will move, not goat, not gander.
Goat droppings are fresh in the hot dust; not yet the beetle; the sun beats,

*

And under blue shade of the mountain, over blue-braiding sea-shadow,
The gull hangs white; whiter than white against the mountain-mass,
The gull extends motionless on a shelf of air, on the substance of shadow.
The gull, at an eye-blink, will, into the astonishing statement of sun, pass.

All night, next door, the defective child cried; now squats in the dust where the
        lizard goes.
10 The wife of the *gobbo* sits under vine leaves, she suffers, her eyes glare.
The engaged ones sit in the privacy of bemusement, heads bent: the classic
        pose.
Let the beetle work, the gull comment the irrelevant anguish of air,

But at your laughter let the molecular dance of the stone-dark glimmer like joy
        in the stone's dream,
And in that moment of possibility, let *gobbo, gobbo's* wife, and us, and all, take
        hands and sing: *redeem, redeem!*

III. The Child Next Door

The child next door is defective because the mother,
Seven brats already in that purlieu of dirt,
Took a pill, or did something to herself she thought would not hurt,
But it did, and no good, for there came this monstrous other.

The sister is twelve. Is beautiful like a saint.
Sits with the monster all day, with pure love, calm eyes.
Has taught it a trick, to make *ciao,* Italian-wise.
It crooks hand in that greeting. She smiles her smile without taint.

I come, and her triptych beauty and joy stir hate
10 —Is it hate?—in my heart. Fool, doesn't she know that the process
Is not that joyous or simple, to bless, or unbless,
The malfeasance of nature or the filth of fate?

Can it bind or loose, that beauty in that kind,
Beauty of benediction? We must trust our hope to prevail
That heart-joy in beauty be wisdom, before beauty fail
And be gathered like air in the ruck of the world's wind!

I think of your goldness, of joy, but how empires grind, stars are hurled.
I smile stiff, saying *ciao,* saying *ciao,* and think: *This is the world.*

IV. The Flower

Above the beach, the vineyard
Terrace breaks to the seaward
Drop, where the cliffs fail
To a clutter of manganese shale.
Some is purple, some powdery-pale.
But the black lava-chunks stand off
The sea's grind, or indolent chuff.
The lava will withstand
The sea's beat, or insinuant hand,
10 And protect our patch of sand.

It is late. The path from the beach
Crawls up. I take you. We reach
The vineyard, and at that path angle
The hedge obtrudes a tangle
Of leaf and green bulge and a wrangle
Bee-drowsy and blowsy with white bloom,
Scarcely giving the passer-by room.
We know that the blossomy mass
Will brush our heads as we pass,
20 And at knee there's gold gorse and blue clover,
And at ankle, blue *malva* all over—
Plus plants I don't recognize
With my non-botanical eyes.
We approach, but before we get there,
If no breeze stirs that green lair,
The scent and sun-honey of air
Is too sweet comfortably to bear.

I carry you up the hill.
In my arms you are still.
30 We approach your special place,
And I am watching your face
To see the sweet puzzlement grow,
And then recognition glow.
Recognition explodes in delight.
You leap like spray, or like light.
Despite my arm's tightness,
You leap in gold-glitter and brightness.
You leap like a fish-flash in bright air,
And reach out. Yes, I'm well aware
40 That this is the spot, and hour,
For you to demand your flower.

When first we came this way
Up from the beach, that day
That seems now so long ago,
We moved bemused and slow

In the season's pulse and flow.
Bemused with sea, and slow
With June heat and perfume,
We paused here, and plucked you a bloom.
50 So here you always demand
Your flower to hold in your hand,
And the flower must be white,
For you have your own ways to compel
Observance of this ritual.
You hold it and sing with delight.
And your mother, for our own delight,
Picks one of the blue flowers there,
To put in your yellow hair.
That done, we go on our way
60 Up the hill, toward the end of the day.

But the season has thinned out.
From the bay edge below, the shout
Of a late bather reaches our ear,
Coming to the vineyard here
By more than distance thinned.
The bay is in shadow, the wind
Nags the shore to white.
The mountain prepares the night.

By the vineyard we have found
70 No bloom worthily white,
And the few we have found
Not disintegrated to the ground
Are by season and sea-salt browned.
We give the best one to you.
It is ruined, but will have to do.
Somewhat better the blue blossoms fare.
So we find one for your hair,
And you sing as though human need
Were not for perfection. We proceed
80 Past floss-borne or sloughed-off seed,
Past curled leaf and dry pod,
And the blue blossom will nod
With your head's drowsy gold nod.

Let all seasons pace their power,
As this has paced to this hour.
Let season and season devise
Their possibilities.
Let the future reassess
All past joy, and past distress,
90 Till we know Time's deep intent,
And the last integument
Of the past shall be rent
To show how all things bent

Their energies to that hour
When you first demanded your flower.

Yes, in that image let
Both past and future forget,
In clasped communal ease,
Their brute identities.

100 The path lifts up ahead
To the *rocca,* supper, bed.
We move in the mountain's shade.
The mountain is at our back.
But ahead, climbs the coast-cliff track.
The valley between is dim.
Ahead, on the cliff rim,
The *rocca* clasps its height.
It accepts the incipient night.

Just once we look back.
110 On sunset, a white gull is black.
It hangs over the mountain crest.
It hangs on that saffron west.
It makes its outcry.
It slides down the sky.

East now, it catches the light.
Its black has gone again white,
And over the *rocca's* height
It gleams in the last light.

Now it sinks from our sight.
120 Beyond the cliff is night.

It sank on unruffled wing.
We hear the sea rustling.

V. Colder Fire

It rained toward day. The morning came sad and white
With silver of sea-sadness and defection of season.
Our joys and convictions are sure, but in that wan light
We moved—your mother and I—in muteness of spirit past logical reason.

Now sun, afternoon, and again summer-glitter on sea.
As you to a bright toy, the heart leaps. The heart unlocks
Joy, though we know, shamefaced, the heart's weather should not be
Merely a reflex to a solstice, or sport of some aggrieved equinox.

*

No, the heart should be steadfast: I know that.
10 And I sit in the late-sunny lee of the watch-house,
At the fortress point, you on my knee now, and the late
White butterflies over gold thistle conduct their ritual carouse.

In whisperless carnival, in vehemence of gossamer,
Pale ghosts of pale passions of air, the white wings weave.
In tingle and tangle of arabesque, they mount light, pair by pair,
As though that tall light were eternal indeed, not merely the summer's
                reprieve.

You leap on my knee, you exclaim at the sun-stung gyration.
And the upper air stirs, as though the vast stillness of sky
Had stirred in its sunlit sleep and made suspiration,
20 A luxurious languor of breath, as after love, there is a sigh.

But enough, for the highest sun-scintillant pair are gone
Seaward, past rampart and cliff borne, over blue sea-gleam.
Close to my chair, to a thistle, a butterfly sinks now, flight done.
By the gold bloom of thistle, white wings pulse under the sky's dream.

The sky's dream is enormous, I lift up my eyes.
In sunlight a tatter of mist clings high on the mountain-mass.
The mountain is under the sky, and there the gray scarps rise
Past paths where on their appointed occasions men climb, and pass.

Past grain-patch, last apron of vineyard, last terrace of olive,
30 Past chestnut, past cork grove, where the last carts can go,
Past camp of the charcoal maker, where coals glow in the black hive,
The scarps, gray, rise up. Above them is that place I know.

The pines are there, they are large, in a deep recess—
Shelf above scarp, enclave of rock, a glade
Benched and withdrawn in the mountain-mass, under the peak's duress.
We came there—your mother and I—and rested in that severe shade.

Pine-blackness mist-tangled, the peak black above: the glade gives
On the empty threshold of air, the hawk-hung delight
Of distance unspooled and bright space spilled—ah, the heart thrives!
40 We stood in that shade and saw sea and land lift in the far light.

Now the butterflies dance, time-tattered and disarrayed.
I watch them. I think how above that far scarp's sunlit wall
Mist threads in silence the darkness of boughs, and in that shade
Condensed moisture gathers at a needle-tip. It glitters, will fall.

I cannot interpret for you this collocation
Of memories. You will live your own life, and contrive
The language of your own heart, but let that conversation,
In the last analysis, be always of whatever truth you would live.

*

For fire flames but in the heart of a colder fire.
50 All voice is but echo caught from a soundless voice.
Height is not deprivation of valley, nor defect of desire,
But defines, for the fortunate, that joy in which all joys should rejoice.

Promises

To Gabriel

I. What Was the Promise That Smiled from the Maples at Evening?

What was the promise that smiled from the maples at evening?
Smiling dim from the shadow, recessed? What language of leaf-lip?
And the heels of the fathers click on the concrete, returning,
Each aware of his own unspecified burden, at sun-dip.
In first darkness hydrangeas float white in their spectral precinct.
Beneath pale hydrangeas the first firefly utters cold burning.
The sun is well down, the first star has now winked.

What was the promise when bullbats dizzied the sunset?
They skimmer and skitter in gold light at great height.
10 The guns of big boys on the common go *boom,* past regret.
Boys shout when the bullbat spins down in that gold light.
"Too little to shoot"—but next year you'll be a big boy.
So shout now and pick up the bird—why, that's blood, it is wet.
Its eyes are still open, your heart in the throat swells like joy.

What was the promise when, after the last light had died,
Children gravely, down walks, in spring dark, under maples, drew
Trains of shoe boxes, empty, with windows, with candles inside,
Going *chuck-chuck,* and blowing for crossings, lonely, *oo-oo?*
But on impulse you fled, and they called, called across the dark lawn,
20 Long calling your name, who now lay in the darkness to hide,
While the sad little trains glimmer on under maples, and on.

What was the promise when, after the dying was done,
All the long years before, like burnt paper, flared into black,
And the house shrunk to silence, the odor of flowers near gone?
Recollection of childhood was natural: cold gust at the back.
What door on the dark flings open, then suddenly bangs?
Yes, something was lost in between, but it's long, the way back.
You sleep, but in sleep hear a door that creaks where it hangs.

Long since, in a cold and coagulate evening, I've stood
30 Where they slept, the long dead, and the farms and far woods fled away,
And a gray light prevailed and both landscape and heart were subdued.
Then sudden, the ground at my feet was like glass, and I say

What I saw, saw deep down—with their fleshly habiliments rent,
But their bones in a phosphorus of glory agleam, there they lay,
Side by side, Ruth and Robert. But quickly that light was spent.

Earth was earth, and in earth-dark the glow died, therefore I lifted
My gaze to that world which had once been the heart's familiar,
Swell of woods and far field-sweep, in dusk by stream-gleams now wefted,
Railroad yonder and coal chute, town roofs far under the first star.
40 Then her voice, long forgotten, calm in silence, said: "Child."
And his, with the calm of a night field, or far star:
"We died only that every promise might be fulfilled."

II. Court-martial

Under the cedar tree,
He would sit, all summer, with me:
An old man and small grandson
Withdrawn from the heat of the sun.

Captain, cavalry, C.S.A.,
An old man, now shrunken, gray,
Pointed beard clipped the classic way,
Tendons long gone crank and wry,
And long shrunken the cavalryman's thigh
10 Under the pale-washed blue jean.
His pipe smoke lifts, serene
Beneath boughs of the evergreen,
With sunlight dappling between.
I see him now, as once seen.

Light throbs the far hill.
The boughs of the cedar are still.

His years like landscape lie
Spread to the backward eye
In life's long irony.
20 All the old hoofbeats fade
In the calm of the cedar shade,
Where only the murmur and hum
Of the far farm, and summer, now come.
He can forget all—forget
Even mortgage and lien and debt,
Cutworm and hail and drouth,
Bang's disease, hoof-and-mouth,
Barn sagging and broken house.
Now in the shade, adrowse,
30 At last he can sit, or rouse
To light a pipe, or say to me

Some scrap of old poetry—
Byron or Burns—and idly
The words glimmer and fade
Like sparks in the dark of his head.

In the dust by his chair
I undertook to repair
The mistakes of his old war.
Hunched on that toy terrain,
40 Campaign by campaign,
I sought, somehow, to untie
The knot of History,
For in our shade I knew
That only the Truth is true,
That life is only the act
To transfigure all fact,
And life is only a story
And death is only the glory
Of the telling of the story,
50 And the *done* and the *to-be-done*
In that timelessness were one,
Beyond the poor *being done*.

The afternoon stood still.
Sun dazzled the far hill.

It was only a chance word
That a chance recollection had stirred.
"Guerrilla—what's that?" I said.
"Bushwhackers, we called 'em," he said.
"Were they on the Yankee side?"
60 "Son, they didn't have any side.
Just out to plunder and ride
And hell-rake the pore countryside.
Just out for themselves, so, son,
If you happened to run across one,
Or better, laid hand to a passel,
No need to be squeamish, or wrestle
Too long with your conscience. But if—"
He paused, raised his pipe, took a whiff—
"If your stomach or conscience was queasy,
70 You could make it all regular, easy.

"By the road, find some shade, a nice patch.
Even hackberry does, at a scratch.
Find a spring with some cress fresh beside it,
Growing rank enough to nigh hide it.
Lord, a man can sure thirst when you ride.
Yes, find you a nice spot to bide.
Bide sweet when you can when you ride.
Order halt, let the heat-daze subside.

Put your pickets, vedettes out, dismount.
80 Water horses, grease gall, take count,
And while the men rest and jaw,
You and two lieutenants talk law.
Brevitatem justitia amat.
Time is short—hell, a rope is—that's that."

That was that, and the old eyes were closed.
On a knee one old hand reposed,
Fingers crooked on the cob pipe, where
The last smoke raveled blue up the air.
Every tale ravels out to an end.
90 But smoke rose, did not waver or bend.
It unspooled, wouldn't stop, wouldn't end.

"By God—" and he jerked up his head.
"By God, they deserved it," he said.
"Don't look at me that way," he said.
"By God—" and the old eyes glared red.
Then shut in the cedar shade.

The head slept in that dusk the boughs made.
The world's silence made me afraid.
Then a July-fly, somewhere,
100 Like silk ripping, ripped the bright air.
Then stopped. Sweat broke in my hair.

I snatched my gaze away.
I swung to the blazing day.
Ruined lawn, raw house swam in light.
The far woods swam in my sight.
Throbbing, the fields fell away
Under the blaze of day.

Calmly then, out of the sky,
Blotting the sun's blazing eye,
110 He rode. He was large in the sky.
Behind, shadow massed, slow, and grew
Like cloud on the sky's summer blue.
Out of that shade-mass he drew.
To the great saddle's sway, he swung,
Not old now, not old now—but young,
Great cavalry boots to the thigh,
No speculation in eye.
Then clotting behind him, and dim,
Clot by clot, from the shadow behind him,
120 They took shape, enormous in air.
Behind him, enormous, they hung there:

*

Ornaments of the old rope,
Each face outraged, agape,
Not yet believing it true—
The hairy jaw askew,
Tongue out, out-staring eye,
And the spittle not yet dry
That was uttered with the last cry.

The horseman does not look back.
130 Blank-eyed, he continues his track,
Riding toward me there,
Through the darkening air.

The world is real. It is there.

III. School Lesson Based on Word of Tragic Death of Entire Gillum Family

They weren't so bright, or clean, or clever,
    And their noses were sometimes imperfectly blown,
But they always got to school the weather whatever,
    With old lard pail full of fried pie, smoked ham, and corn pone.

Tow hair was thick as a corn-shuck mat.
    They had milky blue eyes in matching pairs,
And barefoot or brogan, when they sat,
    Their toes were the kind that hook round the legs of chairs.

They had adenoids to make you choke,
10   And buttermilk breath, and their flannels asteam,
And sat right mannerly while teacher spoke,
    But when book-time came their eyes were glazed and adream.

There was Dollie-May, Susie-May, Forrest, Sam, Brother—
    Thirteen down to eight the stairsteps ran.
They had popped right natural from their big fat mother—
    The clabber kind that can catch just by honing after a man.

In town, Gillum stopped you, he'd say: "Say, mister,
    I'll name you what's true fer folks, ever-one.
Human-man ain't much more'n a big blood blister.
20   All red and proud-swole, but one good squeeze and he's gone.

"Take me, ain't wuth lead and powder to perish,
    Just some spindle bone stuck in a pair of pants,
But a man's got his chaps to love and to cherish,
    And raise up and larn 'em so they kin git they chance."

*

So mud to the hub, or dust to the hock,
    God his helper, wet or dry,
Old Gillum swore by God and by cock,
    He'd git 'em larned before his own time came to die.

That morning blew up cold and wet,
30   All the red-clay road was curdled as curd,
And no Gillums there for the first time yet.
    The morning drones on. Stove spits. Recess. Then the word.

Dollie-May was combing Susie-May's head.
    Sam was feeding, Forrest milking, got nigh through.
Little Brother just sat on the edge of his bed.
    Somebody must have said:"Pappy, now what you aimin' to do?"

An ice pick is a subtle thing.
    The puncture's small, blood only a wisp.
It hurts no more than a bad bee sting.
40   When the sheriff got there the school-bread was long burned to a crisp.

In the afternoon silence the chalk would scrape.
    We sat and watched the windowpanes steam,
Blur the old corn field and accustomed landscape.
    Voices came now faint in our intellectual dream.

Which shoe—yes, which—was Brother putting on?
    That was something, it seemed, you just had to know.
But nobody knew, all afternoon,
    Though we studied and studied, as hard as we could, to know,

Studying the arithmetic of losses,
50   To be prepared when the next one,
By fire, flood, foe, cancer, thrombosis,
    Or Time's slow malediction, came to be undone.

We studied all afternoon, till getting on to sun.
There would be another lesson, but we were too young to take up that one.

IV. Summer Storm (Circa 1916), and God's Grace

Toward sun, the sun flared suddenly red.
    The green of woods was doused to black.
    The cattle bellowed by the haystack.
Redder than ever, red clay was red.
    Up the lane the plowhands came pelting back.

*

Astride and no saddle, and they didn't care
    If a razor-back mule at a break-tooth trot
    Was not the best comfort a man ever got,
But came huddling on, with jangling gear,
10   And the hat that jounced off stayed off, like as not.

In that strange light all distance died.
    You know the world's intensity.
    Field-far, you can read the aphid's eye.
The mole, in his sod, can no more hide,
    And weeps beneath the naked sky.

Past silence, sound insinuates
    Past ear into the inner brain.
    The toad's asthmatic breath is pain,
The cutworm's tooth grinds and grates,
20   And the root, in earth, screams, screams again,

But no cloud yet. No wind, though you,
    A half a county off, now spy
    The crow that, laboring zenith-high,
Is suddenly, with wings askew,
    Snatched, and tumbled down the sky.

And so you wait. You cannot talk.
    The creek-side willows shudder gray.
    The oak leaves turn the other way,
Gray as fish-belly. Then, with a squawk,
30   The henhouse heaves, and flies away,

And darkness rides in on the wind.
    The pitchfork lightning tosses the trees,
    And God gets down on hands and knees
To peer and cackle and commend
    His own sadistic idiocies.

Next morning you stood where the bridge had washed out.
    A drowned cow bobbled down the creek.
    Raw-eyed, men watched. They did not speak.
Till one shrugged, said he guessed he'd make out.
40   Then turned, took the woods-path up the creek.

V. Founding Fathers, Nineteenth-Century Style, Southeast U. S. A.

They were human, they suffered, wore long black coat and gold watch chain.
They stare from daguerreotype with severe reprehension,
Or from genuine oil, and you'd never guess any pain
In those merciless eyes that now remark our own time's sad declension.

Some composed declarations, remembering Jefferson's language.
Knew pose of the patriot, left hand in crook of the spine or
With finger to table, while right invokes the Lord's just rage.
There was always a grandpa, or cousin at least, who had been a real Signer.

Some were given to study, read Greek in the forest, and these
10 Longed for an epic to do their own deeds right honor;
Were Nestor by pigpen, in some tavern brawl played Achilles.
In the ring of Sam Houston they found, when he died, one word engraved:
                    Honor.

Their children were broadcast, like millet seed flung in a wind-flare.
Wives died, were dropped like old shirts in some corner of country.
Said, "Mister," in bed, the child-bride; hadn't known what to find there;
Wept all next morning for shame; took pleasure in silk; wore the keys to the
                    pantry.

"Will die in these ditches if need be," wrote Bowie, at the Alamo.
And did, he whose left foot, soft-catting, came forward, and breath hissed:
Head back, gray eyes narrow, thumb flat along knife-blade, blade low.
"Great gentleman," said Henry Clay, "and a patriot." Portrait by Benjamin
20   West.

Or take those, the nameless, of whom no portraits remain,
No locket or seal ring, though somewhere, broken and rusted,
In attic or earth, the long Decherd, stock rotten, has lain;
Or the mold-yellow Bible, God's Word, in which, in their strength, they also
                    trusted.

Some wrestled the angel, and took a fall by the corncrib.
Fought the brute, stomp-and-gouge, but knew they were doomed in that glory.
All night, in sweat, groaned; fell at last with spit red and a cracked rib.
How sweet then the tears! Thus gentled, they roved the dark land with the old
                    story.

Some prospered, had black men and acres, and silver on table,
30 But remembered the owl call, the smell of burnt bear fat on dusk-air.
Loved family and friends, and stood it as long as able—
"But money and women, too much is ruination, am Arkansas-bound." So went
                    there.

One of mine was a land shark, or so the book with scant praise
Denominates him."A man large and shapeless,
Like a sack of potatoes set on a saddle," it says,
"Little learning but shrewd, not well trusted." Rides thus out of history, neck fat
        and napeless.

One fought Shiloh and such, got cranky, would fiddle all night.
The boys nagged for Texas. "God damn it, there's nothing, God damn it,
In Texas" —but took wagons, went, and to prove he was right,
Stayed a year and a day— "hell, nothing in Texas"— had proved it, came back
40   to black vomit,

And died, and they died, and are dead, and now their voices
Come thin, like the last cricket in frost-dark, in grass lost,
With nothing to tell us for our complexity of choices,
But beg us only one word to justify their own old life-cost.

So let us bend ear to them in this hour of lateness,
And what they are trying to say, try to understand,
And try to forgive them their defects, even their greatness,
For we are their children in the light of humanness, and under the shadow of
        God's closing hand.

VI. Infant Boy at Midcentury

1. When the Century Dragged

When the century dragged, like a great wheel stuck at dead center;
When the wind that had hurled us our half-century sagged now,
And only velleity of air somewhat snidely nagged now,
With no certain commitment to compass, or quarter: then you chose to enter.

You enter an age when the neurotic clock-tick
Of midnight competes with the heart's pulsed assurance of power.
You have entered our world at scarcely its finest hour,
And smile now life's gold Apollonian smile at a sick dialectic.

You enter at the hour when the dog returns to his vomit,
And fear's moonflower spreads, white as girl-thigh, in our dusk of
10   compromise;
When posing for pictures, arms linked, the same smile in their eyes,
Good and Evil, to iron out all differences, stage their meeting at summit.

You come in the year when promises are broken,
And petal fears the late, as fruit the early frost-fall;
When the young expect little, and the old endure total recall,
But discover no logic to justify what they had taken, or forsaken.

*

But to take and forsake now you're here, and the heart will compress
Like stone when we see that rosy heel learn,
With its first step, the apocalyptic power to spurn
20 Us, and our works and days, and onward, prevailing, pass

To pause, in high pride of unillusioned manhood,
At the gap that gives on the new century, and land,
And with calm heart and level eye command
That dawning perspective and possibility of human good.

2. Modification of Landscape

There will, indeed, be modification of landscape,
And in margin of natural disaster, substantial reduction.
There will be refinement of principle, and purified action,
And expansion, we trust, of the human heart-hope, and hand-scope.

But is it a meanness of spirit and indulgence of spite
To suggest that your fair time, and friends, will mirror our own,
And ourselves, for the flesh will yet grieve on the bone,
And the heart need compensation for its failure to study delight?

Some will take up religion, some discover the virtue of money.
10 Some will find liberal causes the mask for psychic disturbance.
Some will expiate ego with excessive kindness to servants,
And some make a cult of honor, though having quite little, if any.

Some, hating all humans, will cultivate love for cats,
And some from self-hate will give children a morbid devotion.
Some will glorify friendship, but watch for the slightest motion
Of eyelid, or lip-twitch, and the longed-for betrayal it indicates.

Success for the great will be heart-bread, and the soul's only ease.
For some it will stink, like mackerel shining in moonlight.
At the mere thought of failure some will wet their sheets in the night,
20 Though some wear it proud as a medal, or manhood's first social disease.

The new age will need the old lies, as our own more than once did;
For death is ten thousand nights—yes, it's only the process
Of accommodating flesh to idea, but there's natural distress
In learning to face Truth's glare-glory, from which our eyes are long hid.

3. Brightness of Distance

You will read the official histories—some true, no doubt.
Barring total disaster, the record will speak from the shelf.
And if there's disaster, disaster will speak for itself.
So all of our lies will be truth, and the truth vindictively out.

Remember our defects, we give them to you gratis.
But remember that ours is not the worst of times.
Our country's convicted of follies rather than crimes—
We throw out baby with bath, drop the meat in the fire where the fat is.

And in even such stew and stink as Tacitus
10 Once wrote of, his generals, gourmets, pimps, poltroons,
He found persons of private virtue, the old-fashioned stout ones
Who would bow the head to no blast; and we know that such are yet with us.

He was puzzled how virtue found perch past confusion and wrath;
How even Praetorian brutes, blank of love, as of hate,
Proud in their craftsman's pride only, held a last gate,
And died, each back unmarred as though at the barracks bath.

And remember that many among us wish you well;
And once, on a strange shore, an old man, toothless and through,
Groped a hand from the lattice of personal disaster to touch you.
20 He sat on the sand for an hour; said *ciao, bello,* as evening fell.

And think, as you move past our age that grudges and grieves,
How eyes, purged of envy, will follow your sunlit chance.
Eyes will brighten to follow your brightness and dwindle of distance.
From privacy of fate, eyes will follow, as though from the shadow of leaves.

VII. Dragon Country: To Jacob Boehme

This is the dragon's country, and these his own streams.
The slime on the railroad rails is where he has crossed the track.
On a frosty morning, that field mist is where his great turd steams,
And there are those who have gone forth and not come back.

I was only a boy when Jack Simms reported the first depredation,
What something had done to his hog pen. They called him a God-damn liar.
Then said it must be a bear, after some had viewed the location,
With fence rails, like matchwood, splintered, and earth a bloody mire.

But no bear had been seen in the county in fifty years, they knew.
10 It was something to say, merely that, for people compelled to explain
What, standing in natural daylight, they couldn't believe to be true;
And saying the words, one felt in the chest a constrictive pain.

*

At least, some admitted this later, when things had got to the worst—
When, for instance, they found in the woods the wagon turned on its side,
Mules torn from trace chains, and you saw how the harness had burst.
Spectators averted the face from the spot where the teamster had died.

But that was long back, in my youth, just the first of case after case.
The great hunts fizzled. You followed the track of disrepair,
Ruined fence, blood-smear, brush broken, but came in the end to a place
20   With weed unbent and leaf calm—and nothing, nothing, was there.

So what, in God's name, could men think when they couldn't bring to bay
That belly-dragging earth-evil, but found that it took to air?
Thirty-thirty or buckshot might fail, but then at least you could say
You had faced it—assuming, of course, that you had survived the affair.

We were promised troops, the Guard, but the Governor's skin got thin
When up in New York the papers called him Saint George of Kentucky.
Yes, even the Louisville reporters who came to Todd County would grin.
Reporters, though rarely, still come. No one talks. They think it unlucky.

If a man disappears—well, the fact is something to hide.
30   The family says, gone to Akron, or up to Ford, in Detroit.
When we found Jebb Johnson's boot, with the leg, what was left, inside,
His mother said, no, it's not his. So we took it out to destroy it.

Land values are falling, no longer do lovers in moonlight go.
The rabbit, thoughtless of air gun, in the nearest pasture cavorts.
Now certain fields go untended, the local birth rate goes low.
The coon dips his little black paw in the riffle where he nightly resorts.

Yes, other sections have problems somewhat different from ours.
Their crops may fail, bank rates rise, loans at rumor of war be called,
But we feel removed from maneuvers of Russia, or other great powers,
40   And from much ordinary hope we are now disenthralled.

The Catholics have sent in a mission, Baptists report new attendance.
But all that's off the point! We are human, and the human heart
Demands language for reality that has not the slightest dependence
On desire, or need—and in church fools pray only that the Beast depart.

But if the Beast were withdrawn now, life might dwindle again
To the ennui, the pleasure, and the night sweat, known in the time before
Necessity of truth had trodden the land, and our hearts, to pain,
And left, in darkness, the fearful glimmer of joy, like a spoor.

VIII. Ballad of a Sweet Dream of Peace

1. And Don't Forget Your Corset Cover, Either

And why, in God's name, is that elegant bureau
Standing out here in the woods and dark?
Because, in God's name, it would create a furor
If such a Victorian piece were left in the middle of Central Park,
To corrupt the morals of young and old
With its marble top and drawer pulls gilt gold
And rosewood elaborately scrolled,
And would you, in truth, want your own young sister to see it in the Park?
But she knows all about it, her mother has told her,
10 *And besides, these days, she is getting much older,*
And why, in God's name, is that bureau left in the woods?
All right, I'll tell you why.
It has as much right there as you or I,
For the woods are God's temple, and even a bureau has moods.
But why, in God's name, is that elegant bureau left all alone in the woods?

It is left in the woods for the old lady's sake,
For there's privacy here for a household chore,
And Lord, I can't tell you the time it can take
To apply her own mixture of beeswax and newt-oil to bring out the gloss once
                                    more.
20 For the poor old hands move slower each night,
And can't manage to hold the cloth very tight,
And it's hard without proper light.
But why, in God's name, all this privacy for a simple household chore?
In God's name, sir! would you simply let
Folks see how naked old ladies can get?
Then let the old bitch buy some clothes like other folks do.
She once had some clothes, I am told,
But they're long since ruined by the damp and mold,
And the problem is deeper when bones let the wind blow through.
30 Besides it's not civil to call her a bitch—and her your own grandma, too.

2. Keepsakes

Oh, what brings her out in the dark and night?
She has mislaid something, just what she can't say,
But something to do with the bureau, all right.
Then why, in God's name, does she polish so much, and not look in a drawer
                                    right away?
Every night, in God's name, she does look there,
But finds only a Book of Common Prayer,
A ribbon-tied lock of gold hair,
A bundle of letters, some contraceptives, and an orris-root sachet.
Well, what is the old fool hunting for?

10 Oh, nothing, oh, nothing that's in the top drawer,
For that's left by late owners who had their own grief to withstand,
And she tries to squinch and frown
As she peers at the Prayer Book upside down,
And the contraceptives are something she can't understand,
And oh, how bitter the tears she sheds, with some stranger's old letters in
          hand!

You're lying, you're lying, she can't shed a tear!
Not with eyeballs gone, and the tear ducts, too.
You are trapped in a vulgar error, I fear,
For asleep in the bottom drawer is a thing that may prove instructive to you:

20 Just an old-fashioned doll with a china head,
And a cloth body naked and violated
By a hole through which sawdust once bled,
But drop now by drop, on a summer night, from her heart it is treacle bleeds
          through.
In God's name, what!—Do I see her eyes move?
Of course, and she whispers,"I died for love,"
And your grandmother whines like a dog in the dark and shade,
For she's hunting somebody to give
Her the life they had promised her she would live,
And I shudder to think what a stink and stir will be made
When some summer night she opens the drawer and finds that poor self she'd
30   mislaid.

3. Go It, Granny—Go It, Hog!

Out there in the dark, what's that horrible chomping?
Oh, nothing, just hogs that forage for mast,
And if you call, "Hoo-pig!" they'll squeal and come romping,
For they'll know from your voice you're the boy who slopped them in dear,
          dead days long past.
Any hogs that I slopped are long years dead,
And eaten by somebody and evacuated,
So it's simply absurd, what you said.
You fool, poor fool, all Time is a dream, and we're all one Flesh, at last,
And the hogs know that, and that's why they wait,
10 Though tonight the old thing is a little bit late,
But they're mannered, these hogs, as they wait for her creaky old tread.
Polite, they will sit in a ring,
Till she finishes work, the poor old thing:
Then old bones get knocked down with a clatter to wake up the dead,
And it's simply absurd how loud she can scream with no shred of a tongue in
          her head.

4. Friends of the Family, or Bowling a Sticky Cricket

Who else, in God's name, comes out in these woods?
Old friends of the family, whom you never saw,
Like yon cranky old coot, who mumbles and broods,
With yachting cap, rusty frock coat, and a placard proclaiming, "I am the
      Law!"
What makes him go barefoot at night in God's dew?
In God's name, you idiot, so would you
If you'd suffered as he had to
When expelled from his club for the horrible hobby that taught him the nature
      of law.
They learned that he drowned his crickets in claret.
10 The club used cologne, and so couldn't bear it.
But they drown them in claret in Buckingham Palace!
Fool, law is inscrutable, so
Barefoot in dusk and dew he must go,
And at last each cries out in a dark stone-glimmering place,
"I have heard the voice in the dark, seeing not who utters. Show me Thy
      face!"

5. You Never Knew Her Either, Though You Thought You Did

Why now, in God's name, is the robe de nuit
Of that girl so torn, and what is that stain?
It's only dried blood, in God's name, that you see.
*But why does she carry that leaf in her hand? Will you try, in God's name, to
      explain?*
It's a burdock leaf under which she once found
Two toads in coitu on the bare black ground,
So now she is nightly bound
To come forth to the woods to embrace a thorn tree, to try to understand pain,
And then wipes the blood on her silken hair,
10 And cries aloud, "Oh, we need not despair,
For I bleed, oh, I bleed, and God lives!" And the heart may stir
Like water beneath wind's tread
That wanders whither it is not said.
Oh, I almost forgot—will you please identify her?
She's the afternoon one who to your bed came, lip damp, the breath like
      myrrh.

6. I Guess You Ought to Know Who You Are

Could that be a babe crawling there in night's black?
Why, of course, in God's name, and birth-blind, but you'll see
How to that dead chestnut he'll crawl a straight track,
Then give the astonishing tongue of a hound with a coon treed up in a tree.
Well, who is the brat, and what's he up to?
He's the earlier one that they thought would be you,
And perhaps, after all, it was true,
For it's hard in these matters to tell sometimes. *But look, in God's name, I am*
            me!
If you are, there's the letter a hog has in charge,
10 With a gold coronet and your own name writ large,
And in French, most politely, "Répondez s'il vous plaît."
Now don't be alarmed we are late.
What's time to a hog? We'll just let them wait.
But for when you are ready, our clients usually say
That to shut the eyes tight and get down on the knees is the quickest and easiest
            way.

7. Rumor Unverified Stop Can You Confirm Stop

Yes, clients report it the tidiest way,
For the first time at least, when all is so strange
And the helpers get awkward sometimes with delay.
But later, of course, you can try other methods that fancy suggests you arrange.
There are clients, in fact, who, when ennui gets great,
Will struggle, or ingeniously irritate
The helpers to acts I won't state:
For Reality's all, and to seek it, some welcome, at whatever cost, any change.
But speaking of change, there's a rumor astir
10 That the woods are sold, and the Purchaser
Soon comes, and if credulity's not now abused,
Will, on this property, set
White foot-arch familiar to violet,
And heel that, smiting stone, is not what is bruised,
And subdues to sweetness the pathside garbage, or thing body had refused.

IX. Lullaby: A Motion like Sleep

Under the star and beech-shade braiding,
Past the willow's dim solicitudes,
Past hush of oak-dark and a stone's star-glinted upbraiding,
Water moves, in a motion like sleep,
Along the dark edge of the woods.
So, son, now sleep.

*

Sleep, and feel how now, at woods-edge,
The water, wan, moves under starlight,
Before it finds that dark of its own deepest knowledge,
10   And will murmur, in motion like sleep,
In that leaf-dark languor of night.
So, son, sleep deep.

Sleep, and dream how deep and dreamless
The covered courses of blood are:
And blood, in a motion like sleep, moves, gleamless,
By alleys darkened deep now
In the leafage of no star.
So, son, sleep now.

Sleep, for sleep and stream and blood-course
20   Are a motion with one name,
And all that flows finds end but in its own source,
And a circuit of motion like sleep,
And will go as once it came.
So, son, now sleep

Till the clang of cock-crow, and dawn's rays,
Summon your heart and hand to deploy
Their energies to know, in the excitement of day-blaze,
How like a wound, and deep,
Is Time's irremediable joy.
30   So, son, now sleep.

from You, Emperors, and Others

Two Pieces after Suetonius

I. Apology for Domitian

He was not bad, as emperors go, not really—
Not like Tiberius cruel, or poor Nero silly.
The trouble was only that omens said he would die,
So what could he, mortal, do? Not worse, however, than you might, or I.

Suppose from long back you had known the very hour—
"Fear the fifth hour"—and yet for all your power
Couldn't strike it out from the day, or the day from the year,
Then wouldn't you have to strike something at least? If you did, would it seem
        so queer?

Suppose you were proud of your beauty, but baldness set in?
10 Suppose your good leg were dwindling to spindly and thin?
Wouldn't you, like Domitian, try the classic bed-stunt
To prove immortality on what was propped to bear the imperial brunt?

Suppose you had dreamed a gold hump sprouted out of your back,
And such a prosperous burden oppressed you to breath-lack;
Suppose lightning scorched the sheets in your own bedroom;
And from your own statue a storm yanked the name plate and chucked it into a
        tomb—

Well, it happened to him. Therefore, there's little surprise
That for hours he'd lock himself up to pull wings from flies.
Fly or man, what odds? He would wander his hall of moonstone,
20 Mirror-bright so he needn't look over his shoulder to see if he was alone.

Let's stop horsing around—it's not Domitian, it's you
We mean, and the omens are bad, very bad, and it's true
That virtue comes hard vis-à-vis the assiduous clock,
And music, at sunset, faint as a dream, is heard from beyond the burdock,

And as for Domitian, the first wound finds the groin,
And he claws like a cat, but the blade continues to go in,
And the body is huddled forth meanly, and what ritual
It gets is at night, and from his old nurse, a woman poor, nonpolitical.

II. Tiberius on Capri

(a)

All is nothing, nothing all:
To tired Tiberius soft sang the sea thus,
Under his cliff-palace wall.
The sea, in soft approach and repulse,
Sings thus, and Tiberius,
Sea-sad, stares past the dusking sea-pulse
Yonder, where come,
One now by one, the lights, far off, of Surrentum.
He stares in the blue dusk-fall,
10   For all is nothing, nothing all.

Let darkness up from Asia tower.
On that darkening island behind him *spintriae* now stir.
In grot and scented bower,
They titter, yawn, paint lip, grease thigh,
And debate what role each would prefer
When they project for the Emperor's eye
Their expertise
Of his Eastern lusts and complex Egyptian fantasies.
But darkward he stares in that hour,
20   Blank now in totality of power.

(b)

There once, on that goat island, I,
As dark fell, stood and stared where Europe stank.
Many were soon to die—
From acedia snatched, from depravity, virtue,
Or frolic, not knowing the reason, in rank
On rank hurled, or in bed, or in church, or
Dishing up supper,
Or in a dark doorway, loosening the girl's elastic to tup her,
While high in the night sky,
10   The murderous tear dropped from God's eye;

And faintly forefeeling, forefearing, all
That to fulfill our time, and heart, would come,
I stood on the crumbling wall
Of that foul place, and my lungs drew in
Scent of dry gorse on the night air of autumn,
And I seized, in dark, a small stone from that ruin,
And I made outcry
At the paradox of powers that would grind us like grain, small and dry.
Dark down, the stone, in its fall,
20   Found the sea: I could do that much, after all.

Mortmain

I. After Night Flight Son Reaches Bedside of Already Unconscious Father, Whose Right Hand Lifts in a Spasmodic Gesture, as Though Trying to Make Contact: 1955

In Time's concatenation and
Carnal conventicle, I,
Arriving, being flung through dark and
The abstract flight-grid of sky,
Saw rising from the sweated sheet and
Ruck of bedclothes ritualistically
Reordered by the paid hand
Of mercy—saw rising the hand—

Christ, start again! What was it I,
10 Standing there, travel-shaken, saw
Rising? What could it be that I,
Caught sudden in gut- or conscience-gnaw,
Saw rising out of the past, which I
Saw now as twisted bedclothes? Like law,
The hand rose cold from History
To claw at a star in the black sky,

But could not reach that far—oh, cannot!
And the star horribly burned, burns,
For in darkness the wax-white clutch could not
20 Reach it, and white hand on wrist-stem turns,
Lifts in last tension of tendon, but cannot
Make contact—*oh, oop-si-daisy,* churns
The sad heart, *oh, atta-boy, daddio's got
One more shot in the locker, peas-porridge hot*—

But no. Like an eyelid the hand sank, strove
Downward, and in that darkening roar,
All things—all joy and the hope that strove,
The failed exam, the admired endeavor,
Prizes and prinkings, and the truth that strove,
30 And back of the Capitol, boyhood's first whore—
Were snatched from me, and I could not move,
Naked in that black blast of his love.

II. A Dead Language: Circa 1885

Mother dead, land lost, stepmother haggard with kids,
Big Brother skedaddling off to Mexico
To make his fortune, gold or cattle or cards,
What could he do but what we see him doing?
Cutting crossties for the first railroad in the region,
Sixteen and strong as a man—was a man, by God!—
And the double-bit bit into red oak, and in that rhythm,
In his head, all day, marched the Greek paradigm:
That was all that was his, and all he could carry all day with him.

10 Λέγω, λέγεις, λέγα, and the axe swung.
That was that year, and the next year we see him
Revolve in his dream between the piece goods and cheese,
In a crossroads store, between peppermint candy and plow-points,
While the eaves drip, and beyond the black trees of winter
Last light grays out, and in the ruts of the lane
Water gleams, sober as steel. That was that land,
And that was the life, and he reached out and
Took the dime from the gray-scaled palm of the Negro plowhand's hand.

'Εν ἀρχῇ ἦν ὁ λόγος: in the beginning
20 Was the word, but in the end was
What? At the mirror, lather on chin, with a razor
Big as a corn-knife, or, so to the boy it seemed,
He stood, and said: 'Εν ἀρχῇ ἦν ὁ λόγος.
And laughed. And said: "That's Greek, now you know how it sounds!"
And laughed, and waved the bright blade like a toy.
And laughing from the deep of a dark conquest and joy,
Said: "Greek—but it wasn't for me. Let's get to breakfast, boy."

III. Fox-fire: 1956

Years later, I find the old grammar, yellowed. Night
Is falling. Ash flakes from the log. The log
Glows, winks, wanes. Westward, the sky,
In one small area redeemed from gray, bleeds dully.
Beyond my window, athwart that red west,
The spruce bough, though snow-burdened, looks black,
Not white. The world lives by the trick of the eye, the trick
Of the heart. I hold the book in my hand, but God
—In what mercy, if mercy?—will not let me weep. But I
10 Do not want to weep. I want to understand.

Oh, let me understand what is that sound,
Like wind, that fills the enormous dark of my head.
Beyond my head there is no wind, the room

Darkening, the world beyond the room darkening,
And no wind beyond to cleave, unclot, the thickening
Darkness. There must be a way to state the problem.
The statement of a problem, no doubt, determines solution.
If once, clear and distinct, I could state it, then God
Could no longer fall back on His old alibi of ignorance.
20 I hear now my small son laugh from a farther room.

I know he sits there and laughs among his toys,
Teddy bear, letter blocks, yellow dumptruck, derrick, choo-choo—
Bright images, all, of Life's significance.
So I put the Greek grammar on the shelf, beside my own,
Unopened these thirty years, and leave the dark room,
And know that all night, while the constellations grind,
Beings with folded wings brood above that shelf,
Awe-struck and imbecile, and in the dark,
Amid History's vice and velleity, that poor book burns
30 Like fox-fire in the black swamp of the world's error.

IV. In the Turpitude of Time: n.d.

In the turpitude of Time,
Hope dances on the razor edge.
I see those ever healing feet
Tread the honed edge above despair.
I see the song-wet lip and tossing hair.

The leaf unfolds the autumn weather.
The heart spills the horizon's light.
In the woods, the hunter, weeping, kneels,
And the dappled fawn weeps in contrition
10 For its own beauty. I hear the toad's intercession

For us, and all, who do not know
How cause flows backward from effect
To bless the past occasion, and
How Time's tongue lifts only to tell,
Minute by minute, what truth the brave heart will fulfill.

Can we—oh, could we only—believe
What annelid and osprey know,
And the stone, night-long, groans to divulge?
If we only could, then that star
20 That dawnward slants might sing to our human ear,

And joy, in daylight, run like feet,
And strength, in darkness, wait like hands,
And between the stone and the wind's voice
A silence wait to become our own song:
In the heart's last kingdom only the old are young.

V. A Vision: Circa 1880

Out of the woods where pollen is a powder of gold
Shaken from pistil of oak minutely, and of maple,
And is falling, and the tulip tree lifts, not yet tarnished,
The last calyx, in which chartreuse coolness recessed, dew,
Only this morning, lingered till noon—look,
Out of the woods, barefoot, the boy comes. He stands,
Hieratic, complete, in patched britches and that idleness of boyhood
Which asks nothing and is its own fulfilment:
In his hand a wand of peeled willow, boy-idle and aimless.

10 Poised between woods and the pasture, sun-green and green shadow,
Hair sweat-dark, brow bearing a smudge of gold pollen, lips
Parted in some near-smile of boyhood bemusement,
Dangling the willow, he stands, and I—I stare
Down the tube and darkening corridor of Time
That breaks, like tears, upon that sunlit space,
And staring, I know who he is, and would cry out.
Out of my knowledge, I would cry out and say:
Listen! Say: *Listen! I know—oh, I know— let me tell you!*

That scene is in Trigg County, and I see it.
20 Trigg County is in Kentucky, and I have been there,
But never remember the spring there. I remember
A land of cedar-shade, blue, and the purl of limewater,
But the pasture parched, and the voice of the lost joree
Unrelenting as conscience, and sick, and the afternoon throbs,
And the sun's hot eye on the dry leaf shrivels the aphid,
And the sun's heel does violence in the corn-balk.
That is what I remember, and so the scene

I had seen just now in the mind's eye, vernal,
Is altered, and I strive to cry across the dry pasture,
30 But cannot, nor move, for my feet, like dry corn-roots, cleave
Into the hard earth, and my tongue makes only the dry,
Slight sound of wind on the autumn corn-blade. The boy,
With imperial calm, crosses a space, rejoins
The shadow of woods, but pauses, turns, grins once,
And is gone. And one high oak leaf stirs gray, and the air,
Stirring, freshens to the far favor of rain.

Some Quiet, Plain Poems

I. Ornithology in a World of Flux

It was only a bird call at evening, unidentified,
As I came from the spring with water, across the rocky back-pasture;
But I stood so still sky above was not stiller than sky in pail-water.

Years pass, all places and faces fade, some people have died,
And I stand in a far land, the evening still, and am at last sure
That I miss more that stillness at bird-call than some things that were to fail
        later.

II. Holly and Hickory

Rain, all night, taps the holly.
It ticks like a telegraph on the pane.
If awake in that house, meditating some old folly
Or trying to live an old pleasure again,
I could hear it sluicing the ruts in the lane.

Rain beats down the last leaf of hickory,
But where I lie now rain-sounds hint less
At benign sleight of the seasons, or Time's adept trickery,
And with years I feel less joy or distress
10 To hear water moving in wheel ruts, star-glintless,

And if any car comes now up that lane,
It carries nobody I could know,
And who wakes in that house now to hear the rain
May fall back to sleep—as I, long ago,
Who dreamed dawnward; and would rise to go.

III. The Well House

What happened there, it was not much,
But was enough. If you come back,
Not much may be *too much,* even if you have your old knack
Of stillness, and do not touch
A thing, a broken toy or rusted tool or any such
Object you happen to find
Hidden where, uncontrolled, grass and weeds bend.

*

The clematis that latches the door
Of the ruinous well house, you might break it.
10 Though guessing the water foul now, and not thirsting to take it,
With thirst from those years before
You might lean over the coping to stare at the water's dark-glinting floor.
Yes, that might be the event
To change *not much* to *too much,* and more than meant.

Yes, Truth is always in balance, and
Not much can become *too much* so quick.
Suppose you came back and found your heart suddenly sick,
And covered your sight with your hand:
Your tears might mean more than the thing you wept for but did not
          understand.
20 Yes, something might happen there
If you came back—even if you just stood to stare.

IV. In Moonlight, Somewhere, They Are Singing

Under the maples at moonrise—
Moon whitening top leaf of the white oak
That rose from the dark mass of maples and range of eyes—
They were singing together, and I woke

From my sleep to the whiteness of moon-fire,
And deep from their dark maples, I
Could hear the two voices shake silver and free, and aspire
To be lost in moon-vastness of the sky.

My young aunt and her young husband
10 From their dark maples sang, and though
Too young to know what it meant I was happy and
So slept, for I knew I would come to know.

But what of the old man awake there,
As the voices, like vine, climbed up moonlight?
What thought did he think of past time as they twined bright in moon-air,
And veined, with their silver, the moon-flesh of night?

Far off, I recall, in the barn lot,
A mule stamped, once; but the song then
Was over, and for that night, or forever, would not
20 Resume—but should it again,

Now years later, wake me to white moon-fire
On pillow, high oak leaf, and far field,
I should hope to find imaged in whatever new voices aspire
Some faith in life yet, by my years, unrepealed.

V. Debate: Question, Quarry, Dream

Asking what, asking what?—all a boy's afternoon,
Squatting in the canebrake where the muskrat will come.
Muskrat, muskrat, please now, please, come soon.
He comes, stares, goes, lets the question resume.
He has taken whatever answer may be down to his mud-burrow gloom.

Seeking what, seeking what?—foot soft in cedar-shade.
Was that a deer-flag white past windfall and fern?
No, but by bluffside lurk powers and in the fern glade
Tall presences, standing all night, like white fox-fire burn.
The small fox lays his head in your hand now and weeps that you go, not to
10   return.

Dreaming what, dreaming what?— lying on the hill at twilight,
The still air stirred only by moth wing, the last stain of sun
Fading to moth-sky, blood-red to moth-white and starlight,
And Time leans down to kiss the heart's ambition,
While far away, before moonrise, come the town lights, one by one.

Long since that time I have walked night streets, heel-iron
Clicking the stone, and in dark in windows have stared.
Question, quarry, dream—I have vented my ire on
My own heart that, ignorant and untoward,
20 Yearns for an absolute that Time would, I thought, have prepared,

But has not yet. Well, let us debate
The issue. But under a tight roof, clutching a toy,
My son now sleeps, and when the hour grows late,
I shall go forth where the cold constellations deploy
And lift up my eyes to consider more strictly the appalling logic of joy.

Two Studies in Idealism: Short Survey
of American, and Human, History

For Allan Nevins

I. Bear Track Plantation: Shortly after Shiloh

Two things a man's built for, killing and you-know-what.
As for you-know-what, I reckon I taken my share,
Bed-ease or bush-whack, but killing—hell, three's all I got,
And he promised me ten, Jeff Davis, the bastard. 'Taint fair.

It ain't fair, a man rides and knows he won't live forever,
And a man needs something to take with him when he dies.
Ain't much worth taking, but what happens under the cover
Or at the steel-point—yeah, that look in their eyes.

*

That same look, it comes in their eyes when you give 'em the business.
10   It's something a man can hang on to, come black-frost or sun.
Come hell or high water, it's something to save from the mess,
No matter whatever else you never got done.

For a second it seems like a man can know what he lives for,
When those eyelids go waggle, or maybe the eyes pop wide,
And that look comes there. Yeah, Christ, then you know who you are—
And will maybe remember that much even after you've died.

But now I lie worrying what look my own eyes got
When that Blue-Belly caught me off balance. Did my look mean then
That I'd honed for something not killing or you-know-what?
20   Hell, no. I'd lie easy if Jeff had just give me that ten.

II. Harvard '61: Battle Fatigue

I didn't mind dying—it wasn't that at all.
It behooves a man to prove manhood by dying for Right.
If you die for Right that fact is your dearest requital,
But you find it disturbing when others die who simply haven't the right.

Why should they die with that obscene insouciance?
They seem to insult the principle of your own death.
Touch pitch, be defiled: it was hard to keep proper distance
From such unprincipled wastrels of blood and profligates of breath.

I tried to slay without rancor, and often succeeded.
10   I tried to keep the heart pure, though my hand took stain.
But they made it so hard for me, the way they proceeded
To parody with their own dying that Death which only Right should sustain.

Time passed. It got worse. It seemed like a plot against me.
I said they had made their own evil bed and lay on it,
But they grinned in the dark—they grinned—and I yet see
That last one. At woods-edge we held, and over the stubble they came with
          bayonet.

He uttered his yell, he was there!—teeth yellow, some missing.
Why, he's old as my father, I thought, finger frozen on trigger.
I saw the ambeer on his whiskers, heard the old breath hissing.
The puncture came small on his chest. 'Twas nothing. The stain then got
20   bigger.

And he said: "Why, son, you done done it—I figgered I'd skeered ye."
Said: "Son, you look puke-pale. Buck up! If it hadn't been you,
Some other young squirt would a-done it." I stood, and weirdly
The tumult of battle went soundless, like gesture in dream. And I was dead,
          too.

*

Dead, and had died for the Right, as I had a right to,
And glad to be dead, and hold my residence
Beyond life's awful illogic, and the world's stew,
Where people who haven't the right just die, with ghastly impertinence.

from Tale of Time

Tale of Time

I. What Happened

It was October. It was the Depression. Money
Was tight. Hoover was not a bad
Man, and my mother
Died, and God
Kept on, and keeps on,
Trying to tie things together, but

It doesn't always work, and we put the body
Into the ground, dark
Fell soon, but not yet, and
10 Have you seen the last oak leaf of autumn, high,
Not yet fallen, stung
By last sun to a gold
Painful beyond the pain one can ordinarily
Get? What

Was there in the interim
To do, the time being the time
Between the clod's *chunk* and
The full realization, which commonly comes only after
Midnight? That

20 Is when you will go to the bathroom for a drink of water.
You wash your face in cold water.
You stare at your face in the mirror, wondering
Why now no tears come, for
You had been proud of your tears, and so
You think of copulation, of
Fluid ejected, of
Water deeper than daylight, of
The sun-dappled dark of deep woods and
Blood on green fern frond, of
30 The shedding of blood, and you will doubt
The significance of your own experience. Oh,
Desolation—oh, if

You were rich!
You try to think of a new position. Is this

Grief? You pray
To God that this be grief, for
You want to grieve.

This, you reflect, is no doubt the typical syndrome.

But all this will come later.
40   There will also be the dream of the eating of human flesh.

II. The Mad Druggist

I come back to try to remember the faces she saw every day.
She saw them on the street, at school, in the stores, at church.
They are not here now, they have been withdrawn, are put away.
They are all gone now, and have left me in the lurch.

I am in the lurch because they were part of her.
Not clearly remembering them, I have therefore lost that much
Of her, and if I do remember,
I remember the lineaments only beyond the ice-blur and soot-smutch

Of boyhood contempt, for I had not thought they were real.
10   The real began where the last concrete walk gave out
And the smart-weed crawled in the cracks, where the last privy canted to spill
Over flat in the rank-nourished burdock, and would soon, no doubt,

If nobody came to prop it, which nobody would do.
The real began there: field and woods, stone and stream began
Their utterance, and the fox, in his earth, knew
Joy; and the hawk, like philosophy, hung without motion, high, where the
          sun-blaze of wind ran.

Now, far from Kentucky, planes pass in the night, I hear them and all, all is
          real.
Some men are mad, but I know that delusion may be one name for truth.
The faces I cannot remember lean at my bed-foot, and grin fit to kill,
20   For we now share a knowledge I did not have in my youth.

There's one I remember, the old druggist they carried away.
They put him in Hoptown, where he kept on making his list—
The same list he had on the street when he stopped my mother to say:
"Here they are, Miss Ruth, the folks that wouldn't be missed,

"Or this God-durn town would be lucky to miss,
If when I fixed a prescription I just happened to pour
Something in by way of improvement." Then leaned in that gray way of his:
"But you—you always say something nice when you come in my store."

*

In Hoptown he worked on his list, which now could have nothing to do
30 With the schedule of deaths continuing relentlessly,
    To include, in the end, my mother, as well as that list-maker who
    Had the wit to see that she was too precious to die:

A fact some in the street had not grasped—nor the attending physician, nor
        God, nor I.

III. Answer Yes or No

Death is only a technical correction of the market.
Death is only the transfer of energy to a new form.
Death is only the fulfillment of a wish.

Whose wish?

IV. The Interim
1.

Between the clod and the midnight
The time was.
There had been the public ritual and there would be
The private realization,
And now the time was, and

In that time the heart cries out for coherence.
Between the beginning and the end, we must learn
The nature of being, in order
In the end to *be,* so

10 Our feet, in first dusk, took
    Us over the railroad tracks, where
    Sole-leather ground drily against cinders, as when
    Tears will not come. She

Whom we now sought was old. Was
Sick. Was dying. Was
Black. Was.
Was: and was that enough? Is
Existence the adequate and only target
For the total reverence of the heart?

20 We would see her who,
    Also, had held me in her arms.
    She had held me in her arms,
    And I had cried out in the wide
    Day-blaze of the world. But

    *

Now was a time of endings.

What is love?

2.

Tell me what love is, for
The harvest moon, gold, heaved
Over the far woods which were,
On the black land black, and it swagged over
The hill-line. That light
Lay gold on the roofs of Squiggtown, and the niggers
Were under the roofs, and
The room smelled of urine.
A fire burned on the hearth:
10 Too hot, and there was no ventilation, and

You have not answered my question.

3.

Propped in a chair, lying down she
Could not have breathed, dying
Erect, breath
Slow from the hole of the mouth, that black
Aperture in the blackness which
Was her face, but
How few of them are really
Black, but she
Is black, and life
10 Spinning out, spilling out, from
The holes of the eyes: and the eyes are
Burning mud beneath a sky of nothing.
The eyes bubble like hot mud with the expulsion of vision.

I lean, I am the
Nothingness which she
Sees.

Her hand rises in the air.
It rises like revelation.
It moves but has no motion, and
20 Around it the world flows like a dream of drowning.
The hand touches my cheek.
The voice says: *you.*

I am myself.

The hand has brought me the gift of myself.

4.

I am myself, and
Her face is black like cave-blackness, and over
That blackness now hangs death, gray
Like cobweb over the blackness of a cave, but
That blackness which she is, is
Not deficiency like cave-blackness, but is
Substance.
The cobweb shakes with the motion of her breath.

My hand reaches out to part that grayness of cobweb.

10 My lips touch the cheek, which is black.
I do not know whether the cheek is cold or hot, but I
Know that
The temperature is shocking.
I press my lips firmly against that death,
I try to pray.

The flesh is dry, and tastes of salt.

My father has laid a twenty-dollar bill on the table.
Secretly.
He, too, will kiss that cheek.

5.

We stand in the street of Squiggtown.
The moon is high now and the tin roofs gleam.
My brother says: *The whole place smelled of urine.*
My father says: *Twenty dollars—oh, God, what*
Is twenty dollars when
The world is the world it is!

The night freight is passing.
The couplings clank in the moonlight, the locomotive
Labors on the grade.
10 The freight disappears beyond the coal chute westward, and
The red caboose light disappears into the distance of the continent.
It will move all night into distance.

My sister is weeping under the sky.
The sky is enormous in the absoluteness of moonlight.

These are factors to be considered in making any final estimate.

6.

There is only one solution. If
You would know how to live, here
Is the solution, and under
My window, when ice breaks, the boulder now
Groans in the gorge, the foam swirls, and in
The intensity of the innermost darkness of steel
The crystal blooms like a star, and at
Dawn I have seen the delicate print of the coon-hand in silt by the riffle.

Hawk-shadow sweetly sweeps the grain.
10 I would compare it with that fugitive thought which I can find no word for.

7.

Planes pass in the night. I turn
To the right side if the beating
Of my own heart disturbs me.
The sound of water flowing is
An image of Time, and therefore
Truth is all and
Must be respected, and
On the other side of the mirror into which,
At morning, you will stare, History

10 Gathers, condenses, crouches, breathes, waits. History
Stares forth at you through the eyes which
You think are the reflection of
Your own eyes in the mirror.
Ah, Monsieur du Miroir!

Your whole position must be reconsidered.

8.

But the solution: You
Must eat the dead.
You must eat them completely, bone, blood, flesh, gristle, even
Such hair as can be forced. You
Must undertake this in the dark of the moon, but
At your plenilune of anguish.

Immortality is not impossible,
Even joy.

V. What Were You Thinking, Dear Mother?

What were you thinking, a child, when you lay,
At the whippoorwill hour, lost in the long grass,
As sun, beyond the dark cedars, sank?
You went to the house. The lamps were now lit.

What did you think when the mourning dove mourned,
Far off in those sober recesses of cedar?
What relevance did your heart find in that sound?
In lamplight, your father's head bent at his book.

What did you think when the last saffron
10 Of sunset faded beyond the dark cedars,
And on noble blue now the evening star hung?
You found it necessary to go to the house,

And found it necessary to live on,
In your bravery and in your joyous secret,
Into our present maniacal century,
In which you gave me birth, and in

Which I, in the public and private mania,
Have lived, but remember that once I,
A child, in the grass of that same spot, lay,
20 And the whippoorwill called, beyond the dark cedars.

VI. Insomnia

1.

If to that place. Place of grass.
If to hour of whippoorwill, I.
If I now, not a child. To.
If now I, not a child, should come to
That place, lie in
That place, in that hour hear
That call, would
I rise,
Go?

10 Yes, enter the darkness. Of.
Darkness of cedars, thinking
You there, you having entered, sly,
My back being turned, face
Averted, or
Eyes shut, for
A man cannot keep his eyes steadily open
Sixty years.

*

I did not see you when you went away.

Darkness of cedars, yes, entering, but what
20 Face, what
Bubble on dark stream of Time, white
Glimmer un-mooned? Oh,
What age has the soul, what
Face does it wear, or would
I meet that face that last I saw on the pillow, pale?

I recall each item with remarkable precision.

Would the sweat now be dried on the temples?

2.

What would we talk about? The dead,
Do they know all, or nothing, and
If nothing, does
Curiosity survive the long unravelment? Tell me

What they think about love, for I
Know now at long last that the living remember the dead only
Because we cannot bear the thought that they
Might forget us. Or is
That true? Look, look at these—
10 But no, no light here penetrates by which
You might see these photographs I keep in my wallet. Anyway,
I shall try to tell you all that has happened to me.

Though how can I tell when I do not even know?

And as for you, and all the interesting things
That must have happened to you and that
I am just dying to hear about—

But would you confide in a balding stranger
The intimate secret of death?

3.

Or does the soul have many faces, and would I,
Pacing the cold hypothesis of Time, enter
Those recesses to see, white,
Whiter than moth-wing, the child's face
Glimmer in cedar gloom, and so
Reach out that I might offer
What protection I could, saying,
"I am older than you will ever be"—for you
Are the child who once
10 Lay lost in the long grass, sun setting.

Reach out, saying: "Your hand—
Give it here, for it's dark and, my dear,
You should never have come in the woods when it's dark,
But I'll take you back home, they're waiting."
And to woods-edge we come, there I stand.

I watch you move across the open space.
You move under the paleness of new stars.
You move toward the house, and one instant,

A door opening, I see
20 Your small form black against the light, and the door
Is closed, and I

Hear night crash down a million stairs.
In the ensuing silence
My breath is difficult.

Heat lightning ranges beyond the horizon.

That, also, is worth mentioning.

4.

Come,
Crack crust, striker
From darkness, and let seize—let what
Hand seize, oh!—my heart, and compress
The heart till, after pain, joy from it
Spurts like a grape, and I will grind
Teeth on flint tongue till
The flint screams. Truth
Is all. But

10 I must learn to speak it
Slowly, in a whisper.

*

Truth, in the end, can never be spoken aloud,
For the future is always unpredictable.
But so is the past, therefore

At wood's edge I stand, and,
Over the black horizon, heat lightning
Ripples the black sky. After
The lightning, as the eye
Adjusts to the new dark,
20 The stars are, again, born.

They are born one by one.

Homage to Emerson,
On Night Flight to New York

To Peter and Ebie Blume

I. His Smile

Over Peoria we lost the sun:
The earth, by snow like sputum smeared, slides
Westward. Those fields in the last light gleam. Emerson—

The essays, on my lap, lie. A finger
Of light, in our pressurized gloom, strikes down,
Like God, to poke the page, the page glows. There is
No sin. Not even error. Night,

On the glass at my right shoulder, hisses
Like sand from a sand-blast, but
10 The hiss is a sound that only a dog's
Ear could catch, or the human heart. My heart

Is as abstract as an empty
Coca-Cola bottle. It whistles with speed.
It whines in that ammoniac blast caused by
The passage of stars, for
At 38,000 feet Emerson

Is dead right. His smile
Was sweet as he walked in the greenwood.
He walked lightly, his toes out, his body
20 Swaying in the dappled shade, and
His smile never withered a violet. He

*

Did not even know the violet's name, not having
Been introduced, but he bowed, smiling,
For he had forgiven God everything, even the violet.

When I was a boy I had a wart on the right forefinger.

II. The Wart

At 38,000 feet you had better
Try to remember something specific, if
You yourself want to be something specific, I remember
The wart and the old colored man, he said, *Son*
You quit that jack-off, and that thing go way,
And I said *Quit what,* and he giggled *He-he,* and he
Said, *You is got white skin and hair red as a ter-mater, but*
You is human-kind, but

At 38,000 feet that is hard to remember.

III. The Spider

The spider has more eyes than I have money.
I used to dream that God was a spider, or

Vice versa, but it is easier
To dream of a funnel, and you
The clear liquid being poured down it, forever.

You do not know what is beyond the little end of the funnel.

The liquid glimmers in darkness, you
Are happy, it pours easily, without fume.

All you have to do is not argue.

IV. One Drunk Allegory

Not argue, unless, that is, you are the kind
That needs to remember something specific
In order to be, at 38,000 feet, whatever you are, and once
In New Orleans, in French Town, in
Front of the Old Absinthe House, and it
Was Saturday night, was 2 A.M., a drunk

Crip slipped, and the air was full of flying crutches
Like a Texas tornado exploding with chicken feathers and
Split boards off busted hen-houses, and bingo!—
10   It was prize money flat on its you-know-what, it
Was like a box of spilled spaghetti, but
I managed to reassemble everything and prop it

Against a lamp post. *Thank you,*
It said in its expensive Harvard-cum-cotton
Voice, then bingo!—
Flat on its you-know-what, on the pavement,
And ditto the crutches. *Prithee,* the voice

Expensively said, *do not trouble yourself*
Further. This is as good a position as any
20   *From which to watch the stars.* Then added:
Until, of course, the cops come. I
Had private reasons for not wanting to be
There when the cops came. So wasn't.

Emerson thought that significance shines through everything,

And at that moment I was drunk enough to think all this was allegory.
If it was, it was sure-God one drunk allegory, and
Somewhere in the womb-gloom of the DC-8

A baby is crying. The cry seems to have a reality
Independent of the baby. The cry
30   Is like a small white worm in my brain.

It nibbles with tiny, insistent assiduity. Its teeth
Are almost too soft. Sometimes it merely tickles.

To my right, far over Kentucky, the stars are shining.

V. Multiplication Table

If the Christmas tree at Rockefeller Center were
A billion times bigger, and you laid it
Flat down in the dark, and
With a steam roller waist-high to God and heavy as
The Rocky Mountains, flattened it out thin as paper, but
Never broke a single damned colored light bulb, and they were all
Blazing in the dark, that would be the way it is, but

Beyond the lights it is dark, and one night in winter, I
Stood at the end of a pier at Coney Island, while
10 The empty darkness howled like a dog, but no wind, and far down
The boardwalk what must have been a cop's flashlight
Jiggled fitfully over what must have been locked store-fronts, then,
Of a sudden, went out. The stars were small and white, and I heard

The sea secretly sucking the piles of the pier with a sound like
An old woman sucking her teeth in the dark before she sleeps.

The nose of the DC-8 dips, and at this point
The man sitting beside me begins, quite audibly, to recite
The multiplication table.

                          Far below,
Individual lights can be seen throbbing like nerve ends.
20 I have friends down there, and their lives have strange shapes
Like eggs splattered on the kitchen floor. Their lives shine
Like oil-slicks on dark water. I love them, I think.

In a room, somewhere, a telephone keeps ringing.

VI. Wind

The wind comes off the Sound, smelling
Of ice. It smells
Of fish and burned gasoline. A sheet
Of newspaper drives in the wind across
The great distance of cement that bleeds
Off into blackness beyond the red flares. The air

Shivers, it shakes like Jello with
The roar of jets—yes, why
Is it you think you can hear the infinitesimal scrape
10 Of that newspaper as it slides over the black cement, forever?

The wind gouges its knuckles into my eye. No wonder there are tears.

VII. Does the Wild Rose?

When you reach home tonight you will see
That the envelope containing the policy
Of your flight insurance is waiting, unopened,
On the table. All had been in order,
In case—but can you tell me,

> *Does the wild rose know your secret*
> *As the summer silence breathes?*

Eastward, the great waters stretch in darkness.
Do you know how gulls sleep when they can't make it home?

10   *Tell me, tell me, does the wild rose*— tell me, for

Tonight I shall dream of small white stars
Falling forever in darkness like dandruff, but

Now let us cross that black cement which so resembles the arctic ice of
Our recollections. There is the city, the sky
Glows, glows above it, there must be

A way by which the process of living can become Truth.

Let us move toward the city. Do you think you could tell me
What constitutes the human bond? Do you ever think
Of a face half in shadow, tears—
20 As it would seem from that muted glitter—in the
Eyes, but

The lips do not tremble.

Is it merely a delusion that they seem about to smile?

from Incarnations

Island of Summer

I. What Day Is

In Pliny, *Phoenice.* Phoenicians,
Of course. Before that, Celts.
Rome, in the end, as always:
A handful of coins, a late emperor.
Hewn stone, footings for what?
Irrigation, but now not easy
To trace a flume-line.

                Later,
Monks, Moors, murderers,
The Mediterranean flotsam, not
10 Excluding the English, they cut
Down olives, plucked vines up, burnt
The chateau.

            All day, cicadas,
At the foot of infinity, like
A tree, saw. The sawdust
Of that incessant effort,
Like filings of brass, sun-brilliant,
Heaps up at the tree-foot. That
Is what day is.

           Do not
Look too long at the sea, for
20 That brightness will rinse out your eyeballs.

They will go gray as dead moons.

II. Where the Slow Fig's Purple Sloth

Where the slow fig's purple sloth
Swells, I sit and meditate the
Nature of the soul, the fig exposes,
To the blaze of afternoon, one haunch
As purple-black as Africa, a single
Leaf the rest screens, but through it, light
Burns, and for the fig's bliss
The sun dies, the sun
Has died forever—far, oh far—
10 For the fig's bliss, thus.

                The air
Is motionless, and the fig,
Motionless in that imperial and blunt
Languor of glut, swells, and inward
The fibers relax like a sigh in that
Hot darkness, go soft, the air
Is gold.

        When you
Split the fig, you will see
Lifting from the coarse and purple seed, its
Flesh like flame, purer
20 Than blood.

        It fills
The darkening room with light.

III. Natural History

Many have died here, but few
Have names, it is like the world, bodies
Have been eaten by dogs, gulls, rodents, ants,
And fish, and Messire Jean le Maingre,
He struck them, and they fled.

             Et les Sarrasins
se retirèrent en une ile qui est devant
le dict chastel—

        but little good that, for
The *Maréchal* was hot on them, and

                  des leurs
y perdirent plus de quatre cent hommes,
10 *que morts, que affolez,*

*

and the root
Of the laurel has profited, the leaf
Of the live-oak achieves a new luster, the mouth
Of the mullet is agape, and my ten-year-old son,
In the island dump, finds a helmet, Nazi—from left
To right, entering at the temple, small and
Perfectly round at the point of entry, neat, but
At egress large, raw, exploding outward, desperate for
Light, air, and openness after
The hot enclosure and intense dark of
20   That brief transit: this
The track of the missile. Death
Came quick, for history,
Like nature, may have mercy,
Though only by accident. Neither
Has tears.

            But at dusk
From the next island, from its pad at
Le centre de recherche d'engins spéciaux, the rocket
Rises, the track of fume now feathers white—spins out, oh whiter—
Rises beyond the earth's shadow, in
30   Full light aspires. Then,
With no sound, the expected explosion. The glitters
Of flame fall, like shreds of bright foil, ice-bright, from
A Christmas tree, die in earth's shadow, but
The feathers of fume yet hang high, dissolve
White in that last light. The technicians
Now go to dinner.

            Beauty
Is the fume-track of necessity. This thought
Is therapeutic.

            If, after several
Applications, you do not find
40   Relief, consult your family physician.

IV. Riddle in the Garden

My mind is intact, but the shapes
of the world change, the peach
has released the bough and at last
makes full confession, its *pudeur*
has departed like peach-fuzz wiped off, and

*

We now know how the hot sweet-
ness of flesh and the juice-dark hug
the rough peach-pit, we know its most
suicidal yearnings, it wants
10   to suffer extremely, it

Loves God, and I warn you, do not
touch that plum, it will burn you, a blister
will be on your finger, and you will
put the finger to your lips for relief—oh, do
be careful not to break that soft

Gray bulge of blister like fruit-skin, for
exposing that inwardness will
increase your pain, for you
are part of the world. You think
20   I am speaking in riddles. But I am not, for

The world means only itself.

V. Paul Valéry Stood on the Cliff And
Confronted the Furious Energies of Nature

Where dust gritty as
        Hot sand was hurled by
        Sea-wind on the cliff-track
        To burnish the holly-leaf, he

Walked, and white the far sail
        Heeled off from windward, and white
        Cat's paws up the channel flicked.
        He paused to look, and far down,

Surf, on the Pointe du Cognet,
10   Boomed, and clawed white,
        Like vine incessant, up
        That glitter and lattice of air.

Far down, far down, below
        The stone where his foot hung, a gull
        Wheeled white in the flame of
        Air. The white wing scythed

The bright stalks of altitude
        Down, they were cut at the root,
        And the sky keeps falling down,
20   Forever it falls down with

*

A clatter like glass, or delight,
  And his head, like a drum, throbs,
  His eyes, they fly away,
  They scream like gulls, and

Over Africa burn all night,
  But Time is not time, therefore
  His breath stops in his throat
  And he stands on the cliff, his white

Panama hat in hand,
30 For he is Monsieur le Poète,
  Paul Valéry is his name,
  On a promenade by the sea, so

He sways high against the blue sky,
  While in the bright intricacies
  Of wind, his mind, like a leaf,
  Turns. In the sun, it glitters.

VI. Treasure Hunt

Hunt, hunt again. If you do not find it, you
Will die. But I tell you this much, it
Is not under the stone at the foot
Of the garden, nor by the wall at the fig tree.
I tell you this much to save you trouble, for I
Have looked, I know. But hurry, for

The terror is, all promises are kept.

Even happiness.

VII. Myth on Mediterranean Beach: Aphrodite as Logos

From left to right, she leads the eye
Across the blaze-brightness of sea and sky

That is the background of her transit.

Commanded thus, from left to right,
As by a line of print on that bright

Blankness, the eye will follow, but

*

There is no line, the eye follows only
That one word moving, it moves in lonely

And absolute arrogance across the blank

10 Page of the world, the word burns, she is
The word, all faces turn. Look!—this

Is what she is: old hunchback in bikini.

A contraption of angles and bulges, an old
Robot with pince-nez and hair dyed gold,

She heaves along beneath the hump.

The breasts hang down like saddle-bags,
To balance the hump the belly sags,

And under the belly-bulge, the flowers

Of the gee-string garland the private parts.
20 She grinds along by fits and starts

Beside the margin of the sea,

Past children and sand-castles and
The lovers strewn along the sand.

Her pince-nez glitter like contempt

For all delusion, and the French lad
Who exhibitionistically had

Been fondling the American college girl

Loses his interest. Ignoring him,
The hunchback stares at the horizon rim,

30 Then slowly, as compulsion grows,

She foots the first frail lace of foam
That is the threshold of her lost home,

And moved by memory in the blood,

Enters that vast indifferency
Of perfection that we call the sea.

How long, how long, she lingers there

She may not know, somnambulist
In that realm where no Time may subsist,

*

But in the end will again feel

40 The need to rise and re-enact
The miracle of the human fact.

She lifts her head, looks toward the shore.

She moves toward us, abstract and slow,
And watching, we feel the slow knowledge grow—

How from the breasts the sea recedes,

How the great-gashed navel's cup
Pours forth the ichor that had filled it up.

How the wavelets sink to seek, and seek,

Then languishing, sink to lave the knees,
50 And lower, to kiss the feet, as these

Find the firm ground where they must go.

The last foam crisps about the feet.
She shivers, smiles. She stands complete

In Botticellian parody.

Bearing her luck upon her back,
She turns now to take the lifeward track,

And lover by lover, on she moves

Toward her own truth, and does not stop.
Each foot stumps flat with the big toe up,

60 But under the heel, the damp-packed sand,

With that compression, like glory glows,
And glory attends her as she goes.

In rapture now she heaves along,

The pince-nez glitter at her eyes,
The flowers wreathe her moving thighs,

For she treads the track the blessèd know

To a shore far lonelier than this
Where waits her apotheosis.

She passes the lovers, one by one,

70 And passing, draws their dreams away,
And leaves them naked to the day.

VIII. The Ivy

The ivy assaults the wall. The ivy
    says: "I will pull you down." Time
    is nothing to the ivy. The ivy

Does not sweat at night, for like the sea
    it dreams a single dream, it
    is its own dream. Therefore,

Peace is the dream's name. The wall
    is stone, and all night the stone,
    where no stars may come, dreams.

10 Night comes. You sleep. What is your dream?

IX. Where Purples Now the Fig

Where purples now the fig, flame in
    Its inmost flesh, a leaf hangs
    Down, and on it, gull-droppings, white
    As chalk, show, for the sun has

Burned all white, for the sun, it would
    Burn our bones to chalk—yes, keep
    Them covered, oh flesh, oh sweet
    Integument, oh frail, depart not

And leave me thus exposed, like Truth.

X. The Red Mullet

The fig flames inward on the bough, and I,
Deep where the great mullet, red, lounges in
Black shadow of the shoal, have come. Where no light may

Come, he the great one, like flame, burns, and I
Have met him, eye to eye, the lower jaw horn,
Outthrust, arched down at the corners, merciless as

Genghis, motionless and mogul, and the eye of
The mullet is round, bulging, ringed like a target
In gold, vision is armor, he sees and does not

10 Forgive. The mullet has looked me in the eye, and forgiven
Nothing. At night I fear suffocation, is there
Enough air in the world for us all, therefore I

*

Swim much, dive deep to develop my lung-case, I am
Familiar with the agony of will in the deep place. Blood
Thickens as oxygen fails. Oh, mullet, thy flame

Burns in the shadow of the black shoal.

XI. A Place Where Nothing Is

I have been in a place where
nothing is, it is not
silence, for there are voices, not
emptiness, for there is
a great fullness, it is
populated with nothingness, nothing-
ness presses on the ribs like
elbows angry, and the lump
of nothingness sticks
10 in the throat like the hard
phlegm, and if, in that dark,
you cough, there is, in that
land of nothingness, no
echo, for the dark has
no walls, or if there is echo,
it is, whatever the original
sound, a laugh. A lamp
by each bed burns, but
gives no light.

         Earlier,
20 I have warned you not to look
too long at the brightness of
the sea, but now—yes—
I retract my words, for
the brightness of that nothing-
ness which is the sea is
not nothingness, but is
like the inestimable sea of

Nothingness Plotinus dreamed.

XII. Masts at Dawn

Past second cock-crow yacht masts in the harbor go slowly white.

No light in the east yet, but the stars show a certain fatigue.
They withdraw into a new distance, have discovered our unworthiness. It is
    long since

The owl, in the dark eucalyptus, dire and melodious, last called, and

Long since the moon sank and the English
Finished fornicating in their ketches. In the evening there was a strong swell.

Red died the sun, but at dark wind rose easterly, white sea nagged the black
    harbor headland.

When there is a strong swell, you may, if you surrender to it, experience
A sense, in the act, of mystic unity with that rhythm. Your peace is the sea's
    will.

10 But now no motion, the bay-face is glossy in darkness, like

An old window pane flat on black ground by the wall, near the ash heap. It
    neither
Receives nor gives light. Now is the hour when the sea

Sinks into meditation. It doubts its own mission. The drowned cat

That on the evening swell had kept nudging the piles of the pier and had
    seemed
To want to climb out and lick itself dry, now floats free. On that surface a slight
    convexity only, it is like

An eyelid, in darkness, closed. You must learn to accept the kiss of fate, for

The masts go white slow, as light, like dew, from darkness
Condensed on them, on oiled wood, on metal. Dew whitens in darkness.

I lie in my bed and think how, in darkness, the masts go white.

20 The sound of the engine of the first fishing dory dies seaward. Soon
In the inland glen wakes the dawn-dove. We must try

To love so well the world that we may believe, in the end, in God.

XIII. The Leaf

[A]

Here the fig lets down the leaf, the leaf
Of the fig five fingers has, the fingers
Are broad, spatulate, stupid,
Ill-formed, and innocent—but of a hand, and the hand,

To hide me from the blaze of the wide world, drops,
Shamefast, down. I am
What is to be concealed. I lurk
In the shadow of the fig. Stop.
Go no further. This is the place.

10 To this spot I bring my grief.
Human grief is the obscenity to be hidden by the leaf.

[B]

We have undergone ourselves, therefore
What more is to be done for Truth's sake? I

Have watched the deployment of ants, I
Have conferred with the flaming mullet in a deep place.

Near the nesting place of the hawk, among
Snag-rock, high on the cliff, I have seen
The clutter of annual bones, of hare, vole, bird, white
As chalk from sun and season, frail
As the dry grass stem. On that

10 High place of stone I have lain down, the sun
Beat, the small exacerbation
Of dry bones was what my back, shirtless and bare, knew. I saw

The hawk shudder in the high sky, he shudders
To hold position in the blazing wind, in relation to
The firmament, he shudders and the world is a metaphor, his eye
Sees, white, the flicker of hare-scut, the movement of vole.

Distance is nothing, there is no solution, I
Have opened my mouth to the wind of the world like wine, I wanted
To taste what the world is, wind dried up

20 The live saliva of my tongue, my tongue
Was like a dry leaf in my mouth.

Destiny is what you experience, that
Is its name and definition, and is your name, for

The wide world lets down the hand in shame:
Here is the human shadow, there, of the wide world, the flame.

[C]

The world is fruitful. In this heat
The plum, black yet bough-bound, bursts, and the gold ooze is,
Of bees, joy, the gold ooze has striven
Outward, it wants again to be of
The goldness of air and—blessèdly—innocent. The grape
Weakens at the juncture of the stem. The world

Is fruitful, and I, too,
In that I am the father
Of my father's father's father. I,
10 Of my father, have set the teeth on edge. But
By what grape? I have cried out in the night.

From a further garden, from the shade of another tree,
My father's voice, in the moment when the cicada ceases, has called to me.

[D]

The voice blesses me for the only
Gift I have given: *teeth set on edge.*

In the momentary silence of the cicada,
I can hear the appalling speed,
In space beyond stars, of
Light. It is

A sound like wind.

Audubon: A Vision

To Allen and Helen Tate

Thou tellest my wanderings: put thou my tears into thy bottle: are they not in thy book?

Psalm 56:8

I caught at his strict shadow and the shadow
released itself with neither haste nor anger. But
he remained silent.

Carlos Drummond de Andrade:
"Travelling in the Family"
Translated by Elizabeth Bishop

Jean Jacques Audubon, whose name was anglicized when, in his youth, he was sent to America, was early instructed in the official version of his identity: that he was the son of the sea captain Jean Audubon and a first wife, who died shortly after his birth in Santo Domingo, and that the woman who brought him up in France was a second wife. Actually, he was the son of Jean Audubon and his mistress during the period when Jean Audubon was a merchant and slave-dealer in Santo Domingo, and the woman who raised him was the wife his father had left behind him in France while he was off making his fortune. By the age of ten Audubon knew the true story, but prompted, it would seem, by a variety of impulses, including some sound practical ones, he encouraged the other version, along with a number of flattering embellishments. He was, indeed, a fantasist of talent, but even without his help, legends accreted about him. The most famous one—that he was the lost Dauphin of France, the son of the feckless Louis XVI and Marie Antoinette—did not, in fact, enter the picture until after his death, in 1851.

Audubon: A Vision

I. Was Not the Lost Dauphin

[A]

Was not the lost dauphin, though handsome was only
Base-born and not even able
To make a decent living, was only
Himself, Jean Jacques, and his passion—what
Is man but his passion?

        Saw,
Eastward and over the cypress swamp, the dawn,
Redder than meat, break;
And the large bird,
Long neck outthrust, wings crooked to scull air, moved
10 In a slow calligraphy, crank, flat, and black against
The color of God's blood spilt, as though
Pulled by a string.

        Saw
It proceed across the inflamed distance.

Moccasins set in hoar frost, eyes fixed on the bird,
Thought: "On that sky it is black."
Thought: "In my mind it is white."
Thinking: "*Ardea occidentalis,* heron, the great one."

Dawn: his heart shook in the tension of the world.

Dawn: and what is your passion?

[B]

October: and the bear,
Daft in the honey-light, yawns.

The bear's tongue, pink as a baby's, out-crisps to the curled tip,
It bleeds the black blood of the blueberry.

The teeth are more importantly white
Than has ever been imagined.

The bear feels his own fat
Sweeten, like a drowse, deep to the bone.

Bemused, above the fume of ruined blueberries,
10 The last bee hums.

*

The wings, like mica, glint
In the sunlight.

He leans on his gun. Thinks
How thin is the membrane between himself and the world.

II. The Dream He Never Knew the End Of
[A]

Shank-end of day, spit of snow, the call,
A crow, sweet in distance, then sudden
The clearing: among stumps, ruined cornstalks yet standing, the spot
Like a wound rubbed raw in the vast pelt of the forest. There
Is the cabin, a huddle of logs with no calculation or craft:
The human filth, the human hope.

                    Smoke,
From the mud-and-stick chimney, in that air, greasily
Brims, cannot lift, bellies the ridgepole, ravels
White, thin, down the shakes, like sputum.

                    He stands,
10 Leans on his gun, stares at the smoke, thinks: "Punk-wood."
Thinks: "Dead-fall half-rotten." Too sloven,
That is, to even set axe to clean wood.

                    His foot,
On the trod mire by the door, crackles
The night-ice already there forming. His hand
Lifts, hangs. In imagination, his nostrils already
Know the stench of that lair beyond
The door-puncheons. The dog
Presses its head against his knee. The hand
Strikes wood. No answer. He halloos. Then the voice.

[B]

What should he recognize? The nameless face
In the dream of some pre-dawn cock-crow—about to say what,
Do what? The dregs
Of all nightmare are the same, and we call it
Life. He knows that much, being a man,
And knows that the dregs of all life are nightmare.

Unless.

Unless what?

[C]

The face, in the air, hangs. Large,
Raw-hewn, strong-beaked, the haired mole
Near the nose, to the left, and the left side by firelight
Glazed red, the right in shadow, and under the tumble and tangle
Of dark hair on that head, and under the coarse eyebrows,
The eyes, dark, glint as from the unspecifiable
Darkness of a cave. It is a woman.

She is tall, taller than he.
Against the gray skirt, her hands hang.

10 "Ye wants to spend the night? Kin ye pay?
Well, mought as well stay then, done got one a-ready,
And leastwise, ye don't stink like no Injun."

[D]

The Indian,
Hunched by the hearth, lifts his head, looks up, but
From one eye only, the other
An aperture below which blood and mucus hang, thickening slow.

"Yeah, a arrow jounced back off his bowstring.
Durn fool—and him a Injun." She laughs.

                                         The Indian's head sinks.
So he turns, drops his pack in a corner on bearskin, props
The gun there. Comes back to the fire. Takes his watch out.
Draws it bright, on the thong-loop, from under his hunter's-frock.
10 It is gold, it lives in his hand in the firelight, and the woman's
Hand reaches out. She wants it. She hangs it about her neck.

And near it the great hands hover delicately
As though it might fall, they quiver like moth-wings, her eyes
Are fixed downward, as though in shyness, on that gleam, and her face
Is sweet in an outrage of sweetness, so that
His gut twists cold. He cannot bear what he sees.

Her body sways like a willow in spring wind. Like a girl.

The time comes to take back the watch. He takes it.
And as she, sullen and sunken, fixes the food, he becomes aware
20 That the live eye of the Indian is secretly on him, and soundlessly
The lips move, and when her back is turned, the Indian
Draws a finger, in delicious retardation, across his own throat.

*

After food, and scraps for his dog, he lies down:
In the corner, on bearskins, which are not well cured,
And stink, the gun by his side, primed and cocked.

Under his hand he feels the breathing of the dog.

The woman hulks by the fire. He hears the jug slosh.

[E]

The sons come in from the night, two, and are
The sons she would have. Through slit lids
He watches. Thinks: "Now."

                The sons
Hunker down by the fire, block the firelight, cram food
Into their large mouths, where teeth
Grind in hot darkness, their breathing
Is heavy like sleep, he wants to sleep, but
The head of the woman leans at them. The heads
Are together in firelight.

10 He hears the jug slosh.

              Then hears,
Like the whisper and *whish* of silk, that other
Sound, like a sound of sleep, but he does not
Know what it is. Then knows, for,
Against firelight, he sees the face of the woman
Lean over, and the lips purse sweet as to bestow a kiss, but
This is not true, and the great glob of spit
Hangs there, glittering, before she lets it fall.

The spit is what softens like silk the passage of steel
On the fine-grained stone. It whispers.

20 When she rises, she will hold it in her hand.

[F]

With no sound, she rises. She holds it in her hand.
Behind her the sons rise like shadow. The Indian
Snores. Or pretends to.

      He thinks: "Now."

                 And knows
He has entered the tale, knows
He has entered the dark hovel
In the forest where trees have eyes, knows it is the tale
They told him when he was a child, knows it
Is the dream he had in childhood but never
Knew the end of, only
10 The scream.

[G]

But no scream now, and under his hand
The dog lies taut, waiting. And he, too, knows
What he must do, do soon, and therefore
Does not understand why now a lassitude
Sweetens his limbs, or why, even in this moment
Of fear—or is it fear?—the saliva
In his mouth tastes sweet.

"Now, now!" the voice in his head cries out, but
Everything seems far away, and small.

10 He cannot think what guilt unmans him, or
Why he should find the punishment so precious.

It is too late. Oh, oh, the world!

Tell me the name of the world.

[H]

The door bursts open, and the travelers enter:
Three men, alert, strong, armed. And the Indian
Is on his feet, pointing.

           He thinks
That now he will never know the dream's ending.

[I]

Trussed up with thongs, all night they lie on the floor there.
The woman is gagged, for she had reviled them.
All night he hears the woman's difficult breath.

Dawn comes. It is gray. When he eats,
The cold corn pone grinds in his throat, like sand. It sticks there.

Even whiskey fails to remove it. It sticks there.

The leg-thongs are cut off the tied-ones. They are made to stand up.
The woman refuses the whiskey. Says: "What fer?"
The first son drinks. The other
10 Takes it into his mouth, but it will not go down.

The liquid drains, slow, from the slack of the mouth.

[J]

They stand there under the long, low bough of the great oak.
Eastward, low over the forest, the sun is nothing
But a circular blur of no irradiation, somewhat paler
Than the general grayness. Their legs
Are again bound with thongs.

They are asked if they want to pray now. But the woman:
"If'n it's God made folks, then who's to pray to?"
And then: "Or fer?" And bursts into laughing.

For a time it seems that she can never stop laughing.

10 But as for the sons, one prays, or tries to. And one
Merely blubbers. If the woman
Gives either a look, it is not
Pity, nor even contempt, only distance. She waits,

And is what she is,

And in the gray light of morning, he sees her face. Under
The tumbled darkness of hair, the face
Is white. Out of that whiteness
The dark eyes stare at nothing, or at
The nothingness that the gray sky, like Time, is, for
20 There is no Time, and the face
Is, he suddenly sees, beautiful as stone, and

So becomes aware that he is in the manly state.

[K]

The affair was not tidy: bough low, no drop, with the clients
Simply hung up, feet not much clear of the ground, but not
Quite close enough to permit any dancing.
The affair was not quick: both sons long jerking and farting, but she,
From the first, without motion, frozen
In a rage of will, an ecstasy of iron, as though
This was the dream that, lifelong, she had dreamed toward.

                                                    The face,
Eyes a-glare, jaws clenched, now glowing black with congestion
Like a plum, had achieved,
10 It seemed to him, a new dimension of beauty.

[L]

There are tears in his eyes.
He tries to remember his childhood.
He tries to remember his wife.
He can remember nothing.

His throat is parched. His right hand,
Under the deerskin frock, has been clutching the gold watch.

The magic of that object had been,
In the secret order of the world, denied her who now hangs there.

He thinks: "What has been denied me?"
10 Thinks: "There is never an answer."

Thinks: "The question is the only answer."

He yearns to be able to frame a definition of joy.

[M]

And so stood alone, for the travelers
Had disappeared into the forest and into
Whatever selves they were, and the Indian,
Now bearing the gift of a gun that had belonged to the hanged-ones,
Was long since gone, like smoke fading into the forest,
And below the blank and unforgiving eye-hole
The blood and mucus had long since dried.

He thought: "I must go."

*

                              But could not, staring
        At the face, and stood for a time even after
10   The first snowflakes, in idiotic benignity,
        Had fallen. Far off, in the forest and falling snow,
        A crow was calling.

                              So stirs, knowing now
        He will not be here when snow
        Drifts into the open door of the cabin, or,
        Descending the chimney, mantles thinly
        Dead ashes on the hearth, nor when snow thatches
        These heads with white, like wisdom, nor ever will he
        Hear the infinitesimal stridor of the frozen rope
        As wind shifts its burden, or when

20   The weight of the crow first comes to rest on a rigid shoulder.

III. We Are Only Ourselves

We never know what we have lost, or what we have found.
We are only ourselves, and that promise.
Continue to walk in the world. Yes, love it!

He continued to walk in the world.

IV. The Sign Whereby He Knew
[A]

His life, at the end, seemed—even the anguish—simple.
Simple, at least, in that it had to be,
Simply, what it was, as he was,
In the end, himself and not what
He had known he ought to be. The blessedness!—

To wake in some dawn and see,
As though down a rifle barrel, lined up
Like sights, the self that was, the self that is, and there,
Far off but in range, completing that alignment, your fate.

10   Hold your breath, let the trigger-squeeze be slow and steady.

The quarry lifts, in the halo of gold leaves, its noble head.

This is not a dimension of Time.

[B]

In this season the waters shrink.

The spring is circular and surrounded by gold leaves
Which are fallen from the beech tree.

Not even a skitter-bug disturbs the gloss
Of the surface tension. The sky

Is reflected below in absolute clarity.
If you stare into the water you may know

That nothing disturbs the infinite blue of the sky.

[C]

Keep store, dandle babies, and at night nuzzle
The hazelnut-shaped sweet tits of Lucy, and
With the piratical mark-up of the frontier, get rich.

But you did not, being of weak character.

You saw, from the forest pond, already dark, the great trumpeter swan
Rise, in clangor, and fight up the steep air where,
At the height of last light, it glimmered, like white flame.

The definition of love being, as we know, complex,
We may say that he, after all, loved his wife.

10   The letter, from campfire, keelboat, or slum room in New Orleans,
Always ended, "God bless you, dear Lucy." After sunset,

Alone, he played his flute in the forest.

[D]

Listen! Stand very still and,
Far off, where shadow
Is undappled, you may hear

The tusked boar grumble in his ivy-slick.

Afterward, there is silence until
The jay, sudden as conscience, calls.

The call, in the infinite sunlight, is like
The thrill of the taste of—on the tongue—brass.

[E]

The world declares itself. That voice
Is vaulted in—oh, arch on arch—redundancy of joy, its end
Is its beginning, necessity
Blooms like a rose. Why,

Therefore, is truth the only thing that cannot
Be spoken?

It can only be enacted, and that in dream,
Or in the dream become, as though unconsciously, action, and he stood,

At dusk, in the street of the raw settlement, and saw
10 The first lamp lit behind a window, and did not know
What he was. Thought: "I do not know my own name."

He walked in the world. He was sometimes seen to stand
In perfect stillness, when no leaf stirred.

Tell us, dear God—tell us the sign
Whereby we may know the time has come.

V. The Sound of That Wind
[A]

He walked in the world. Knew the lust of the eye.

Wrote: "Ever since a Boy I have had an astonishing desire
            to see Much of the World and particularly
            to acquire a true knowledge of the Birds of North America."

He dreamed of hunting with Boone, from imagination painted his portrait.
He proved that the buzzard does not scent its repast, but sights it.
He looked in the eye of the wounded white-headed eagle.

Wrote: "... the Noble Fellow looked at his Ennemies
            with a Contemptible Eye."

10 At dusk he stood on a bluff, and the bellowing of buffalo
Was like distant ocean. He saw
Bones whiten the plain in the hot daylight.

He saw the Indian, and felt the splendor of God.

Wrote: "... for there I see the Man Naked from his
            hand and yet free from acquired Sorrow."

*

Below the salt, in rich houses, he sat, and knew insult.
In the lobbies and couloirs of greatness he dangled,
And was not unacquainted with contumely.

Wrote: "My Lovely Miss Pirrie of Oackley Passed by Me
20   this Morning, but did not remember how beautifull
                I had rendered her face once by Painting it
                at her Request with Pastelles."

Wrote: ". . . but thanks to My humble talents I can run
                the gantlet throu this World without her help."

And ran it, and ran undistracted by promise of ease,
Nor even the kind condescension of Daniel Webster.

Wrote: ". . . would give me a fat place was I willing to
                have one; but I love indepenn and piece more
                than humbug and money."

30 And proved same, but in the end, entered
On honor. Far, over the ocean, in the silken salons,
With hair worn long like a hunter's, eyes shining,
He whistled the bird-calls of his distant forest.

Wrote: ". . . in my sleep I continually dream of birds."

And in the end, entered into his earned house,
And slept in a bed, and with Lucy.

                                        But the fiddle
Soon lay on the shelf untouched, the mouthpiece
Of the flute was dry, and his brushes.

                                His mind
Was darkened, and his last joy
40 Was in the lullaby they sang him, in Spanish, at sunset.

He died, and was mourned, who had loved the world.

Who had written: ". . . a world which though wicked enough
                in all conscience is *perhaps* as good
                as worlds unknown."

[B]

So died in his bed, and
Night leaned, and now leans,
Off the Atlantic, and is on schedule.
Grass does not bend beneath that enormous weight
That with no sound sweeps westward. In the Mississippi,
On a mud bank, the wreck of a great tree, left
By flood, lies, the root-system and now-stubbed boughs
Lifting in darkness. It
Is white as bone. That whiteness
10 Is reflected in dark water, and a star
Thereby.

     Later,
In the shack of a sheep-herder, high above the Bitterroot,
The candle is blown out. No other
Light is visible.

The Northwest Orient plane, New York to Seattle, has passed, winking
       westward.

[C]

For everything there is a season.

But there is the dream
Of a season past all seasons.

In such a dream the wild-grape cluster,
High-hung, exposed in the gold light,
Unripening, ripens.

Stained, the lip with wetness gleams.

I see your lip, undrying, gleam in the bright wind.

I cannot hear the sound of that wind.

VI. Love and Knowledge

Their footless dance
Is of the beautiful liability of their nature.
Their eyes are round, boldly convex, bright as a jewel,
And merciless. They do not know
Compassion, and if they did,
We should not be worthy of it. They fly
In air that glitters like fluent crystal
And is hard as perfectly transparent iron, they cleave it
With no effort. They cry
10   In a tongue multitudinous, often like music.

He slew them, at surprising distances, with his gun.
Over a body held in his hand, his head was bowed low,
But not in grief.

He put them where they are, and there we see them:
In our imagination.

What is love?

One name for it is knowledge.

VII. Tell Me a Story
[A]

Long ago, in Kentucky, I, a boy, stood
By a dirt road, in first dark, and heard
The great geese hoot northward.

I could not see them, there being no moon
And the stars sparse. I heard them.

I did not know what was happening in my heart.

It was the season before the elderberry blooms,
Therefore they were going north.

The sound was passing northward.

[B]

Tell me a story.

In this century, and moment, of mania,
Tell me a story.

Make it a story of great distances, and starlight.

The name of the story will be Time,
But you must not pronounce its name.

Tell me a story of deep delight.

from Or Else

I. The Nature of a Mirror

The sky has murder in the eye, and I
Have murder in the heart, for I
Am only human.
We look at each other, the sky and I.
We understand each other, for

The solstice of summer has sagged, I stand
And wait. Virtue is rewarded, that
Is the nightmare, and I must tell you

That soon now, even before
10 The change from Daylight Saving Time, the sun,
Beyond the western ridge of black-burnt pine stubs like
A snaggery of rotten shark teeth, sinks
Lower, larger, more blank, and redder than
A mother's rage, as though
F.D.R. had never run for office even, or the first vagina
Had not had the texture of dream. Time

Is the mirror into which you stare.

II. Natural History

In the rain the naked old father is dancing, he will get wet.
The rain is sparse, but he cannot dodge all the drops.

He is singing a song, but the language is strange to me.

The mother is counting her money like mad, in the sunshine.
Like shuttles her fingers fly, and the sum is clearly astronomical.

Her breath is sweet as bruised violets, and her smile sways like daffodils
           reflected in a brook.

The song of the father tells how at last he understands.
That is why the language is strange to me.

*

That is why clocks all over the continent have stopped.

10 The money the naked old mother counts is her golden memories of love.
That is why I see nothing in her maniacally busy fingers.

That is why all flights have been canceled out of Kennedy.

As much as I hate to, I must summon the police.
For their own good, as well as that of society, they must be put under
          surveillance.

They must learn to stay in their graves. That is what graves are for.

III. Time as Hypnosis

For I. A. Richards

White, white in that dawnlight, the world was exploding, white
Light bursting from whiteness. What
Is the name of the world?—for

Whiteness, all night from the black sky unfeathering,
Had changed the world's name, and maybe
My own, or maybe it was all only
A dream I was having, but did not
Know it, or maybe the truth was that I,
Huddling tight in the blankets and darkness and self,
10   Was nothing, was nothing but what
The snow dreamed all night. Then light:

Two years and no snow in our section, and two years
Is a long time when you are twelve. So,

All day in a landscape that had been
Brown fields and black woods but was now
White emptiness and arches,
I wandered. The white light
Filled all the vertiginous sky, and even
My head until it
20   Spread bright and wide like another sky under which I
Wandered. I came
To a place where the woods were, stood under
A crazed geometry of boughs black but
Snow-laden and criss-crossed with light, and between
Banks of humped snow and whiteness of ice-fret, saw
Black water slide slow, and glossy as sleep.

*

I stared at the water, and staring, wondered
What the white-bellied minnow, now deep in
Black leaf-muck and mud, thought.
30 I thought of the muskrat dim in his mud-gloom.

Have you ever seen how delicately
Etched the print of the field mouse's foot in fresh snow is?
I saw the tracks. But suddenly, none. Nothing
But the wing-flurried snow. Then, small as a pin-head, the single
Bright-frozen, red bead of a blood-drop. Have you ever
Stared into the owl's eyes? They blink slow, then burn:
Burn gold in the dark inner core of the snow-shrouded cedar.

There was a great field that tilted
Its whiteness up to the line where the slant, blue knife-edge of sky
40 Cut it off. I stood
In the middle of that space. I looked back, saw
My own tracks march at me. Mercilessly,
They came at me and did not stop. Ahead,
Was the blankness of white. Up it rose. Then the sky.

Evening came, and I sat by the fire, and the flame danced.

All day, I had wandered in the glittering metaphor
For which I could find no referent.

All night, that night, asleep, I would wander, lost in a dream
That was only what the snow dreamed.

IV. Blow, West Wind

I know, I know—though the evidence
Is lost, and the last who might speak are dead.
Blow, west wind, blow, and the evidence, O,

Is lost, and wind shakes the cedar, and O,
I know how the kestrel hung over Wyoming,
Breast reddened in sunset, and O, the cedar

Shakes, and I know how cold
Was the sweat on my father's mouth, dead.
Blow, west wind, blow, shake the cedar, I know

10 How once I, a boy, crouching at creekside,
Watched, in the sunlight, a handful of water
Drip, drip, from my hand. The drops—they were bright!

But you believe nothing, with the evidence lost.

Interjection #1:

Caveat

For John Crowe Ransom

Necessarily, we must think of the
world as continuous, for if it were
not so I would have told you, for I have
bled for this knowledge, and every man
is a sort of Jesus, but in any
case, if it were not so, you wouldn't know
you are in the world, or even that the
world exists at all—

              but only, oh, on-
ly, in discontinuity, do we
10 know that we exist, or that, in the deep-
est sense, the existence of anything
signifies more than the fact that it is
continuous with the world.

              A new high-
way is under construction. Crushed rock has
been spread for miles and rolled down. On Sunday,
when no one is there, go and stand on the
roadbed. It stretches before your eyes in-
to distance. But fix your eyes firmly on
one fragment of crushed rock. Now, it only
20 glows a little, inconspicuously
one might say. But soon, you will notice a
slight glittering. Then a marked vibration
sets in. You brush your hand across your eyes,
but, suddenly, the earth underfoot is
twitching. Then, remarkably, the bright sun
jerks like a spastic, and all things seem to
be spinning away from the univer-
sal center that the single fragment of
crushed rock has ineluctably become.

30 At this point, while there is still time and will,
I advise you to detach your gaze from
that fragment of rock. Not all witnesses
of the phenomenon survive unchanged
the moment when, at last, the object screams

in an ecstasy of

being.

V. I Am Dreaming of a White Christmas:
The Natural History of a Vision

For Andrew Vincent Corry

[1]

No, not that door—never! But,
Entering, saw. Through
Air brown as an old daguerreotype fading. Through
Air that, though dust to the tongue, yet—
Like the inward, brown-glimmering twilight of water—
Swayed. Through brown air, dust-dry, saw. Saw
It.

    The bed

        Where it had
Been. Now was. Of all
Covering stripped, the mattress
10 Bare but for old newspapers spread.
Curled edges. Yellow. On yellow paper dust,
The dust yellow. No! Do not.

           Do not lean to
Look at that date. Do not touch
That silken and yellow perfection of Time that
Dust is, for
There is no Time. I,
Entering, see.

      I,
Standing here, breathe the dry air

[2]

            See
Yonder the old Morris chair bought soon
After marriage, for him to rest after work in, the leather,
Once black, now browning, brown at the dry cracks, streaked
With a fungoid green. Approaching,
See.

    See it.

      The big head. Propped,
Erect on the chair's leather pillow, bald skin
Tight on skull, not white now, brown
Like old leather lacquered, the big nose

10 Brown-lacquered, bold-jutting yet, but with
Nostril-flanges gone tattered. I have not
Yet looked at the eyes. Not
Yet.

     The eyes
Are not there. But,
Not there, they stare at what
Is not there.

[3]

     Not there, but
In each of the appropriate twin apertures, which are
Deep and dark as a thumb-gouge,
Something that might be taken for
A mulberry, large and black-ripe long back, but
Now, with years, dust-dried. The mulberries,
Desiccated, each out of
Its dark lurking-place, stare out at
Nothing.

     His eyes
10 Had been blue.

[4]

     Hers brown. But
Are not now. Now staring,
She sits in the accustomed rocker, but with
No motion. I cannot
Be sure what color the dress once was, but
Am sure that the fabric now falls decisively away
From the Time-sharpened angle of knees. The fabric
Over one knee, the left, has given way. And
I see what protrudes.

     See it.

     Above,
10 The dry fabric droops over breastlessness.

Over the shrouded femurs that now are the lap, the hands,
Palm-down, lie. The nail of one forefinger
Is missing.

*

On the ring-finger of the left hand
There are two diamond rings. On that of the right,
One. On Sundays, and some evenings
When she sat with him, the diamonds would be on the fingers.

The rings. They shone.

Shine now.

In the brown air.

20 On the brown-lacquered face
There are now no
Lips to kiss with.

[5]

The eyes had been brown. But
Now are not where eyes had been. What things
Now are where eyes had been but
Now are not, stare. At the place where now
Is not what once they
Had stared at.

There is no fire, on the cold hearth now,
To stare at.

[6]

On
The ashes, gray, a piece of torn orange peel.
Foil wrappings of chocolates, silver and crimson and gold,
Yet gleaming from grayness. Torn Christmas paper,
Stamped green and red, holly and berries, not
Yet entirely consumed, but warped
And black-gnawed at edges. I feel
Nothing. A red
Ribbon, ripped long ago from some package of joy,
10 Winds over the gray hearth like
A fuse that failed. I feel
Nothing.

Not even
When I see the tree.

*

Why had I not seen the tree before?
Why, on entering, had I not seen it?
It must have been there, and for
A long time, for
The boughs are, of all green, long since denuded.
That much is clear. For the floor
20 Is there carpeted thick with the brown detritus of cedar.

Christmas trees in our section were always cedar.

[7]

Beneath the un-greened and brown-spiked tree,
On the dead-fall of brown frond-needles, are,
I see, three packages. Identical in size and shape.
In bright Christmas paper. Each with red bow, and under
The ribbon, a sprig of holly.

But look!

The holly

Is, clearly, fresh.

I say to myself:

The holly is fresh.

And

My breath comes short. For I am wondering
Which package is mine.

Oh, which?

10 I have stepped across the hearth and my hand stretches out.

But the voice:

No presents, son, till the little ones come.

[8]

What shadow of tongue, years back unfleshed, in what
Darkness locked in a rigid jaw, can lift and flex?

The man and the woman sit rigid. What had been
Eyes stare at the cold hearth, but I
Stare at the three chairs. Why—
Tell me why—had I not observed them before? For
They are here.

    The little red chair,
For the baby. The next biggest chair
For my little sister, the little red rocker. Then,
10 The biggest, my own, me the eldest.

The chairs are all empty.

      But
I am thinking a thought that is louder than words.
Thinking:

   They're empty, they're empty, but me—oh, I'm here!

And that thought is not words, but a roar like wind, or
The roar of the night-freight beating the rails of the trestle,
And you under the trestle, and the roar
Is nothing but darkness alive. Suddenly,
Silence.

   And no
Breath comes.

[9]

    Where I was,
Am not. Now am
Where the blunt crowd thrusts, nudges, jerks, jostles,
And the eye is inimical. Then,
Of a sudden, know:

    Times Square, the season
Late summer and the hour sunset, with fumes
In throat and smog-glitter at sky-height, where
A jet, silver and ectoplasmic, spooks through
The sustaining light, which
10 Is yellow as acid. Sweat,
Cold in arm-pit, slides down flesh.

 *

What year it is, I can't, for the life of me,
Guess, but know that,
Far off, south-eastward, in Bellevue,
In a bare room with windows barred, a woman,
Supine on an iron cot, legs spread, each ankle
Shackled to the cot-frame,
Screams.

She keeps on screaming because it is sunset.

20   Her hair has been hacked short.

[10]

Clerks now go home, night watchmen wake up, and the heart
Of the taxi-driver, just coming on shift,
Leaps with hope.

All is not in vain.

Old men come out from the hard-core movies.
They wish they had waited till later.

They stand on the pavement and stare up at the sky.
Their drawers are drying stiff at the crotch, and

The sky dies wide. The sky
10   Is far above the first hysteria of neon.

Soon they will want to go and get something to eat.

Meanwhile, down the big sluice of Broadway,
The steel logs jerk and plunge
Until caught in the rip, snarl, and eddy here before my face.

A mounted policeman sits a bay gelding. The rump
Of the animal gleams expensively. The policeman
Is some sort of dago. His jowls are swart.
His eyes are bright with seeing.

He is as beautiful as a law of chemistry.

[11]

In any case,
I stand here and think of snow falling. But am
Not here. Am
Otherwhere, for already,
This early and summer not over, in west Montana—
Or is it Idaho?—in
The Nez Perce Pass, tonight
It will be snowing.

The Nez Perce is more than 7,000 feet, and I
10   Have been there. The first flakes,
Large, soft, sparse, come straight down
And with enormous deliberation, white
Out of unbreathing blackness. Snow
Does not yet cling, but the tall stalk of bear-grass
Is pale in darkness. I have seen, long ago,
The paleness of bear-grass in darkness.

                                   But tell me, tell me,
Will I never know
What present there was in that package for me,
Under the Christmas tree?

[12]

All items listed above belong in the world
In which all things are continuous,
And are parts of the original dream which
I am now trying to discover the logic of. This
Is the process whereby pain of the past in its pastness
May be converted into the future tense

Of joy.

Interjection #2:
I Know a Place Where All is Real

For Austin Warren

I know a place where all is real. I
have been there, therefore
know. Access is not easy, the way
rough, and visibility extremely poor, especially
among the mountains. Maps
show only the blank space, somewhere
northwest of Mania and beyond Delight,
but if you can manage to elude the natives of
intervening zones, who practice
10   ghastly rites and have an appetite for human flesh,
you may find a sly track through
narrow and fog-laced passes. Meanwhile
give little credence to tales told
by returning travelers or those
who pretend to be such. But truth,
sometimes, is even more unacceptable
to the casual hearer, and in bars
I have been laughed at for reporting
the simple facts.

                    In any case,
20   few travelers do return.
Among those who choose to remain and apply
for naturalization, a certain number
find that they cannot stand the altitude, but these,
upon making their way out, sometimes die of an oppressive
pulmonary complaint as soon as they hit the low country.

VI. Chain Saw at Dawn in Vermont In Time of Drouth
1.

Dawn and, distant, the steel-snarl and lyric
Of the chain saw in deep woods:
I wake. Was it
Trunk-scream, bough-rip and swish, then earth-thud?
No—only the saw's song, the saw
Sings: *now!* Sings:
Now, now, now, in the
Lash and blood-lust of an eternal present, the present
Murders the past, the nerve shrieks, the saw

*

10 Sings *now,* and I wake, rising
    From that darkness of sleep which
    Is the past, and is
    The self. It is
    Myself, and I know how,
    Now far off,
    New light gilds the spruce-tops.
    The saw, for a moment, ceases, and under
    Arm-pits of the blue-shirted sawyer sweat
    Beads cold, and
20 In the obscene silence of the saw's cessation,
    A crow, somewhere, calls.

    The crow, in distance, calls with the crystalline beauty
    Of the outraged heart.

    Have I learned how to live?

        2.

    On the other side of the woods, in the village, a man
    Is dying. Wakes
    In dawn to the saw's song, thinks
    How his wife was a good wife, wonders
    Why his boy turned out bad, wonders why
    He himself never managed to pay off the mortgage, thinks
    Of dawn and the first light spangling the spruces, and how
    He leaned on the saw and the saw
    Sang. But had not known what
10 The saw sang. So now thinks:
    I have not learned how to die, but

    For that thought has no language, has only
    The saw's song, in distance: glee of steel and the
    Sun-shriek, the scream of castration, the whirl-tooth hysteria
    Of *now, now, now!* So
    Sweats. What

    Can I tell him? I
    Cannot tell him how to die because
    I have not learned how to live—what man
20 Has learned how to live?—and I lie

    In the dawn, and the thin sheet of summer
    Lies on me, and I close my eyes, for
    The saw sings, and I know
    That soon I must rise and go out in the world where
    The heel of the sun's foot smites horridly the hill,
    And the stalk of the beech leaf goes limp,
    And the bright brook goes gray among boulders,
    And the saw sings, for

    *

I must endeavor to learn what
30 I must learn before I must learn
The other thing. If
I learn even a little, I may,
By evening, be able
To tell the man something.

Or he himself may have learned by then.

VII. Small White House

The sun of July beats down on the small white house.
The pasture is brown-bright as brass, and like brass, sings with heat.
Halt! And I stand here, hills shudder, withdraw into distance,
Leprous with light. And a child's cry comes from the house.

Tell me, oh, where, in what state, did I see the small white house,
Which I see in my mind?—And the wax-wing's beak slices the blue
            cedar-berry,
Which is as blue as distance. The river, far off, shrinks
Among the hot boulders, no glister, looks dead as a discarded snake-skin
            rubbed off on stone. The house

Swims in that dazzle of no-Time. The child's cry comes from the house.

VIII. Forever O'Clock

[1]

A clock is getting ready to strike forever o'clock.
I do not know where the clock is, but it is somewhere.
I know it is somewhere, for I can hear it trying to make up its mind to strike.
Somewhere is the place where it is while it is trying to make up its mind.
The sound it makes trying to make up its mind is purely metaphysical.
The sound is one you hear in your bloodstream and not your ear.
You hear it the way a man tied to a post in the yard of the State Penitentiary of
            Utah
Could hear the mind of the Deputy Warden getting ready to say, "Fire!"
You hear it the way you hear your wife's breathing back in a dark room at
            home, when
You are away on a trip and wake up in some hotel bedroom, and do not know
            offhand where you are and do not know whose breath you do
10   hear there beside you.

[2]

The clock is taking time to make up its mind and that is why I have time
To think of some things that are not important but simply are.
A little two-year-old Negro girl-baby, with hair tied up in spindly little tits with
    strings of red rag,
Sits in the red-clay dust. Except for some kind of rag around her middle, she is
    naked, and black as a ripe plum in sunshine.
Behind the child is a gray board shack, and from the mud-chimney a twist of
    blue smoke is motionless against the blue sky.
The fields go on forever, and what had been planted there is not there now. The
    drouth does not see fit to stop even now.
The pin-oak in the yard has been dead for years. The boughs are black stubs
    against the blue sky.
Nothing alive is here but the child and a dominecker hen, flattened puff-belly
    down, under the non-shade of the pin-oak.

Inside the gray feathers, the body of the hen pants with heat.
The yellow beak of the hen is open, and the flattened string-thin tongue looks
10   black and dry and sharp as a pin.
The naked child with plum-black skin is intensely occupied.
From a rusted tin snuff can in the right hand, the child pours red dust over the
    spread fingers of the left hand held out prone in the bright air.
The child stares at the slow-falling red dust. Some red dust piles precariously
    up on the back of the little black fingers thrust out. Some does
    not.
The sun blazes down on the naked child in the mathematical center of the
    world. The sky glitters like brass.
A beat-up old 1931 Studebaker, of a kind you are too young ever to have seen,
    has recently passed down the dirt road, and a plume of red dust
    now trails it toward the horizon.
I watch the car that I know I am the man driving as it recedes into distance and
    approaches the horizon.

[3]

I have now put on record one thing that is not important but simply is.
I watch the beat-up old green Studebaker moving like a dot into distance
    trailing its red plume of dust toward the horizon.
I wonder if it will ever get there. The wondering throbs like a bruise inside my
    head.
Perhaps it throbs because I do not want to know the answer to my wondering.
The sun blazes down from the high center of the perfect concavity of sky. The
    sky glitters like brass.

A clock somewhere is trying to make up its mind to strike forever o'clock.

IX. Rattlesnake Country

For James Dickey

1.

Arid that country and high, anger of sun on the mountains, but
One little patch of cool lawn:

     Trucks
Had brought in rich loam. Stonework
Held it in place like a shelf, at one side backed
By the length of the house porch, at one end
By rock-fall. Above that, the mesquite, wolf-waiting. Its turn
Will, again, come.

    Meanwhile, wicker chairs, all day,
Follow the shimmering shade of the lone cottonwood, the way that
Time, sadly seeking to know its own nature, follows
10 The shadow on a sun-dial. All day,
The sprinkler ejects its misty rainbow.

     All day,
The sky shivers white with heat, the lake,
For its fifteen miles of distance, stretches
Tight under the white sky. It is stretched
Tight as a mystic drumhead. It glitters like neurosis.
You think it may scream, but nothing
Happens. Except that, bit by bit, the mountains
Get heavier all afternoon.

    One day,
When some secret, high drift of air comes eastward over the lake,
20 Ash, gray, sifts minutely down on
Our lunch-time ice cream. Which is vanilla, and white.

There is a forest fire on Mount Ti-Po-Ki, which
Is at the western end of the lake.

2.

If, after lunch, at God's hottest hour,
You make love, flesh, in that sweat-drench,
Slides on flesh slicker than grease. To grip
Is difficult.

*

   At drink-time,
The sun, over Ti-Po-Ki, sets
Lopsided, and redder than blood or bruised cinnabar, because of
The smoke there. Later,
If there is no moon, you can see the red eyes of fire
Wink at you from
10 The black mass of the mountain.

At night, in the dark room, not able to sleep, you
May think of the red eyes of fire that
Are winking from blackness. You may,
As I once did, rise up and go from the house. But,
When I got out, the moon had emerged from cloud, and I
Entered the lake. Swam miles out,
Toward moonset. Motionless,
Awash, metaphysically undone in that silvered and
Unbreathing medium, and beyond
20 Prayer or desire, saw
The moon, slow, swag down, like an old woman's belly.

Going back to the house, I gave the now-dark lawn a wide berth.

At night the rattlers come out from the rock-fall.
They lie on the damp grass for coolness.

   3.

I-yee!—
      and the wranglers, they cry on the mountain, and waking
At dawn-streak, I hear it.

               High on the mountain
I hear it, for snow-water there, snow long gone, yet seeps down
To green the raw edges and enclaves of forest
With a thin pasturage. The wranglers
Are driving our horses down, long before daylight, plunging
Through gloom of the pines, and in their joy
Cry out:

         I-yee!

         We ride this morning, and,
10 Now fumbling in shadow for *levis,* pulling my boots on, I hear
That thin cry of joy from the mountain, and what once I have,
Literally, seen, I now in my mind see, as I
Will, years later, in my mind, see it—the horsemen
Plunge through the pine-gloom, leaping
The deadfall—*I-yee!*—
Leaping the boulder—*I-yee!*— and their faces

Flee flickering white through the shadow—*I-yee!*—
And before them,
Down the trail and in dimness, the riderless horses,
20 Like quicksilver spilled in dark glimmer and roil, go
Pouring downward.
                    The wranglers cry out.

                              And nearer.

                                              But,
Before I go for my quick coffee-scald and to the corral,
I hear, much nearer, not far from my open window, a croupy
Gargle of laughter.

                    It is Laughing Boy.

    4.

Laughing Boy is the name that my host—and friend—gives his yard-hand.
Laughing Boy is Indian, or half, and has a hare-lip.
Sometimes, before words come, he utters a sound like croupy laughter.
When he utters that sound his face twists. Hence the name.

Laughing Boy wakes up at dawn, for somebody
Has to make sure the rattlers are gone before
The nurse brings my host's twin baby daughters out to the lawn.
Laughing Boy, who does not like rattlers, keeps a tin can
Of gasoline covered with a saucer on an outer ledge of the porch.
10 Big kitchen matches are in the saucer. This
At the porch-end toward the rock-fall.

The idea is: Sneak soft-foot round the porch-end,
There between rattlers and rock-fall, and as one whips past,
Douse him. This with the left hand, and
At the same instant, with the nail of the right thumb,
Snap a match alight.

                    The flame,
If timing is good, should, just as he makes his rock-hole,
Hit him.

The flame makes a sudden, soft, gaspy sound at
20 The hole-mouth, then dances there. The flame
Is spectral in sunlight, but flickers blue at its raw edge.

Laughing Boy has beautiful coordination, and sometimes
He gets a rattler. You are sure if
The soft, gasping sound and pale flame come before
The stub-buttoned tail has disappeared.

*

Whenever
Laughing Boy really gets a rattler, he makes that sound like
Croupy laughter. His face twists.

Once I get one myself. I see, actually, the stub-buttoned tail
Whip through pale flame down into earth-darkness.

30 "The son-of-a-bitch," I am yelling, "did you see me, I got him!"

I have gotten that stub-tailed son-of-a-bitch.

I look up at the sky. Already, that early, the sky shivers with whiteness.

5.

What was *is* is now *was*. But
Is *was* but a word for wisdom, its price? Some from
That long-lost summer are dead now, two of the girls then young,
Now after their pain and delusions, worthy endeavors and lies, are,
Long since, dead.

The third
Committed her first adultery the next year, her first lover
A creature odd for her choosing, he who
Liked poetry and had no ambition, and
She cried out in his arms, a new experience for her. But
10 There were the twins, and she had, of course,
Grown accustomed to money.

Her second,
A man of high social position, who kept a score-card. With her,
Not from passion this time, just snobbery. After that,
From boredom. Forgot, finally,
The whole business, took up horse-breeding, which
Filled her time and even, I heard, made unneeded money, and in
The old news photo I see her putting her mount to the jump.
Her yet beautiful figure is poised forward, bent elbows
Neat to her tight waist, face
20 Thrust into the cleansing wind of her passage, the face
Yet smooth as a girl's, no doubt from the scalpel
Of the plastic surgeon as well as
From her essential incapacity
For experience.

The husband, my friend,
Would, by this time, be totally cynical. The children
Have been a disappointment. He would have heavy jowls.
Perhaps he is, by this time, dead.

*

As for Laughing Boy, he wound up in the pen. Twenty years.
This for murder. Indians
30   Just ought to leave whiskey to the white folks.

I can't remember the names of the others who came there,
The casual weekend-ers. But remember

What I remember, but do not
Know what it all means, unless the meaning inheres in
The compulsion to try to convert what now is *was*
Back into what was *is.*

                    I remember
The need to enter the night-lake and swim out toward
The distant moonset. Remember
The blue-tattered flick of white flame at the rock-hole
40   In the instant before I lifted up
My eyes to the high sky that shivered in its hot whiteness.

And sometimes—usually at dawn—I remember the cry on the mountain.

All I can do is to offer my testimony.

X. Homage to Theodore Dreiser: Psychological Profile
On the Centennial of his Birth
(August 27, 1871)

Oh, the moon shines fair tonight along the Wabash,
From the fields there comes the breath of new mown hay.
Thro' the sycamores the candle lights are gleaming,
On the banks of the Wabash, far away.

The Refrain of "On the Banks of the Wabash, Far Away"
Words by Theodore Dreiser and Paul Dresser
Music by Paul Dresser

Who is the ugly one slump-slopping down the street?
Who is the chinless wonder with the potato-nose?
Can't you hear the soft *plop* of the pancake-shaped feet?

He floats, like Anchises' son, in the cloud of his fine new clothes,
Safe, safe at last, from the street's sneer, toward a queen who will fulfill
The fate devised him by Venus—but where, oh when! That is what he never
                    knows.

Born with one hand in his pants and one in the till,
He knows that the filth of self, to be loved, must be clad in glory,
So once stole twenty-five dollars to buy a new coat, and that is why still

*

10 The left eye keeps squinting backward—yes, history
Is gum-shoeing closer behind, with the constable-hand that clutches.
Watch his mouth, how it moves without sound, he is telling himself his own old
      story.

Full of screaming his soul is, and a stench like live flesh that scorches.
It's the screaming, and stench, of a horse-barn aflame,
And the great beasts rear and utter, their manes flare up like torches.

From lies, masturbation, vainglory, and shame,
He moves in his dream of ladies swan-necked, with asses ample and sweet,
But knows that no kiss heals his soul, it is always the same.

The same—but a brass band plays in the distance, and the midnight cricket,
20 Though thinly, asseverates his name. He seeks amid the day's traffic a sign—
Some horseshoe or hunchback or pin—that now, at last, at the end of this street

He will enter upon his reality: but enters only in-
To your gut, or your head, or your heart, to enhouse there and stay,
And in that hot darkness lie lolling and swell—like a tumor, perhaps benign.

May I present Mr. Dreiser? He will write a great novel, someday.

XI. Flaubert In Egypt

For Dorothea Tanning

Winterlong, off La Manche, wind leaning. Gray stones of the gray
    city sluiced by gray rain. And he dreamed

Of desert and distance, sunlight like murder, lust and new colors whose
    names exploded the spectrum like dynamite,
    or cancer. So went there,

Who did not know what he was, or could be, though hoping he might
    find there his fate. Found
    what he found: with head shaven,

One lock at the occiput left, red tarboosh wind-flaunted, rode hard at
10   the Sphinx, at the "Father of Terrors," which,
    in that perspective and distance, lifted slow from
    the desert, like a great ship from hull-down.
    At its height,
    it swung. His cry burst forth.

In the white-washed room, by the light of wicks in three oil-glasses and to
    the merciless *screak* of the rebec, with musicians
    blind-folded, the dancer, her breasts
    cruelly bound to bulge upward and bare, above
    pink trousers, flesh rippling in bronze, danced
20   the dance which

  *

He recalls from the oldest Greek vases—the leap on one foot with
　　　the free foot crossed over, the fingers
　　　aquiver, face calm, and
　　　slow centuries sifting like shadow. Light
　　　flickers on whitewash. He finds
　　　the *mons veneris* shaven, arse noble.
　　　That night three *coups,* and once
　　　performs cunnilingus. Fingers clutching her necklace,
　　　he lies. He remembers his boyhood. Her fingers
30　　　and naked thighs twitch in sleep.

By day, on the minaret-top, the stork clacked its beak. At the edge of
　　　the carrion-field, the wild dog,
　　　snout blue from old blood,
　　　skulked, and camel bells in the distance.
　　　On the voyage down-Nile, on the slave-boat, old women,
　　　black and slaves too, who had seen all of life, tried
　　　to persuade the young girls, market-bound,
　　　to smile. But once,

On the height of Gebel Abusir, looking down on the Cataract, where
40　　　the Nile flung itself to white froth on black granite, he
　　　cried out: "Eureka—the name, it is Emma!"
　　　And added: "Bovary." Pronouncing the *o,*
　　　as recorded by his companion, quite short.

So home, and left Egypt, which was: palms black, sky red, and the river
　　　like molten steel, and the child's hand
　　　plucking his sleeve—*"Baksheesh,*
　　　and I'll get you my mother to fuck"– and the bath-boy
　　　he buggered, this in a clinical spirit and as
　　　a tribute to the host-country. And the chancre, of course,
50　　　bright as a jewel on his member, and borne
　　　home like a trophy.

But not to be omitted: on the river at Thebes, having long stared
　　　at the indigo mountains of sunset, he let
　　　eyes fix on the motion of three wave-crests that,
　　　in unison, bowed beneath the wind, and his heart
　　　burst with a solemn thanksgiving to God for
　　　the fact he could perceive the worth of the
　　　world with such joy.

Years later, death near, he remembered the palm fronds—
60　　　how black against a bright sky!

XII. Vision Under the October Mountain:
A Love Poem

Golding from green, gorgeous the mountain
high hangs in gold air, how
can stone float, it is

the image of authority, of reality—or, is it?—floating
with no weight, and glows, did we
once in the womb dream, dream
a gold mountain in gold
air floating, we in the

pulse and warm slosh of
10 that unbreathing bouillon, lulled in
the sway of that sweet
syllogism—oh, unambiguous—swung
in the tide of that bliss unbreathed, bathed in
un-self which was self, did we
dream a gold mountain, did
it glow in that faceless unfatuous
dark, did
it glow in gold air in the airless
abstraction of dark, floating high
20 above our blind eyes with

no lashes yet, unbrined by grief yet, we
seeing nothing, but
what did we dream—a
gold mountain,
floating?

I want to understand the miracle
of your presence here by my side, your
gaze on the mountain. I want

to hear the whole story of how
30 you came here, with
particular emphasis on the development of

the human scheme of values.

XIII. Stargazing

The stars are only a backdrop for
The human condition, the stars
Are brilliant above the black spruces,
And fall comes on. Wind

Does not move in the star-stillness, wind
Is afraid of itself, as you have been afraid in
Those moments when destruction and revelation
Have spat at each other like cats, and the mirror
Showed no breath, ha, ha, and the wind,

10 Far off in arctic starlight, is afraid
To breathe, and waits, huddled in
Sparse blackness of spruces, black glitter in starlight, in
A land, north, where snow already is, and waits:

And the girl is saying, "You do not look
At the stars," for I did not look at
The stars, for I know they are there, know
That if I look at the stars, I

Will have to live over again all I have lived
In the years I looked at stars and
20 Cried out, "O reality!" The stars
Love me. I love them. I wish they

Loved God, too. I truly wish that.

XIV. Little Boy and Lost Shoe

The little boy lost his shoe in the field.
Home he hobbled, not caring, with a stick whipping goldenrod.
Go find that shoe—I mean it, right now!
And he went, not now singing, and the field was big.

Under the sky he walked and the sky was big.
Sunlight touched the goldenrod, and yellowed his hair,
But the sun was low now, and oh, he should know
He must hurry to find that shoe, or the sun will be down.

Oh, hurry, boy, for the grass will be tall as a tree.
10 Hurry, for the moon has bled, but not like a heart, in pity.
Hurry, for time is money and the sun is low.
Yes, damn it, hurry, for shoes cost money, you know.

*

I don't know why you dawdle and do not hurry.
The mountains are leaning their heads together to watch.
How dilatory can a boy be, I ask you?

                                   Off in Wyoming,
The mountains lean. They watch. They know.

XV. Composition in Gold and Red-Gold

Between the event and the word, golden
The sunlight falls, between
The brown brook's braiding and the mountain it
Falls, in pitiless plenitude, and every leaf
On the ruined apple tree is gold, and the apples all
Gold, too, especially those

On the ground. The gold of apples
That have fallen flushes to flame, but
Gold is the flame. Gold
10 Goes red-gold—and the scene:

A chipmunk is under the apple tree, sits up
Among gold apples, is
Golden in gold light. The chipmunk
Wriggles its small black nose
In the still center of the world of light.

The hair of the little girl is as brown-gold as
Brook water braiding in sunlight.

The cat, crouching by the gray stone, is gold, too.
The tail of the cat, half-Persian, weaves from side to side,
20 In infinite luxury, gold plume
Of sea-weed in that tide of light.
That is a motion that puts
The world to sleep.

The eyes of the cat are gold, and

I want to sleep. But
The event: the tiny
Shriek unstitches the afternoon, the girl
Screams, the sky
Tingles crystalline like a struck wine glass, and you
30 Feel the salt thickening, like grit, in your secret blood. Afterward

*

There is a difference in the quality of silence.
Every leaf, gold, hangs motionless on the tree, but
There is a difference in the quality of
Motionlessness: unverbed, unverved, they
Hang. On the last day will the sun
Explode? Or simply get too tired?

The chipmunk lies gold among the apples.
It is prone and totally relaxed like ripe
Fruit fallen, and,
40   Upon closer inspection, you can see
The faint smear of flame-gold at the base
Of the skull. This effect
Completes the composition.

The little girl
Holds the cat in her arms,
Crooning, "Baby, oh, baby." She weeps under
The powerful flood of gold light.

Somewhere, in the shade of alders, a trout
Hangs steady, head against a current like ice.

50   The eagle I had earlier seen climbing
The light tall above the mountain is

Now beyond sight.

XVI. There's a Grandfather's Clock in the Hall

There's a grandfather's clock in the hall, watch it closely. The minute hand
            stands still, then it jumps, and in between jumps there is
            no-Time,
And you are a child again watching the reflection of early morning sunlight on
            the ceiling above your bed,

Or perhaps you are fifteen feet under water and holding your breath as you
            struggle with a rock-snagged anchor, or holding your breath just
            long enough for one more long, slow thrust to make the orgasm
            really intolerable,
Or you are wondering why you really do not give a damn, as they trundle you
            off to the operating room,

Or your mother is standing up to get married and is very pretty, and excited and
            is a virgin, and your heart overflows, and you watch her with
            tears in your eyes, or
She is the one in the hospital room and she is really dying.

*

They have taken out her false teeth, which are now in a tumbler on the bedside
        table, and you know that only the undertaker will ever put them
        back in.
You stand there and wonder if you will ever have to wear false teeth.

She is lying on her back, and God, is she ugly, and
With gum-flabby lips and each word a special problem, she is asking if it is a
        new suit that you are wearing.

You say yes and hate her uremic guts, for she has no right to make you hurt the
        way that question hurts.
You do not know why that question makes your heart hurt like a kick in the
        scrotum,

For you do not yet know that the question, in its murderous triviality, is the last
        thing she will ever say to you,
Nor know what baptism is occurring in a sod-roofed hut or hole on the
        night-swept steppes of Asia, and a million mouths, like ruined
        stars in darkness, make a rejoicing that howls like wind, or
        wolves,

Nor do you know the truth, which is: *Seize the nettle of innocence in both your*
        hands, for this is the only way, and every
Ulcer in love's lazaret may, like a dawn-stung gem, sing—or even burst into
        whoops of, perhaps, holiness.

But, in any case, watch the clock closely. Hold your breath and wait.
Nothing happens, nothing happens, then suddenly, quick as a wink, and slick as
        a mink's prick, Time thrusts through the time of no-Time.

XVII. Reading Late at Night, Thermometer Falling

[1]

The radiator's last hiss and steam-clang done, he,
Under the bare hundred-watt bulb that glares
Like revelation, blanket
Over knees, woolly gray bathrobe over shoulders, handkerchief
On great bald skull spread, glasses
Low on big nose, sits. The book
Is propped on the blanket.

                Thus—
But only in my mind's eye now:

                      and there, in the merciless
Glitter of starlight, the fields, mile
On mile over the county, stretch out and are
Crusted with ice which, whitely,
Answers the glitter of stars.

*

　　　　　　　　The mercury
Falls, the night is windless, mindless, and long, and somewhere,
Deep in the blackness of woods, the tendons
Of a massive oak bough snap with the sound of a
Pistol-shot.

　　　　　　A beam,
Somewhere in the colding house where he sits,
Groans. But his eyes do not lift. Who,
Long back, had said to me:

20　"When I was young I felt like I
Had to try to understand how things are, before I died."

[2]

But lived long.

　　　　　　Lived
Into that purity of being that may
Be had past all ambition and the frivolous hope, but who now
Lives only in my mind's eye,
　　　　　　　　though I

Cannot see what book is propped there under that forever
Marching gaze—Hume's *History of England,* Roosevelt's
Winning of the West, a Greek reader,
Now Greek to him and held in his hands like a prayer, or
Some college text book, or Freud on dreams, abandoned
10　By one of the children. Or, even,
Coke or Blackstone, books forbidding and blackbound, and once I,
Perhaps twelve then, found an old photograph:

　　　　　　　　　　a young man,
In black coat, high collar, and string tie, black, one hand out
To lie with authority on a big book (Coke or Blackstone?), eyes
Lifted into space.

　　　　And into the future.

　　　　　　　Which
Had not been the future. For the future
Was only his voice that, now sudden, said:

"Son, give me that!"

He took the photograph from my hand, said:

20　"Some kinds of foolishness a man is due to forget, son."

　*

Tore it across. Tore
Time, and all that Time had been, across. Threw it
Into the fire. Who,
Years later, would say:

"I reckon I was lucky enough to learn early that a man can be happy in his
              obligations."

Later, I found the poems. Not good.

[3]

The date on the photograph: 1890.

He was very young then. And poor.

Man lives by images. They
Lean at us from the world's wall, and Time's.

[4]

Night of the falling mercury, and ice-glitter.
Drouth-night of August and the horned insect booming
At the window-screen.

Ice-field, dusty road. distance flees.

And he sits there, and I think I hear
The faint click and grind of the brain as
It translates the perception of black marks on white paper into
Truth.

      Truth is all.

         We must love it.

And he loved it, who once said:

10 "It is terrible for a man to live and not know."

Every day he walked out to the cemetery to honor his dead.
That was truth, too.

[5]

Dear Father—Sir—the "Sir" being
The sometimes disturbed recollection
Of the time when you were big, and not dead, and I
Was little, and all boys, of that time and place, automatically
Said that to their fathers, and to any other grown man,
White of course, or damned well got their blocks
Knocked off.

        So, Sir, I,
Who certainly could never have addressed you on a matter
As important as this when you were not dead, now
10 Address you on it for the last time, even though
Not being, after all my previous and sometimes desperate efforts,
Sure what a son can ever say to a father, even
A dead one.

        Indecipherable passion and compulsion—well,
Wouldn't it be sad to see them, of whatever
Dark root, dwindle into mere
Self-indulgence, habit, tic of the mind, or
The picking of a scab. Reality
Is hard enough to come by, but even
In its absence we need not blaspheme
20 It.

   Not that
You ever could, God knows. Though I,
No doubt, have, and even now
Run the risk of doing so when I say
That I live in a profound, though
Painful, gratitude to you for what
You could not help but be: i.e., yourself.

Who, aged eighty, said:

"I've failed in a lot of things, but I don't think anybody can say that I didn't
        have guts."

Correct.

    And I,
30 In spite of my own ignorance and failures,
Have forgiven you all your virtues.

          Even your valor.

[6]

Who, aged eighty-six, fell to the floor,
Unconscious. Two days later,
Dead. Thus they discovered your precious secret:
A prostate big as a horse-apple. Cancer, of course.

No wonder you, who had not spent a day in bed,
Or uttered a single complaint, in the fifty years of my life,
Cried out at last.

You were entitled to that. It was only normal.

[7]

So disappeared.

        Simply not there.

                And the seasons,
Nerve-tingling heat or premonitory chill, swung
Through the year, the years swung,

                    and the past, great
Eater of dreams, secrets, and random data, and
Refrigerator of truth, moved
Down what green valley at a glacier's
Massive pace,

        moving
At a pace not to be calculated by the trivial sun, but by
A clock more unforgiving that, at
10 Its distance of mathematical nightmare,
Glows forever. The ice-mass, scabbed
By earth, boulders, and some strange vegetation, moves
So imperceptibly that it seems
Only more landscape.

        Until,
In late-leveling light, some lunkhead clodhopper,
The clodhopper me,
The day's work done, now trudging home,
Stops.

      Stares.

        And there it is.

           It looms.

*

The bulk of the unnamable and de-timed beast is now visible,
20 Erect, in the thinly glimmering shadow of now sun-thinned ice.

                                        Somehow yet

Alive.

        The lunkhead
Stares.

        The beast,
From his preternatural height, unaware of
The cringe and jaw-dropped awe crouching there below, suddenly,
As if that shimmer of ice-screen had not even been there, lifts,

Into distance,

                    the magisterial gaze.

        [8]

The mercury falls. Tonight snow is predicted. This,
However, is another country. Found in a common atlas

XVIII. Folly on Royal Street before the Raw Face of God

Drunk, drunk, drunk, amid the blaze of noon,
Irrevocably drunk, total eclipse or,
At least, almost, and in New Orleans once,
In French Town, spring,
Off the Gulf, without storm warnings out,
Burst, like a hurricane of
Camellias, sperm, cat-squalls, fish-smells, and the old
Pain of fulfillment-that-is-not-fulfillment, so
Down Royal Street—Sunday and the street
10 Blank as my bank account
With two checks bounced—we—
C. and M. and I, every
Man-jack skunk-drunk—
Came.

        A cat,
Gray from the purple shadow of bougainvillaea,
Fish-head in dainty jaw-clench,
Flowed fluid as thought, secret as sin, across
The street. Was gone. We,
In the shock of that sudden and glittering vacancy, rocked
20 On our heels.

    *

                        A cop,
Of brachycephalic head and garlic breath,
Toothpick from side of mouth and pants ass-bagged and holster low,
From eyes the color of old coffee grounds,
Regarded with imperfect sympathy
La condition humaine—
Which was sure-God what we were.

We rocked on our heels.

                        At sky-height—
Whiteness ablaze in dazzle and frazzle of light like
A match flame in noon-glare—a gull
30 Kept screaming above the doomed city.
It screamed for justice against the face of God.

Raw-ringed with glory like an ulcer, God's
Raw face stared down.

                        And winked.

                                        We
Mouthed out our Milton for magnificence.

For what is man without magnificence?

Delusion, delusion!

                        But let
Bells ring in all the churches.
Let likker, like philosophy, roar
In the skull. Passion
40 Is all. Even
The sleaziest.

                        War
Came. Among the bed-sheet Arabs, C.
Sported his gold oak leaf. Survived.
Got back. Back to the bank. But
One morning was not there. His books,
However, were in apple-pie order. His suits,
All dark, hung in the dark closet. Drawn up
In military precision, his black shoes,
Though highly polished, gave forth
50 No gleam in that darkness. In Mexico,
He died.

                For M.,
Twenty years in the Navy. Retired,
He fishes. Long before dawn, the launch slides out.
Land lost, he cuts the engine. The launch

Lifts, falls, in the time of the sea's slow breath.
Eastward, first light is like
A knife-edge honed to steel-brightness
And laid to the horizon. Sometimes,
He comes back in with no line wet.

60 As for the third, the tale
Is short. But long,
How long the art, and wisdom slow!—for him who
Once rocked on his heels, hearing the gull scream,
And quoted Milton amid the blaze of noon.

XIX. Sunset Walk in Thaw-Time in Vermont

1.

Rip, whoosh, wing-whistle: and out of
The spruce thicket, beating the snow from
Black spruce boughs, it
Bursts. The great partridge cock, black against flame-red,
Into the red sun of sunset, plunges. Is
Gone.

      In the ensuing
Silence, abrupt in
Back-flash and shiver of that sharp startlement, I
Stand. Stare. In mud-streaked snow,
10 My feet are. I,
Eyes fixed past black spruce boughs on the red west, hear,
In my chest, as from a dark cave of
No-Time, the heart
Beat.

      Where
Have the years gone?

2.

All day the stream, thaw-flooding, foamed down its gorge.
Now, skyless but for the high-tangled spruce night, it
Moves, and the bulge and slick twining of muscular water, foam-
Slashed and white-tettered, glints now only in
The cold, self-generating light of snow
Strong yet in the darkness of rock-banks.

*

　　　　　　　　　　　　　　　The boulder
Groans in the stream, the stream heaves
In the deep certainty of its joy, like
Doom, and I,
10　Eyes fixed yet on the red west, begin to hear—though
Slow and numb as upon waking—
The sound of water that moves in darkness.

I stand, and in my imagination see
The slick heave of water, blacker than basalt, and on it
The stern glint, like steel, of snow-darkness.

　　　3.

On the same spot in summer, at thrush-hour, I,
As the last light fails, have heard that full
Shadow-shimmered and deep-glinting liquidity, and
Again will; but not now.

　　　　　　　　　　Now
Here stare westward, and hear only
The movement of darkening water, and from
Whatever depth of being I am, ask
To be made worthy of my human failures and folly, and
Worthy of my human ignorance and anguish, and of
10　What soul-stillness may be achieved as I
Stand here with the cold exhalation of snow
Coiling high as my knees.

　　　　　　　　Meanwhile,
On the mountain's east hump, darkness coagulates, and
Already, where sun has not touched for hours, the new
Ice-crystal frames its massive geometry.

　　　4.

When my son is an old man, and I have not,
For some fifty years, seen his face, and, if seeing it,
Would not even be able to guess what name it wore, what
Blessing should I ask for him?

That some time, in thaw-season, at dusk, standing
At woodside and staring
Red-westward, with the sound of moving water
In his ears, he
Should thus, in that future moment, bless,
10　Forward into that future's future,
An old man who, as he is mine, had once
Been his small son.
　　　*

For what blessing may a man hope for but
An immortality in
The loving vigilance of death?

XX. Birth of Love

Season late, day late, sun just down, and the sky
Cold gunmetal but with a wash of live rose, and she,
From water the color of sky except where
Her motion has fractured it to shivering splinters of silver,
Rises. Stands on the raw grass. Against
The new-curdling night of spruces, nakedness
Glimmers and, at bosom and flank, drips
With fluent silver. The man,

Some ten strokes out, but now hanging
10   Motionless in the gunmetal water, feet
Cold with the coldness of depth, all
History dissolving from him, is
Nothing but an eye. Is an eye only. Sees

The body that is marked by his use, and Time's,
Rise, and in the abrupt and unsustaining element of air,
Sway, lean, grapple the pond-bank. Sees
How, with that posture of female awkwardness that is,
And is the stab of, suddenly perceived grace, breasts bulge down in
The pure curve of their weight and buttocks
20   Moon up and, in that swelling unity,
Are silver, and glimmer. Then

The body is erect, she is herself, whatever
Self she may be, and with an end of the towel grasped in each hand,
Slowly draws it back and forth across back and buttocks, but
With face lifted toward the high sky, where
The over-wash of rose color now fails. Fails, though no star
Yet throbs there. The towel, forgotten,
Does not move now. The gaze
Remains fixed on the sky. The body,

30   Profiled against the darkness of spruces, seems
To draw to itself, and condense in its whiteness, what light
In the sky yet lingers or, from
The metallic and abstract severity of water, lifts. The body,
With the towel now trailing loose from one hand, is
A white stalk from which the face flowers gravely toward the high sky.
This moment is non-sequential and absolute, and admits
Of no definition, for it
Subsumes all other, and sequential, moments, by which
Definition might be possible. The woman,

*

40 Face yet raised, wraps,
   With a motion as though standing in sleep,
   The towel about her body, under the breasts, and,
   Holding it there, hieratic as lost Egypt and erect,
   Moves up the path that, stair-steep, winds
   Into the clamber and tangle of growth. Beyond
   The lattice of dusk-dripping leaves, whiteness
   Dimly glimmers, goes. Glimmers and is gone, and the man,

   Suspended in his darkling medium, stares
   Upward where, though not visible, he knows
50 She moves, and in his heart he cries out that, if only
   He had such strength, he would put his hand forth
   And maintain it over her to guard, in all
   Her out-goings and in-comings, from whatever
   Inclemency of sky or slur of the world's weather
   Might ever be. In his heart
   He cries out. Above

   Height of the spruce-night and heave of the far mountain, he sees
   The first star pulse into being. It gleams there.

   I do not know what promise it makes to him.

XXI. A Problem in Spatial Composition
[1]

Through the high window, upright rectangle of distance:

Over the green interstices and shambling glory, yet bright, of forest,
Distance flees westward, the sun low.

Beyond the distance of forest, hangs that which is blue:
Which is, in knowledge, a tall scarp of stone, gray, but now is,
In the truth of perception, stacked like a mass of blue cumulus.
Blue deepens.

       What we know, we know, and
Sun now down, flame, above blue, dies upward forever in
Saffron: pure, pure and forever, the sky
10 Upward is. The lintel of the high window, by interruption,

Confirms what the heart knows: *beyond is forever—*

                  and nothing moves
Across the glister of saffron, and under the
Window the brook that,
After lalling and lounging daylong by shallow and reach,
Through dapple to glitter, now recessed in
Its premature leaf-night, utters a deeper-toned meditation.

[2]

While out of the green, up-shining ramshackle of leaf, set
In the lower right foreground, the stub
Of a great tree, gaunt-blasted and black, thrusts.

           A single
Arm jags upward, higher goes, and in that perspective, higher
Than even the dream-blue of distance that is
The mountain.

    Then
Stabs, black, at the infinite saffron of sky.

All is ready.

    The hawk,
Entering the composition at the upper left frame
10 Of the window, glides,
In the pellucid ease of thought and at
His breathless angle,
Down.

   Breaks speed.

      Hangs with a slight lift and hover.

           Makes contact.

The hawk perches on the topmost, indicative tip of
The bough's sharp black and skinny jag skyward.

[3]

The hawk, in an eyeblink, is gone.

from Can I See Arcturus From Where I Stand?

A Way to Love God

Here is the shadow of truth, for only the shadow is true.
And the line where the incoming swell from the sunset Pacific
First leans and staggers to break will tell all you need to know
About submarine geography, and your father's death rattle
Provides all biographical data required for the *Who's Who* of the dead.

I cannot recall what I started to tell you, but at least
I can say how night-long I have lain under stars and
Heard mountains moan in their sleep. By daylight,
They remember nothing, and go about their lawful occasions
10 Of not going anywhere except in slow disintegration. At night
They remember, however, that there is something they cannot remember,
So moan. Theirs is the perfected pain of conscience, that
Of forgetting the crime, and I hope you have not suffered it. I have.

I do not recall what had burdened my tongue, but urge you
To think on the slug's white belly, how sick-slick and soft,
On the hairiness of stars, silver, silver, while the silence
Blows like wind by, and on the sea's virgin bosom unveiled
To give suck to the wavering serpent of the moon; and,
In the distance, in *plaza, piazza, place, platz,* and square,
20 Boot heels, like history being born, on cobbles bang.

Everything seems an echo of something else.

And when, by the hair, the headsman held up the head
Of Mary of Scots, the lips kept on moving,
But without sound. The lips,
They were trying to say something very important.

But I had forgotten to mention an upland
Of wind-tortured stone white in darkness, and tall, but when
No wind, mist gathers, and once on the Sarré at midnight,
I watched the sheep huddling. Their eyes
30 Stared into nothingness. In that mist-diffused light their eyes
Were stupid and round like the eyes of fat fish in muddy water,
Or of a scholar who has lost faith in his calling.

*

Their jaws did not move. Shreds
Of dry grass, gray in gray mist-light, hung
From the side of a jaw, unmoving.

You would think that nothing would ever again happen.

That may be a way to love God.

Evening Hawk

From plane of light to plane, wings dipping through
Geometries and orchids that the sunset builds,
Out of the peak's black angularity of shadow, riding
The last tumultuous avalanche of
Light above pines and the guttural gorge,
The hawk comes.

       His wing
Scythes down another day, his motion
Is that of the honed steel-edge, we hear
The crashless fall of stalks of Time.

10   The head of each stalk is heavy with the gold of our error.

Look! look! he is climbing the last light
Who knows neither Time nor error, and under
Whose eye, unforgiving, the world, unforgiven, swings
Into shadow.

      Long now,
The last thrush is still, the last bat
Now cruises in his sharp hieroglyphics. His wisdom
Is ancient, too, and immense. The star
Is steady, like Plato, over the mountain.

If there were no wind we might, we think, hear
20 The earth grind on its axis, or history
Drip in darkness like a leaking pipe in the cellar.

Answer to Prayer

A Short Story That Could Be Longer

In that bad year, in a city to have now no name,
In the already-dark of a winter's day, our feet
Unsteady in slip-tilt and crunch of re-freezing snow as if lame,
And two hands ungloved to clasp closer though cold, down a side street

We moved. Ahead, intersecting, stretched the avenue where
Life clanged and flared like a gaudy disaster under
Whatever the high sky wombed in its dark imperative of air,
And where, to meat and drink set, we might soon pretend, or

At least hope, that sincerity could be bought by pain.
10 But now stopped. She said, "Wait!" And abrupt, was gone
Up the snow-smeared broad stone to dark doors before I could restrain
That sentimental idiocy. Alone,

As often before in a night-street, I raised eyes
To pierce what membrane remotely enclosed the great bubble of light that now
The city inflated against the dark hover of infinities,
And saw how a first frail wavering stipple of shadow

Emerged high in that spectral concavity of light, and drew down to be,
In the end, only snow. Then she, again there, to my question, replied
That she had made a prayer. And I: "For what?" And she:
"Nothing much, just for you to be happy." Then cocking her head to one
20   side,

Looked up and grinned at me, an impudent eye-sparkling grin, as though
She had just pulled the trick of the week, and on a cold-flushed
Cheek, at the edge of the grin for an accent, the single snow-
Flake settled, and gaily in insult she stuck her tongue out, and blood rushed

To my heart. So with hands again nakedly clasped, through the soft veil and
        swish
Of flakes falling, we moved toward the avenue. And later, proceeded,
Beyond swirl and chain-clank of traffic, and a siren's far anguish,
To the unlit room to enact what comfort body and heart needed.

Who does not know the savvy insanity and wit
30 Of history! and how its most savage peripeteia always
Has the shape of a joke—if you find the heart to laugh at it.
In such a world, then, one must be pretty careful how one prays.

Her prayer, yes, was answered, for in spite of my meager desert,
Of a sudden, life—it was bingo! was bells and all ringing like mad,
Lights flashing, fruit spinning, the machine spurting dollars like dirt—
Nevada dollars, that is—but all just a metaphor for the luck I now had.

*

But that was long later, and as answer to prayer long out
Of phase. And now thinking of her, I can know neither what, nor where,
She may be, and even in gratitude, I must doubt
40   That she ever remembers she ever prayed such a prayer.

Or if she remembers, she laughs into the emptiness of air.

Paradox

Running ahead beside the sea,
You turned and flung a smile, like spray.
It glittered like tossed spray in the sunlight.
Yes, well I remember, to this day,
That glittering ambiguity.

I saw, when your foot fulfilled its stride,
How the sand, compressed, burst to silver light,
But when I had reached that aureoled spot
There was only another in further flight:
10   And bright hair, wind-strung, to tease the sun's pride.

Yes, far away and long ago,
In another land, on another shore,
That race you won—even as it was lost,
For if I caught you, one moment more,
You had fled my grasp, up and to go

With glowing pace and the smile that mocks
Pursuit down whatever shore reflects
Our flickering passage through the years,
As we enact our more complex
20   Version of Zeno's paradox.

Midnight Outcry

Torn from the dream-life, torn from the life-dream,
Beside him in darkness, the cry bursts: *Oh!*
Endearment and protest—they avail
Nothing against whatever is so
Much deeper and darker than anything love may redeem.

He lies in the dark and tries to remember
How godlike to strive in passion and sweat,
But fears to awaken and clasp her, lest
Their whole life be lost, for he cannot forget
10   That the depths that cry rose from might shrivel a heart, or member.

*

How bright dawns morning!—how sweetly the face
Inclines over the infant to whom she gives suck.
So his heart leaps in joy, but remembering
That echo of fate beyond faith or luck,
He fixes his studious gaze on the scene to trace

In the least drop spilled between nipple and the ferocious
Little lip-suction, some logic, some white
Spore of the human condition that carries,
In whiteness, the dark need that only at night
20 Finds voice—one only and always strange to us.

The day wore on, and he would ponder,
Lifting eyes from his work, thinking, thinking,
Of the terrible distance in love, and the pain,
Smiling back at the sunlit smile, even while shrinking
From recall of the nocturnal timbre, and the dark wonder.

Old Nigger on One-Mule Cart Encountered Late at Night When Driving Home From Party in the Back Country

Flesh, of a sudden, gone nameless in music, flesh
Of the dancer, under your hand, flowing to music, girl-
Flesh sliding, flesh flowing, sweeter than
Honey, slicker than Essolube, over
The music-swayed, delicate trellis of bone
That is white in secret flesh-darkness. What
The music, it says: *no name, no name!*—only
That movement under your hand, what
It is, and no name, and you shut your eyes, but
10 The music, it stops. O.K. Silence
Rages, it ranges the world, it will
Devour us, for
That sound I do now hear is not external, is
Simply the crinkle and crepitation,
Like crickets gone nuts, of
Booze in the blood. *Goodnight! Goodnight!*

I can't now even remember the name of the dancer, but

I must try to tell you what, in July, in Louisiana,
Night is. No moon, but stars whitely outrageous in
20 Blackness of velvet, the long lane ahead
Whiter than snow, wheels soundless in deep dust, dust
Pluming whitely behind, and ahead all
The laneside hedges and weed-growth

Long since powdered whiter than star-dust, or frost, but air
Hot. The night pants hot like a dog, it breathes
Off the blossoming bayou like the expensive whiff
Of floral tributes at a gangster's funeral in N.O.,
It breathes the smell love makes in darkness, and far off,
In the great swamp, an owl cries,
30 And does not stop. At the sharp right turn,
Hedge-blind, which you take too fast,
There it is: death-trap.

On the fool-nigger, ass-hole wrong side of
The road, naturally: And the mule-head
Thrusts at us, and ablaze in our headlights,
Outstaring from primal bone-blankness and the arrogant
Stupidity of skull snatched there
From darkness and the saurian stew of pre-history.
For an instant—the eyes. The eyes,
40 They blaze from the incandescent magma
Of mule-brain. Thus mule-eyes. Then
Man-eyes, not blazing, white-bulging
In black face, in black night, and man-mouth
Wide open, the shape of an *O,* for the scream
That does not come. Even now,
That much in my imagination, I see. But also
The cargo of junk the black face blooms amidst—
Rusted bed-springs on end, auto axle at God-knows-what
Angle up-canted, barbed wire on a fence rail wound,
50 Lengths of stove pipe beat-up. God-yes,
A death-trap. But
I snatch the wheel left in a dust-skid,
Smack into the ditch, but the ditch
Shallow, and so, not missing a beat, I'm out
And go on, and he's left alone on his cart there
Unmoving, and dust of the car's passage settles
White on sweat-sticky skin, black, of the forehead, and on
The already gray head. This,
Of course, under the high stars.

60 Perhaps he had screamed, after all.

And go on: to the one last drink, sweat-grapple in darkness, then
Sleep. But only until
The hour when small, though disturbing, gastric shifts
Are experienced, the hour when the downy
Throat of the swamp owl vibrates to the last
Predawn cry, the hour
When joy-sweat, or night-sweat, has dried to a microscopic
Crust on the skin, and some
Recollection of childhood brings tears
70 To dark-wide eyes, and the super-ego
Again throws the switch for the old recorded harangue.

Until waking, that is—and I wake to see
Floating in darkness above the bed the
Black face, eyes white-bulging, mouth shaped like an *O,* and so
Get up, get paper and pencil, and whittle away at
The poem. Give up. Back to bed. And remember
Now only the couplet of what
Had aimed to be—Jesus Christ—a sonnet:
     One of those who gather junk and wire to use
80   For purposes that we cannot peruse.

As I said, Jesus Christ. But

Moved on through the years. Am here. Another
Land, another love, and in such latitude, having risen
In darkness, feet bare to cold boards, stare,
Through ice-glitter of glass and air purer
Than absolute zero, into
The white night and star-crackling sky over
The snow-mountain. Have you ever,
At night, stared into the snow-filled forest and felt
90 The impulse to flee there? Enter there? Be
There and plunge naked
Through snow, through drifts floundering, white
Into whiteness, among
Spectral great beech-boles, birch-whiteness, black jag
Of shadow, black spruce-bulks snow-shouldered, floundering
Upward and toward the glacial assertion that
The mountain is? Have you ever
Had the impulse to stretch forth your hand over
The bulge of forest and seize trees like the hair
100 Of a head you would master? Well,
We are entitled to our fantasies, for life
Is only the fantasy that has happened to us, and

In God's name. But

In the lyrical logic and nightmare astuteness that
Is God's name, by what magnet, I demand,
Are the iron and out-flung filings of our lives, on
A sheet of paper, blind-blank as Time, snapped
Into a polarized pattern—and I see,
By a bare field that yearns pale in starlight, the askew
110 Shack. He arrives there. Unhitches the mule.
Stakes it out. Between cart and shack,
Pauses to make water, and while
The soft, plopping sound in deep dust continues, his face
Is lifted into starlight, calm as prayer. He enters
The dark shack, and I see
A match spurt, then burn down, die.

*

The last glow is reflected on the petal-pink
And dark horn-crust of the thumbnail.

And so I say:
120 Brother, Rebuker, my Philosopher past all
Casuistry, will you be with me when
I arrive and leave my own cart of junk
Unfended from the storm of starlight and
The howl, like wind, of the world's monstrous blessedness,
To enter, by a bare field, a shack unlit?
Entering into that darkness to fumble
My way to a place to lie down, but holding,
I trust, in my hand, a name—
Like a shell, a dry flower, a worn stone, a toy—merely
130 A hard-won something that may, while Time
Backward unblooms out of time toward peace, utter
Its small, sober, and inestimable
Glow, trophy of truth.

Can I see Arcturus from where I stand?

from Now and Then

American Portrait: Old Style

I.

Beyond the last house, where home was,
Past the marsh we found the old skull in, all nameless
And cracked in star-shape from a stone-smack,
Up the hill where the grass was tangled waist-high and wind-tousled,
To the single great oak that, in leaf-season, hung like
A thunderhead black against whatever blue the sky had,

And here, at the widest circumference of shade, when shade was,
Ran the trench, six feet long,
And wide enough for a man to lie down in,
10 In comfort, if comfort was still any object. No sign there
Of any ruined cabin or well, so Pap must have died of camp fever,
And the others pushed on, God knows where.

II.

The Dark and Bloody Ground, so the teacher romantically said,
But one look out the window, and woods and ruined cornfields we saw:
A careless-flung corner of country, no hope and no history here.
No hope but the Pullman lights that swept
Night-fields—glass-glint from some farmhouse and flicker of ditches—
Or the night freight's moan on the rise where
You might catch a ride on the rods,
20 Just for hell, or if need had arisen.
No history either—no Harrod or Finley or Boone,
No tale how the Bluebellies broke at the Rebel yell and cold steel.

So we had to invent it all, our Bloody Ground, K and I,
And him the best shot in ten counties and could call any bird-note back,
But school out, not big enough for the ballgame,
And in the full tide of summer, not ready
For the twelve-gauge yet, or even a job, so what
Can you do but pick up your BBs and Benjamin,
Stick corn pone in pocket, and head out
30 "To Rally in the Cane-Brake and Shoot the Buffalo"—
As my grandfather's cracked old voice would sing it

From days of his own grandfather—and often enough
It was only a Plymouth Rock or maybe a fat Dominecker
That fell to the crack of the unerring Decherd.

III.

Yes, imagination is strong. But not strong enough in the face of
The sticky feathers and BBs a mother's hand held out.
But no liberal concern was evinced for a Redskin,
As we trailed and out-tricked the sly Shawnees
In a thicket of ironweed, and I wrestled one naked
40 And slick with his bear grease, till my hunting knife
Bit home, and the tomahawk
Slipped from his hand. And what mother cared about Bluebellies
Who came charging our trench? But we held
To pour the last volley at face-gape before
The tangle and clangor of bayonet.

Yes, a day is merely forever
In memory's shiningness,
And a year but a gust or a gasp
In the summer's heat of Time, and in that last summer
50 I was almost ready to learn
What imagination is—it is only
The lie we must learn to live by, if ever
We mean to live at all. Times change.
Things change. And K up and gone, and the summer
Gone, and I longed to know the world's name.

IV.

Well, what I remember most
In a world long Time-pale and powdered
Like a vision still clinging to plaster
Set by Piero della Francesca
60 Is how K, through lane-dust or meadow,
Seemed never to walk, but float
With a singular joy and silence,
In his cloud of bird dogs, like angels,
With their eyes on his eyes like God,
And the sun on his uncut hair bright
As he passed through the ramshackle town and odd folks there
With coats on and vests and always soft gabble of money—
Polite in his smiling, but never much to say.

V.

To pass through to what? No, not
70 To some wild white peak dreamed westward,
And each sunrise a promise to keep. No, only
The Big Leagues, not even a bird dog,
And girls that popped gum while they screwed.

*

Yes, this was his path, and no batter
Could do what booze finally did:
Just blow him off the mound—but anyway,
He had always called it a fool game, just something
For children who hadn't yet dreamed what
A man is, or barked a squirrel, or raised
80   A single dog from a pup.

VI.

And I, too, went on my way, the winning and losing, or what
Is sometimes of all things the worst, the not knowing
One thing from the other, nor knowing
How the teeth in Time's jaw all snag backward
And whatever enters therein
Has less hope of remission than shark-meat,

And one Sunday afternoon, in the idleness of summer,
I found his farm, and him home there,
With the bird dogs crouched round in the grass
90   And their eyes on his eyes as he whispered
Whatever to bird dogs it was.
Then yelled: "Well, for Christ's sake—it's you!"

Yes, me, for Christ's sake, and some sixty
Years blown like a hurricane past! But what can you say—
Can you say—when *all-to-be-said* is the *done?*
So our talk ran to buffalo-hunting, and the look on his mother's face,
When she held the BBs out.

And the sun sank slow as he stood there,
All Indian-brown from waist up, who never liked tops to his pants,
100   And standing nigh straight, but the arms and the pitcher's
Great shoulders, they were thinning to old-man thin.
Sun low, all silence, then sudden:
"But, Jesus," he cried, "what makes a man do what he does—
Him living until he dies!"

Sure, all of us live till we die, but bingo!
Like young David at brookside, he swooped down,
Snatched a stone, wound up, and let fly,
And high on a pole over yonder the big brown insulator
Simply exploded. "See—I still got control!" he said.

VII.

110   Late, late, toward sunset, I wandered
Where old dreams had once been Life's truth, and where
I saw the trench of our valor, now nothing
But a ditch full of late-season weed-growth,
Beyond the rim of shade.

*

There was nobody there, hence no shame to be saved from, so I
Just lie in the trench on my back and see high,
Beyond the tall ironweed stalks, or oak leaves
If I happen to look that way,
How the late summer's thinned-out sky moves,
120 Drifting on, drifting on, like forever,
From *where* on to *where,* and I wonder
What it would be like to die,
Like the nameless old skull in the swamp, lost,
And know yourself dead lying under
The infinite motion of sky.

VIII.

But why should I lie here longer?
I am not dead yet, though in years,
And the world's way is yet long to go,
And I love the world even in my anger,
130 And that's a hard thing to outgrow.

Boy Wandering in Simms' Valley

Through brush and love-vine, well blooded by blackberry thorn
Long dry past prime, under summer's late molten light
And past the last rock-slide at ridge-top and stubborn,
Raw tangle of cedar, I clambered, breath short and spit white

From lung-depth. Then down the lone valley, called Simms' Valley still,
Where Simms, long back, had nursed a sick wife till she died.
Then turned out his spindly stock to forage at will,
And took down his twelve-gauge, and simply lay down by her side.

No kin they had, and nobody came just to jaw.
10 It was two years before some straggling hunter sat down
On the porch-edge to rest, then started to prowl. He saw
What he saw, saw no reason to linger, so high-tailed to town.

A dirt-farmer needs a good wife to keep a place trim,
So the place must have gone to wrack with his old lady sick.
And when I came there, years later, old furrows were dim,
And dimmer in fields where grew maples and such, a span thick.

So for years the farm had contracted: now barn down, and all
The yard back to wilderness gone, and only
The house to mark human hope, but ready to fall.
20 No buyer at tax-sale, it waited, forgotten and lonely.

*

I stood in the bedroom upstairs, in lowering sun,
And saw sheets hang spiderweb-rotten, and blankets a mass
Of what weather and leaves from the broken window had done,
Not to mention the rats. And thought what had there come to pass.

But lower was sinking the sun. I shook myself,
Flung a last glance around, then suddenly
Saw the old enameled bedpan, high on a shelf.
I stood still again, as the last sun fell on me,

And stood wondering what life is, and love, and what they may be.

Orphanage Boy

From the orphanage Al came to
Work on the farm as what you'd call
Hired boy if he got enough to
Call hire. Back at the woodpile chop-
ping stove-lengths, he taught me all the
Dirty words I'd never heard of
Or learned from farm observation,
And generally explained how
Folks went in for fun, adding that
10   A farm was one hell of a place
For finding fun.

          Polite enough,
He'd excuse himself after sup-
per and go sit on the stile with
Bob, the big white farm bulldog, close
At his side, and watch the sun sink
Back of the barn or, maybe in
The opposite direction, the
Moon rise.

        It was a copperhead
Bit Bob, and nothing, it looked like,
20   Would make him better. Just after
Supper one night my uncle stood
On the front porch and handed a
Twelve-gauge to Al, and said, "Be sure
You do it right back of the head."
He never named Bob's name.

          Al's face
Was white as clabber, but he took
The gun, not saying a word, just
Walking away down the lane to-

ward sunset, Bob too, me follow-
30 ing. Then, in the woods where it was
Nigh dark, he did it. He gave me
The gun, smoke still in the muzzle,
Said, "Git away, you son-a-bitch,"
And I got away and he lay
On the dead leaves crying even
Before I was gone.

          That night he
Never came home and the Sheriff
Never found him.

         It was six months
Before I went back in the woods
40 To the place. There was a real grave
There. There was a wood cross on the
Grave. He must have come back to the
Barn for the shovel and hammer,
And back again to hang them up.

It must have taken nigh moonset.

Red-Tail Hawk and Pyre of Youth

To Harold Bloom

1.

Breath clamber-short, face sun-peeled, stones
Loose like untruth underfoot, I
Had just made the ridge crest, and there,
Opening like joy, the unapprehensible purity
Of afternoon flooded, in silver,
The sky. It was
The hour of stainless silver just before
The gold begins.

Eyes, strangely heavy like lead,
10 Drew down to the .30-30 hung on my hand
As on a crooked stick, in growing wonder
At what it might really be. It was as though
I did not know its name. Nor mine. Nor yet had known
That all is only
All, and part of all. No wind
Moved the silver light. No movement,

*

Except for the center of
That convex perfection, not yet
A dot even, nameless, no color, merely
20 A shadowy vortex of silver. Then,
In widening circles—oh, nearer!
And suddenly I knew the name, and saw,
As though seeing, it come toward me,
Unforgiving, the hot blood of the air:
Gold eyes, unforgiving, for they, like God, see all.

2.

There was no decision in the act,
There was no choice in the act—the act impossible but
Possible. I screamed, not knowing
From what emotion, as at that insane range
30 I pressed the cool, snubbed
Trigger. Saw
The circle
Break.

3.

Heart leaping in joy past definition, in
Eyes tears past definition, by rocky hill and valley
Already dark-devoured, the bloody
Body already to my bare flesh embraced, cuddled
Like babe to heart, and my heart beating like love:
Thus homeward.

40 But nobody there.

So at last
I dared stare in the face—the lower beak drooping,
As though from thirst, eyes filmed.
Like a secret, I wrapped it in newspaper quickly
And hid it deep
In the ice chest.

Too late to start now.

4.

Up early next morning, with
My father's old razor laid out, the scissors,
50 Pliers and needles, waxed thread,
The burlap and salt, the arsenic and clay,
Steel rods, thin, and glass eyes
Gleaming yellow. Oh, yes,
I knew my business. And at last a red-tail—

Oh, king of the air!

*

And at that miraculous range.

How my heart sang!

Till all was ready—skull now well scraped
And with arsenic dried, and all flesh joints, and the cape
60 Like a carapace feathered in bronze, and naturally anchored
At beak and at bone joints, and steel
Driven through to sustain wing and bone
And the clay-burlap body there within.
It was molded as though for that moment to take to the air—though,
In God's truth, the chunk of poor wingless red meat,
The model from which all was molded, lay now
Forever earthbound, fit only
For dog tooth, not sky.

5.

Year after year, in my room, on the tallest of bookshelves,
70 Regal, it perched on its bough-crotch to guard
Blake and *Lycidas,* Augustine, Hardy and *Hamlet,*
Baudelaire and Rimbaud, and I knew that the yellow eyes,
Unsleeping, stared as I slept.

Till I slept in that room no more.

6.

Years pass like a dream, are a dream, and time came
When my mother was dead, father bankrupt, and whiskey
Hot in my throat while there for the last

Time I lay, and my heart
Throbbed slow in the
80 Meaningless motion of life, and with
Eyes closed I knew
That yellow eyes somewhere, unblinking, in vengeance stared.

Or *was* it vengeance? What could I know?

Could Nature forgive, like God?

7.

That night in the lumber room, late,
I found him—the hawk, feathers shabby, one
Wing bandy-banged, one foot gone sadly
Askew, one eye long gone—and I reckoned
I knew how it felt with one gone.

*

90 And all relevant items I found there: my first book of Milton,
The *Hamlet,* the yellow, leaf-dropping Rimbaud, and a book
Of poems friends and I had printed in college, not to mention
The collection of sexual Japanese prints—strange sex
Of mechanical sexlessness. And so made a pyre for
The hawk that, though gasoline-doused and wing-dragging,
Awaited, with what looked like pride,
The match.

8.

Flame flared. Feathers first, and I flinched, then stood
As the steel wire warped red to defend
100 The shape designed godly for air. But
It fell with the mass, and I
Did not wait.

What left
To do but walk in the dark, and no stars?

9.

Some dreams come true, some no.
But I've waked in the night to see
High in the late and uncurdled silver of summer
The pale vortex appear once again—and you come
And always the rifle swings up, though with
110 The weightlessness now of dream,
The old .30-30 that knows
How to bind us in air-blood and earth-blood together
In our commensurate fate,
Whose name is a name beyond joy.

10.

And I pray that in some last dream or delusion,
While hospital wheels creak beneath
And the nurse's soles make their *squeak-squeak* like mice,
I'll again see the first small silvery swirl
Spin outward and downward from sky-height
120 To bring me the truth in blood-marriage of earth and air—
And all will be as it was
In that paradox of unjoyful joyousness,
Till the dazzling moment when I, a last time, must flinch
From the regally feathered gasoline flare
Of youth's poor, angry, slapdash, and ignorant pyre.

Youth Stares at Minoan Sunset

On the lap of the mountain meadow,
At the break of the Cretan cliff-quarry where
Venetians had once sawed their stone, soft
Nag of surf far below foot, he
Stares seaward the distance to sunset.

The sky is rose-hearted, immense, undisturbed.
In that light the youth's form is black, without motion,
And birds, gull nor other, have no transaction
In the inflamed emptiness of sky. Mountainward,
10 No bird cries. We had called once,
But we were too far, too far.

Molten and massy, of its own weight flattened,
The sun accelerates downward, the sea,
From general slate-blue, flaming upward.
Contact is made at the horizon line.

On that line, one instant, one only,
The great coin, flame-massy and with
The frail human figure thereon minted black,
Balances. Suddenly is gone. A gull
20 Defiles at last the emptiness of air.

We are closer now. The black
Silhouette, yet small, stares seaward. To our cry
It does not turn. Later,
It will, and turning, see us with a slow
And pitying happiness of recognition born of
A knowledge we do not yet have. Or have forgotten.

He spreads his arms to the sky as though he loves it—and us.

He is so young.

Ah, Anima!

Watch the great bough lashed by wind and rain. Is it
A metaphor for your soul—or Man's—or even

Mine in the hurricane of Time? Now,
In the gray and splintered light, in the scything

Tail of the hurricane, miles of forest around us
Heave like the sea, and the gray underside of leaf is exposed

*

Of every tree, non-coniferous. The tall
Pines blackly stagger. Beyond,

The bulk and backdrop of mountain is
10   Obscured. Can you locate yourself

On the great chart of history?
In the distance a tree crashes.

Empires have fallen, and the stream
Gnashes its teeth with the *klang* of boulders.

Later, sleep. Tomorrow, help
Will come. The Governor promises. Roads will be rebuilt,

And houses. Food distributed. But, meanwhile, sleep
Is a disaster area, too. You have lain down

In the shards of Time and the un-roar of the wind of being,
20   And when, in the dark, you wake, with only

The *klang* of distant boulders in your ears,
You may wish that you, even in the wrack and dark pelt of storm,

Had run forth, screaming as wind snatched your breath away
Until you were nameless—oh, anima!—and only

Your mouth, rounded, is in the night there, the utterance gone. Perhaps
That is the only purity—to leave

The husk behind, and leap
Into the blind and antiseptic anger of air.

Unless

All will be in vain unless—unless what? Unless
You realize that what you think is Truth is only

A husk for something else. Which might,
Shall we say, be called energy, as good a word as any. As when

The rattlesnake, among desert rocks
And Freudian cactus tall in moonlight,

Scrapes off the old integument, and flows away,
Clean and lethal and gleaming like water over moon-bright sand,

Unhusked for its mission. Oh, *neo nato!* fanged, unforgiving,
10   We worship you for what you are. In the morning,

*

In the ferocity of daylight, the old skin
Will be translucent and abstract, like Truth. The mountains,

In distance, will glitter like diamonds, or salt.
They too will, in that light, seem abstract.

At night I have stood there, and the wide world
Was flat and circular under the storm of the

Geometry of stars. The mountains, in starlight, were black
And black-toothed to define the enormous circle

Of desert of which I was the center. This
20 Is one way to approach the question.

All is in vain unless you can, motionless, standing there,
Breathe with the rhythm of stars.

You cannot, of course, see your own face, but you know that it,
Lifted, is stripped to white bone by starlight. This is happening.

This is happiness.

Not Quite Like a Top

Did you know that the earth, not like a top on its point,
Spins on an axis that sways, and swings, from its middle?

Well, I didn't know, but do now, and often at night,
After maybe three highballs, I lie in my bed,

In the dark, and try to feel the off-center sensation,
And sometimes if

(In the northern hemisphere, this) my head points north,
I do. Or maybe I do. It is like

So many things they say are true, but you
10 Can't always be sure you feel them,

Even in dark, in bed, head north.
I have, in shameless dark, sometimes

Wept because
I couldn't be sure something precious was true,

Like they say. Examples could be multiplied. But
Once, in a Pullman berth (upper), I desperately prayed

*

To God to exist so that I
Might have the exalted horror of denying

Him. But nothing
20   Came of that project. Nothing. Oh, nothing.

But so young was I then! And maybe the axis of earth
Does not really sway from its center, even if

Ancient Egyptian and modern astronomers say so,
And what good would it do me to have firsthand evidence,

When there's so much that I, lying in darkness, don't know?

Waiting

You will have to wait. Until it. Until
The last owl hoot has quivered to a

Vibrant silence and you realize that there is no breathing
Beside you, and dark curdles toward dawn of no dawn. Until

Drouth breaks, too late to save the corn,
But not too late for flood, and the hobbled cow, stranded

On a sudden islet, gargles in grief in the alder-brake. Until
The doctor enters the waiting room, and

His expression betrays all, and you wish
10   He'd take his goddam hand off your shoulder. Until

The woman you have lived with all the years
Says, without rancor, that life is the way life is, and she cannot

Remember when last she loved you, and had lived the lie only
For the children's sake. Until you become uncertain of French

Irregular verbs, and by a strange coincidence begin to take Catholic
Instruction from Monsignor O'Malley, who chews a hangnail. Until

You realize, to your surprise, that our Savior died for us all,
And as tears gather in your eyes, you burst out laughing,

For the joke is certainly on Him, considering
20   What we are. Until

You pick the last alibi off, like a scab, and
Admire the inwardness, as beautiful as inflamed

*

Flesh, or summer sunrise. Until
You remember that, remarkably, common men have done noble deeds. Until

It grows on you that, at least, God
Has allowed man the grandeur of certain utterances.

True or not. But sometimes true.

The Mission

In the dark kitchen the electric icebox rustles.
It whispers like the interior dialogue of guilt and extenuation,
And I wake from a dream of horses. They do not know
I am dreaming of them. By this time they must be long dead.

Behind barbed wire, in fog off the sea, they stand.
Two clumps of horses, uncavorting, like gray stone, stand,
Heavy manes unrustling in even the gray sea wind.
The sea is gray. Night falls. Later, the manes will rustle,

But ever so little, in new wind lifting off the Bay of Biscay. But no—
10 They are dead. *La boucherie chevaline,* in the village,
Has a gold horse-head above the door. I wake
From my dream, and know that the shadow

Of the great spruce close by my house must be falling
Black on the white roof of winter. The spruce
Wants to hide the house from the moon, for
The moon's intentions have never been quite clear.

The spruce does not know that a secret square of moonlight lies cunningly on
The floor by my bed, and I watch it and think how,
On the snow-locked mountain, deep in a fissure
20 Under the granite ledge, the bear

Huddles inside his fur like an invalid inside
A charity-ward blanket. Fat has thinned on bone, and the fur
Is too big for him now. He stirs in sleep, farts
Gently in the glacial blackness of the cave. The eyes

Do not open. Outside, in moonlight,
The ledges are bearded with ice, and the brook,
Black, crawls under ice. It has a mission, but,
In that blackness, has forgotten what. I, too,

Have forgotten the nature of my own mission. This
30 May be fortunate, for if I stare at the dark ceiling
And try to remember, I do not have to go back to sleep,
And not sleeping, will not again dream

*

Of clumps of horses, fog-colored in sea fog, rumps
To the sea wind, standing like stone primitively hewn,
While the fields, gray, stretch beyond them, and distance dies.
Perhaps that lost mission is to try to understand

The possibility of joy in the world's tangled and hieroglyphic beauty.

When the Tooth Cracks—Zing!

When the tooth cracks—zing!—it
Is like falling in love, or like
Remembering your mother's face when she—and you only
A child—smiled, or like
Falling into Truth. This,
Of course, before the pain
Begins. But even
The pain is something—is, you might say,
For lack of a better word,
10   Reality.

          Do you
Remember that Jacob Boehme saw
Sunlight flash on a pewter platter on
The table, and his life was totally changed?

Is the name of God nothing more than
The accidental flash on a platter? But what is accident?

I have waked in the dark with the heart-throbbing conviction
Of having just seen some masterly
Shape, but without name. The world
Is suddenly different, then
20   The pain begins. Sharp as a snapped tooth, it strikes.
And, again, I have waked knowing
That I have only been dreaming,
In classic and timeless precision, of
Winter moonlight flooding a large room where
No spark now winks on the hearth, a broken
Brandy snifter glitters in moonshine by the coffee table, a
Half-burned cigarette butt beside it. And
A woman's slipper lies on its side
On the moon-bleached rug. In moonshine,
30   Silky as pastel, dust covers all.

It is only a dream, but it must have a name.
Must we totally forget a thing to know it?
Perhaps redemption is nothing more than the way
We learn to live with memories that are no longer remembered.

*

But it is hard to know the end of a story.

We often pray God to let us have Truth.
It is more important to pray God to help us to live with it.

Especially if your memory is not what it used to be.

Love Recognized

There are many things in the world and you
Are one of them. Many things keep happening and
You are one of them, and the happening that
Is you keeps falling like snow
On the landscape of not-you, hiding hideousness, until
The streets and the world of wrath are choked with snow.

How many things have become silent? Traffic
Is throttled. The mayor
Has been, clearly, remiss, and the city
10 Was totally unprepared for such a crisis. Nor
Was I—yes, why should this happen to me?
I have always been a law-abiding citizen.

But you, like snow, like love, keep falling,

And it is not certain that the world will not be
Covered in a glitter of crystalline whiteness.

Silence.

How to Tell a Love Story

There is a story that I must tell, but
The feeling in my chest is too tight, and innocence
Crawls through the tangles of fear, leaving,
Dry and translucent, only its old skin behind like
A garter snake's annual discard in the ground juniper. If only

I could say just the first word with breath
As sweet as a babe's and with no history—but, Christ,
If there is no history there is no story.
And no Time, no word.
10 For then there is nothing for a word to be about, a word

*

Being frozen Time only, and I have dived deep
Where light faded from gold to dark blue, and darker below,
And my chest was filled with a story like innocence,
But I rose, rose up, and plunged into light-blaze brutal as blackness,
And the sky whirled like fireworks. Perhaps I could then have begun it.

If only the first word would come and untwist my tongue!
Then the story might grow like Truth, or a tree, and your face
Would lean at me. If only the story could begin when all truly began,
White surf and a storm of sunlight, you running ahead and a smile
20   Back-flung—but then, how go on? For what would it mean?

Perhaps I can't say the first word till I know what it all means.
Perhaps I can't know till the doctor comes in and leans.

Little Black Heart of the Telephone

That telephone keeps screaming its little black heart out:
Nobody there? Oh, nobody's there!—and the blank room bleeds
For the poor little black bleeding heart of the telephone.
I, too, have suffered. I know how it feels
When you scream and scream, and nobody's there.
I am feeling that way this goddam minute,
If for no particular reason.

Tell the goddam thing to shut up! Only
It's not ringing now at all, but I
10   Can scrutinize it and tell that it's thinking about
Ringing, and just any minute, I know.
So, you demand, *the room's not empty, you're there?*
Yes, I'm here, but it might start screaming just after
I've gone out the door, in my private silence.

Or if I stayed here I mightn't answer, might pretend
Not to be here at all, or just be part of the blankness
The room is, as the blankness
Bleeds for the little bleeding black heart
Of the telephone. If, in fact, it should scream,
20   My heart would bleed too, for I know how pain can't find words.
Or sometimes is afraid to find them.

I tell you because I know you will understand.
I know you have screamed: *Nobody there? Oh, nobody's there!*
You've looked up at stars lost in blankness that bleeds
Its metaphysical blood, but not of redemption.
Have you ever stopped by the roadside at night, and couldn't
Remember your name, and breath
Came short? Or at night waked up with a telephone screaming,
And covered your head, afraid to answer?

*

30 Anyway, in broad daylight, I'm now in the street,
    And no telephone anywhere near, or even
    Thinking about me. But tonight, back in bed, I may dream
    Of a telephone screaming its little black heart out,
    In an empty room, toward sunset,
    While a year-old newspaper, yellowing, lies on the floor, and velvety
    Dust thick over everything, especially
    On the black telephone, on which no thumb-print has,
    For a long time now, been visible.

    In my dream I wonder why, long since, it's not been disconnected.

Last Laugh

    The little Sam Clemens, one night back in Hannibal,
    Peeped through the dining-room keyhole, to see, outspread
    And naked, the father split open, lights, liver, and all
    Spilling out from that sack of mysterious pain, and the head

    Sawed through, where his Word, like God's, held its deepest den,
    And candlelight glimmered on blood-slick, post-mortem steel,
    And the two dead fish-eyes stared steadily ceilingward—well, then,
    If you yourself were, say, twelve, just how would you feel?

    Oh, not that you'd loved him—that ramrod son of Virginia,
10 Though born for success, failing westward bitterly on.
    "Armed truce"—that was all, years later, you could find to say in you.
    But still, when a father's dead, an umbrella's gone

    From between the son and the direful elements.
    No, Sam couldn't turn from the keyhole. It's not every night
    You can see God butchered in such learned dismemberments,
    And when the chance comes you should make the most of the sight.

    Though making the most, Sam couldn't make terms with the fact
    Of the strangely prismatic glitter that grew in his eye,
    Or climbing the stairs, why his will felt detached from the act,
20 Or why stripping for bed, he stared so nakedly

    At the pore little body and thought of the slick things therein.
    Then he wept on the pillow, surprised at what he thought grief,
    Then fixed eyes at darkness while, slow, on his face grew a grin,
    Till suddenly something inside him burst with relief,

    Like a hog-bladder blown up to bust when the hog-killing frost
    Makes the brats' holiday. So took then to laughing and could not
    Stop, and so laughed himself crying to sleep. At last,
    Far off in Nevada, by campfire or sluice or gulch-hut,

    *

Or in roaring S.F., in an acre of mirror and gilt,
30 Where the boys with the dust bellied-up, he'd find words come,
His own face stiff as a shingle, and him little-built.
Then whammo!—the back-slapping riot. He'd stand, looking dumb.

God was dead, for a fact. He knew, in short, the best joke.
He had learned its thousand forms, and since the dark stair-hall
Had learned what was worth more than bullion or gold-dust-plump poke.
And married rich, too, with an extra spin to the ball;

For Livy loved God, and he'd show her the joke, how they lied.
Quite a tussle it was, but hot deck or cold, he was sly
And won every hand but the last. Then at her bedside
40 He watched dying eyes stare up at a comfortless sky,

And was left alone with his joke, God dead, till he died.

Heat Lightning

Heat lightning prowls, pranks the mountain horizon like
Memory. I follow the soundless flicker,

As ridge after ridge, as outline of peak after peak,
Is momentarily defined in the

Pale wash, the rose-flush, of distance. Somewhere—
Somewhere far beyond them—that distance. I think

Of the past and how this soundlessness, no thunder,
Is like memory purged of emotion,

Or even of meaning. I watch
10 The lightning wash pale beyond the night mountains, beyond

Night cumulus, like a stage set. Nothing
Is real, and I think of her, in timelessness: the clutch

In the lightless foyer, the awkward wall-propping, one ear
Cocked for footsteps, all the world

Hates a lover. It seems only a dream, the unsounding
Flicker of memory, even the episode when

Arms, encircling, had clamped arms to sides, the business
Banked on a pillow, head

Back over bed-edge, the small cry of protest—
20 But meanwhile, paradoxically, heels

*

Beating buttocks in deeper demand. Then heels stopping
In shudder and sprawl, only whites

Of eyes showing, like death. What all the tension,
The tingle, twist, tangle, the panting and pain,

What all exploitation of orifices and bruised flesh but
The striving for one death in two? I remember—

Oh, look! in that flash, how the peak
Blackens zenithward—as I said, I remember

     The glutted, slack look on the face once
30 And the faintest blood-smear at the mouth's left corner,

And not till next day did I notice the two
Symmetrical half-moons of blue marks tattooed

On my shoulder, not remembering, even then, the sensation
Of the event; and of course, not now, for heat lightning

Is thunderless. And thunderless, even,
The newspaper obit, years later, I stumbled on. Yes,

How faint that flash! And I sit in the unmooned
Dark of an August night, waiting to see

     The rose-flush beyond the black peaks, and think how far,
40 Far away, down what deep valley, scree, scar,

The thunder redoubled, redoubling, rolls. Here silence.

Inevitable Frontier

Be careful! Slow and careful, for you now approach
The frontier where the password is difficult to utter—or grasp.

Echo among chert peaks and perilously balanced boulders
Has something to do with it, not to mention your early rearing, with

Its naïve logic. For remember now, this is the frontier
Where words coming out of a mouth are always upside-

Down, and all tongues are sloppily cubical, and shadows of nothing are,
Whatever the hour, always something, and tend to bleed

     If stepped on—oh, do keep mindful how
10 Slick the blood of shadow can be, especially

  *

If the shadow is of nothing. As a corollary,
The shadow of something, yourself for instance,

Provides its own peculiar hazards. You may trip
On it, and start falling upward, screaming,

Screaming for somebody to grab you before you are out
Of reach. Your eyes, too, must be readjusted, for

Here people, owl-like, see only by dark, and grope by day. Here,
People eat in shamefaced privacy, but the great Public Square,

Sparsely planted, is full, in daylight, of gut-wheeze and littered with feces
20 Till the carts come, and later, *à l'heure sexuelle,* at noon, waiters wheel out

To the café terraces divans of ingeniously provocative designs,
While clients, now clad in filmy robes, emerge from locker-rooms, laughing

Like children at tag. Food is, of course, forbidden, but scented drinks,
And coffee, are served under awnings. Another item:

Criminality is rare, but those convicted,
Mystically deprived of the memory of their names, are exiled

To the Isles of the Blest, where they usually end by swallowing their tongues,
This from boredom, for in their language *bliss* and *boredom*

Have the same linguistic root. Yes, many things
30 Are different here, and to be happy and well-adjusted, you

Must put out of mind much you have been taught. Among others, the names
Of Plato, St. Paul, Spinoza, Pascal and Freud must not be spoken, and when,

Without warning, by day or night, the appalling
White blaze of God's Great Eye sweeps the sky, History

Turns tail and scuttles back to its burrow
Like a groundhog caught in a speeding sportscar's headlight.

Heart of the Backlog

Snug at hearthside, while heart of the backlog
Of oak simmers red in the living pulse of its own
Decay, you sit. You count
Your own heartbeat. How steady, how
Firm! What, ah, is Time! And sometimes

It is hard, after all, to decide
If the ticking you now hear is
A whisk of granules of snow,
Hard and belated on panes, or simply
10   The old organ, fist-size and resolute,
Now beastlike caught
In your rib-cage, to pace

But go nowhere. It does,
In a ghostly sense, suggest now the sound of
Pacing, as if, in soft litter, curved claws
Were muffled. Or is it
The pace of the muffled old clock in the hall?

You watch the talus-like slide of
Consumed oak from oak yet consuming. Yes, tell me
20   How many the years that burn there. How delicate, dove-gray
The oak-ash that, tiny and talus-like, slides to unwink
The glowing of oak and the years unconsumed!
What is the color of years your fireplace consumes as you sit there?

But think, shut your eyes. Shut your eyes and see only
The wide stretch of world beyond your warm refuge—fields
Windless and white in full moonlight,
Snow past and now steady the stars, and, far off,
The woods-lair of darkness. Listen! is that
The great owl that you, warm at your hearthside, had heard?

30   How feather-frail, think, is the track of the vole
On new snow! How wide is the world! How fleeting and thin
Its mark of identity, breath
In a minuscule issue of whiteness
In air that is brighter than steel! The vole pauses, one paw
Uplifted in whiteness of moonlight.

There is no indication of what angle, or slant,
The great shadow may silkily accent the beauty of snow,
And the vole, Little One, has neither theology nor
Aesthetic—not even what you may call
40   Stoicism, as when the diagnostician pauses, and coughs.
Poor thing, he has only himself. And what do you have

*

When you go to the door, snatch it open, and, cold,
The air strikes like steel down your lungs, and you feel
The Pascalian nausea make dizzy the last stars?
Then shut the door. The backlog burns down. You sit and

Again the owl calls, and with some sadness you wonder
If at last, when the air-scything shadow descends
And needles claw-clamp through gut, heart and brain,
Will ecstasy melting with terror create the last little cry?
50 Is God's love but the last and most mysterious word for death?

Has the thought ever struck you to rise and go forth—yes, lost
In the whiteness—to never look upward, or back, only on,
And no sound but the snow-crunch, and breath
Gone crisp like the crumpling of paper? Listen!
Could that be the creak of a wing-joint gigantic in distance?

No, no—just a tree, far off, when ice inward bites.
No, no, don't look back—oh, I beg you!

I beg you not to look back, in God's name.

Diver

Arrowed, the body flies in light.
The heels flash as water closes.
The board yet quivers where feet struck.
Concentric to the water's wound,
In live geometry the bright-
Born circles widen targetwise
In mathematic accuracy.

Now in the water's inner gleam,
Where no sound comes, and yap and nag
10 Of the world's old currish annoy is stilled,
The body glides. In timeless peace
The mover that shows no movement moves
Behind the prow of a diver's hands,
And in our watching hearts we know
An unsuspected depth and calm
Of identity we had never dreamed.

But look! The face is up, dark hair
Snaps sidewise to show the boyish grin.
And we smile, too, in welcome back
20 To all the joy and anguish of
The earth we walk on, lie down in.

Rather Like a Dream

If Wordsworth, a boy, reached out
To touch stone or tree to confirm
His own reality, that wasn't

So crazy. Or even illogical. For
We have all done the same, or at least
Felt the impulse. Right now I feel it, for

I walk in the mountain woods,
Alone, hour sunset, season
When the first maple leaf falls red, the first

10 Beech leaf gold. Each leaf of each species
Gathers, brooding, beneath it, its film
Of darkness, and waits, and the promise

Of another summer is already a dream. Thus years,
As I stand at this moment, are gathered
In their brooding darkness beneath.

Another summer is now truly a dream
To join those moments, and hours, of joy
That dissolve into glitter, like tears, then gather

Each under a brooding leaf, or join
20 The darkness of conifers, not yet snow-draped.
I stand on stone and am thinking

Of what is no more. Oh, happiness!—often
Unrecognized. But shade hardens, and years
Are darkening under each leaf—old love, old folly,

Old evil and anguish, and the drawstring
Of darkness draws tighter, and the monk-hood
Of darkness grows like a sky over all,

As I stand in the spruce-deep where stars never come.
I stand, hands at sides, and wonder,
30 Wonder if I should put out a hand to touch

Tree or stone—just to know.

Heart of Autumn

Wind finds the northwest gap, fall comes.
Today, under gray cloud-scud and over gray
Wind-flicker of forest, in perfect formation, wild geese
Head for a land of warm water, the *boom,* the lead pellet.

Some crumple in air, fall. Some stagger, recover control,
Then take the last glide for a far glint of water. None
Knows what has happened. Now, today, watching
How tirelessly *V* upon *V* arrows the season's logic,

Do I know my own story? At least, they know
10 When the hour comes for the great wing-beat. Sky-strider,
Star-strider—they rise, and the imperial utterance,
Which cries out for distance, quivers in the wheeling sky.

That much they know, and in their nature know
The path of pathlessness, with all the joy
Of destiny fulfilling its own name.
I have known time and distance, but not why I am here.

Path of logic, path of folly, all
The same—and I stand, my face lifted now skyward,
Hearing the high beat, my arms outstretched in the tingling
20 Process of transformation, and soon tough legs,

With folded feet, trail in the sounding vacuum of passage,
And my heart is impacted with a fierce impulse
To unwordable utterance—
Toward sunset, at a great height.

from Being Here

Speleology

At cliff-foot where great ledges thrust, the cave
Debouches, soil level and rank, where the stream,
Ages back, had come boiling forth, and now from alluvial earth
The last of old virgin forest trees rise to cliff-height,
And at noon twilight reigns. No one comes.

I must have been six when I first found the cave-mouth
Under ledges moss-green, and moss-green the inner dark.
Each summer I came, in twilight peered in, crept further,
Till one summer all I could see was a gray
10 Blotch of light far behind. Ran back. Didn't want to be dead.

By twelve, I was bolder. Besides, now had me a flashlight.
The whole night before couldn't sleep. Daylight. Then breakfast.
The cave wandered on, roof lower and lower except
Where chambers of darkness rose and stalactites down-stabbed
To the heart of my light. Again, lower.

I cut off the light. Knew darkness and depth and no Time.
Felt the cave-cricket crawl up an arm. Switched light on
To see the lone life there, the cave-cricket pale
As a ghost on my brown arm. I thought: *They are blind.*
20 Crept on. Heard, faintly, below

A silken and whispering rustle. Like what? Like water—so swung
The light to one side. I had crawled out
A ledge under which, far down, far down, the water yet channeled
And sang to itself, and answered my high light with swollen
White bursts of bubble. Light out, unmoving, I lay,

Lulled as by song in a dream, knowing
I dared not move in a darkness so absolute.
I thought: *This is me.* Thought: *Me—who am I?* Felt
Heart beating as though to a pulse of darkness and earth, and thought
30 How would it be to be here forever, my heart,

*

In its beat, part of all. Part of all—
But I woke with a scream. The flashlight,
It slipped, but I grabbed it. Had light—
And once more looked down the deep slicing and sluicing
Of limestone where water winked, bubbles like fish-eyes, a song like terror.

Years later, past dreams, I have lain
In darkness and heard the depth of that unending song,
And hand laid to heart, have once again thought: *This is me.*
And thought: *Who am I?* And hand on heart, wondered
40   What would it be like to be, in the end, part of all.

And in darkness have even asked: *Is this all? What is all?*

When Life Begins

Erect was the old Hellenistic head,
White-thatched in that dark cedar shade,
Curl-tangled the beard like skill-carved stone
With chisel-grooved shadow accenting the white.
The blue gaze fixed on a mythic distance.

That distance, a far hill's horizon, bulged
Past woods into the throbbing blue
Of a summer's afternoon. Our silence
Now seemed to have substantial life
10   That was the death of the pulse of Time.

One hand, gnarled, liver-blotched, but sinewed
From wrestling with the sleight of years,
Lay propped on a blue-jeaned knee and wrapped
Around a cob pipe, from which one thread
Of smoke, more blue than distance, rose
To twine into the cedar-dark.

The boy—he felt he wasn't there.
He felt that all reality
Had been cupboarded in that high head,
20   But now was absorbed into the abstractness
Of that blue gaze, so fixed and far,
Aimed lethally past the horizon's fact.

He thought all things that ever lived
Had gone to live behind that brow,
And in their infinite smallness slept
Until the old voice might wake them again
To strive in the past but passionate

*

Endeavor—hoofbeat at night, steel-clang,
Boom of the battery to take,
30 Far smoke seen long before you hear sound,
And before that, too, the gust of grape
Overhead, through oak leaves. Your stallion rears.

Your stallion rears—yes, it is *you!*

With your glasses you spot, from east, from west,
From woods-cover, skirmishers mincing out
On both flanks of that rise. Rifle-fire
Prickles the distance, noiseless, white.
Then a shell bursts over that fanged, far hill,
Single, annunciatory, like
40 A day-star over new Bethlehem.

In the country-quiet, momentarily
After that event renewed, one lone
Quail calls.

       And the old man, once he said
How a young boy, dying, broke into tears.
"Ain't scairt to die"—the boy's words—"it's jist
I ne'er had no chanst to know what tail's like."

Hunger and thirst, and the quavering yell
That more than bugle gave guts to a charge,
And once said: "My Mary, her hands were like silk,
50 But strong—and her mount on his shadow would dance."
Once said: "But things—they can seem like a dream."

Old eyelids shut the horizon out.
The boy sat and wondered when life would begin,
Nor knew that, beyond the horizon's heave,
Time crouched, like a great cat, motionless
But for tail's twitch. Night comes. Eyes glare.

Grackles, Goodbye

Black of grackles glints purple as, wheeling in sun-glare,
The flock splays away to pepper the blueness of distance.
Soon they are lost in the tracklessness of air.
I watch them go. I stand in my trance.

Another year gone. In trance of realization,
I remember once seeing a first fall leaf, flame-red, release
Bough-grip, and seek, through gold light of the season's sun,
Black gloss of a mountain pool, and there drift in peace.

*

Another year gone. And once my mother's hand
10 Held mine while I kicked the piled yellow leaves on the lawn
And laughed, not knowing some yellow-leaf season I'd stand
And see the hole filled. How they spread their obscene fake lawn.

Who needs the undertaker's sick lie
Flung thus in the teeth of Time, and earth's spin and tilt?
What kind of fool would promote that kind of lie?
Even sunrise and sunset convict the half-wit of guilt.

Grackles, goodbye! The sky will be vacant and lonely
Till again I hear your horde's rusty creak high above,
Confirming the year's turn and the fact that only, only,
20 In the name of Death do we learn the true name of Love.

Youthful Truth-Seeker, Half-Naked, at Night, Running down Beach South of San Francisco

In dark, climbing up. Then down-riding the sand sluice
Beachward from dune-head. Running, feet bare on
Sand wet-packed and star-stung. Phlegm in lungs loose.
Though now tide turning, spume yet prickling air on

My chest, which naked, splits darkness. On the right hand,
Palisades of white-crashing breakers renew and stretch on
Into unmooned drama and distance.—To understand
Is impossible now. Flight from what? To what? And alone.

Far behind, the glow of the city of men fades slow.
10 And ahead, white surf and dark dunes in dimness are wed,
While Pacificward, fog, leagues afar, now threatens to grow,
But on I yet run, face up, stars shining above my wet head

Before they are swaddled in grayness, though grayness, perhaps,
Is what waits—after history, logic, philosophy too,
Even rhythm of lines that bring tears to the heart, and scraps
Of old wisdom that like broken bottles in darkness gleam at you.

What was the world I had lived in? Poetry, orgasm, joke:
And the joke the biggest on me, the laughing despair
Of a truth the heart might speak, but never spoke—
20 Like the twilit whisper of wings with no shadow on air.

You dream that somewhere, somehow, you may embrace
The world in its fullness and threat, and feel, like Jacob, at last
The merciless grasp of unwordable grace
Which has no truth to tell of future or past—

*

But only life's instancy, by daylight or night,
While constellations strive, or a warbler whets
His note, or the ice creaks blue in white-night Arctic light,
Or the maniac weeps—over what he always forgets.

So lungs aflame now, sand raw between toes,
30 And the city grows dim, dimmer still,
And the grind of breath and of sand is all one knows
Of what a man flees to, or from, in his angry need to fulfill

What?—On the beach flat I fall by the foam-frayed sea,
Which now and then brushes an outflung hand, as though
In tentative comfort, yet knowing itself to be
As ignorant as I, and as feckless also.

So I stare at the stars that remain, shut eyes, in dark press an ear
To sand, cold as cement, to apprehend,
Not merely the grinding of shingle and sea-slosh near,
40 But the groaning miles of depth where light finds its end.

Below all silken soil-slip, all crinkling earth-crust,
Far deeper than ocean, past rock that against rock grieves,
There at the globe's deepest dark and visceral lust,
Can I hear the *groan-swish* of magma that churns and heaves?

No word? No sign? Or is there a time and place—
Ice-peak or heat-simmered distance—where heart, like eye,
May open? But sleep at last—it has sealed up my face,
And last foam, retreating, creeps from my hand. It will dry,

While fog, star by star, imperially claims the night.
50 How long till dawn flushes dune-tops, or gilds beach-stones?
I stand up. Stand thinking, I'm one poor damn fool, all right.
Then ask, if years later, I'll drive again forth under stars, on tottering bones.

Snowshoeing Back to Camp in Gloaming

Scraggle and brush broken through, snow-shower jarred loose
To drape shoulders, dead boughs, snow-sly and trap-laid,
Snatching thongs of my snowshoes, I
Stopped. At the edge of the high mountain mowing,
I stood. Westward stared
At the half mile of white alabaster unblemished
To the blackness of spruce forest lifting
In a long scree-climb to cliff-thrust,
Where snow, in level striation of ledges, stretched, and the sun,
10 Unmoving, hung
Clear yet of the peak-snagged horizon—
The sun, by a spectral spectrum belted,
Pale in its ghost-nimb.

*

The shadow of spruces, magenta,
Bled at me in motionlessness
Across unmarred white of the mowing.

Time died in my heart.

So I stood on that knife-edge frontier
Of Timelessness, knowing that yonder
20   Ahead was the life I might live
Could I but move
Into the terror of unmarred whiteness under
The be-nimbed and frozen sun.

While behind, I knew,
In the garrote of perfect knowledge, that
The past flowed backward: trees bare
As though of all deeds unleafed, and
Dead leaves lost are only
Old words forgotten in snowdrifts.

30   But the crow in distance called, and I knew
He spoke truth, for

Higher a wash of pale pink suddenly tinted the mowing,
And from spruce-blackness magenta
Leaped closer. But at
That instant, sun-nimb
Made contact with jag-heave of mountain.
Magenta lapped suddenly gray at my feet,
With pink, farther up,
Going gray.

40   Hillward and sky-thrust, behind me,
Leafless and distanced to eastward, a huge
Beech clung to its last lone twinge
Of pink on the elephant-gray—far under
One star.

Now the track, gone pale in tree-night,
Downward floated before me, to darkness,

So starward I stared
To the unnamed void where Space and God
Flinch to come, and where
50   Un-Time roars like a wind that only
The dead, unweeping, hear.

Oh, Pascal!
What does a man need to forget?

*

But moved on, however, remembering
That somewhere—somewhere, it seemed—
Beautiful faces above a hearthstone bent
Their inward to an outward glow.

Remembering, too, that when a door upon dark
Opens, and I, fur-prickled with frost,
60 Against the dark stand, one gaze
Will lift and smile with sudden sheen
Of a source far other than firelight—or even

Imagined star-glint.

Sila

Sila, for the Eskimo, "is the air, not the sky; movement, not wind; the very breath of life, but not physical life; he is clear-sighted energy, activating intelligence; the powerful fluid circulating 'all around' and also within each individual . . . "

Larousse World Mythology

Upgrade, past snow-tangled bramble, past
Deadfall snow-buried, there—
The ruin of old stonework, where man-heart
Long ago had once lifted
In joy, and back muscles strained. "Stay, Sila!" the boy
Commanded the tawny great husky, broad-chested,
That in harness yet stood, forward-leaning. The boy
Stamped his cross-countries. Stared
At the ruin. Thought:
10 *Two hundred years back—and it might
Have been me.*

And wondered what name the man
Might have had. Thought:
*Well, summer, I'll come
And hunt for the gravestones.* Then thought
How letters that crude must be weathered away—how deeper
A skull must be pulping to earth, and now grinless.
But thought: *At least, I can touch it, whatever
It is, stone or skull.*

20 *Was young,* then he thought, *young as me, maybe.*

Then felt muscles tighten and clinch
At a sudden impulse of surprise
To find here the old mark of life that for life
Once had sung, while the axe-edge glittered in sunlight.

*

Oh, what are the years! his heart cried, and he felt
His own muscles pulsing in joy, just as when
Hands clasp for the lift of the beauty of butt-swell.

Land is benched here, great beeches,
Gray, leafless, arising parklike and artful
30 From snow artificial as Christmas.
"Stay, Sila!" he called, and on level ground now
Slick-glided to where the blue gleam of ice-eyes
Looked up in his own, with a knowledge deeper than words.
He snapped harness loose, slipped out of cross-countries,
Wrapped cords at his waist, and—
The dog exploded.

From behind a beech deadfall, the doe, it had leaped,
Cow-awkward on earth, but magically airy in flight,
And weightless as wind, forelegs airward prowing
40 To seem as frail as a spider's, but hooves aglitter like glass
To cleave sunlight. Then,
Suddenly knifing the ice-crust as deep
As a trap, while the husky's wide paw-spread
Had opened like snowshoes behind.
Five leaps—and first blood, at a haunch,
Flesh laid back as though in a hunter's thin knife-slice.

Again, two more leaps, and white slash at belly—
Red line drawn clean on the curve. The boy's order
No use now: "Stay! Damn it, stay!" Until
50 Hand on harness, at last and too late, for
Red blood dripped now from white fang
To whiteness of snow, and eyes blue as steel drove into
The boy's eyes brain-deep, while, that instant,
All eons of friendship fled.
Then dog-eyes go earthward. The guts
Of the doe slip forth blue on the ice-crust.

The husky, stiff as in bronze cast, waits.

Only one thing to do. Who'd leave the doe there,
Dying slow into sunset, while all the small teeth—
60 Fox, field mouse, and wildcat—emerge
For their nocturnal feast? So the boy's knees bend,
Break the snow-crust like prayer,
And he cuddles the doe's head, and widening brown eyes
Seem ready, almost, to forgive.

He longs for connection, to give explanation. Sudden,
The head, now helpless, drops back on his shoulder. Twin eyes
Hold his own entrapped in their depth,
But his free hand, as though unaware,

Slides slow back
70   To grope for the knife-sheath.

The boy could not shut his eyes to the task,
As some fool girl might, but set
Eyes deeper in eyes, as he cradled the head, and gently
Held up the soft chin
To tauten the fullness of throat, and then,
As scrupulous as a well-trained tailor, set
The knife's needle point where acuteness
Would enter without prick of pain, and
Slashed in a single, deep motion.

80   He was sure that the doe
Never twitched.

On snow unconsciously heaped, he let down the head,
Aware even yet of the last embracement of gaze.
He watched, bewitched by the beauty, how blood flowed,
Red petal by petal, a great rose that bloomed where he stood.
How petal on petal, curve swelling past curve,
Gleamed forth at his feet on the snow,
And each petal sparkled with flicker of ice through the crimson,
As rays of last sun found a special glory in smallness.

90   He lifted his head, knife yet in hand, and westward
Fixed eyes beyond beech-bench to the snow-hatched
Stone thrust of the mountain, above which sky, too,
More majestically bloomed, but petals paler as higher—
The rose of the blood of the day. Still as stone,
So he stood. Then slowly—so slowly—
He raised the blade of the knife he loved honing, and wiped
The sweet warmness and wetness across his own mouth,
And set tongue to the edge of the silk-whetted steel.

He knew he knew something at last
100 That he'd never before known.
No name for it—no!

He snow-cleaned the knife. Sheathed it. Called: "Come!"
The dog, now docile, obeyed. With bare hands full of snow,
The boy washed him of blood and, comblike,
With fingers ennobled the ruff.

Then suddenly clasping the creature, he,
Over raw fur, past beeches, the mountain's snow-snag,
And the sky's slow paling of petals,
Cries out into vastness
110 Of silence: "Oh, world!"

He felt like a fool when tears came.

*

Some sixty years later, propped on death's pillow,
Again will he see that same scene, and try,
Heart straining, to utter that cry?—But
Cannot, breath short.

Vision

The vision will come—the Truth be revealed—but
Not even its vaguest nature you know—ah, truth

About what? But deep in the sibilant dark
That conviction irregularly

Gleams like fox-fire in sump-woods where,
In distance, lynx-scream or direful owl-stammer

Freezes the blood in a metaphysical shudder—which
Might be the first, feather-fine brush of Grace. Such

An event may come with night rain on roof, season changing
10   And bed too wide; or, say, when the past is de-fogged

And old foot tracks of folly show fleetingly clear before
Rationalization again descends, as from seaward.

Or when the shadow of pastness teasingly
Lifts and you recollect having caught—when, when?—

A glint of the nature of virtue like
The electrically exposed white of a flicker's

Rump feathers at the moment it flashes for the black thicket.
Or when, even, in a section of the city

Where no acquaintance would ever pass,
20   You watch snowflakes slash automobile lights

As you move toward the first
Illicit meeting, naturally at a crummy

Café. Your pace slows. You see her
Slip from the cab, dash for the door, dark fur coat

Collar up, head down. Inside,
As you order two highballs,

All eyes seem to focus on you. Drinks come, but
There is nothing to say. Hands

*

Do, damply, clasp—though no bed yet. Each stares
30 Into the other's eyes, desire like despair, and doom

Grows slow, and fat, and dark, like a burgundy begonia.
Soon you will watch the pale silken flash

Of well-turned ankles beneath dark fur,
As she hurries away on her stolen time, cab-hunting, and the future

Scarcely breathes. Your chest is a great clot. Perhaps then.
Oh, no. It may not happen, in fact, until

A black orderly, white-coated, on rubber soles, enters at 5 A.M.
The hospital room, suds and razor in hand, to shave,

With no word of greeting, the area the surgeon
40 Will penetrate. The robot departs. No one

Comes yet. Do not give up hope.
There is still time. Watch dawn blur the window.

Can it be that the vision has, long back, already come—
And you just didn't recognize it?

Part of What Might Have Been a Short Story, Almost Forgotten

(octosyllabics)

Fifty-odd years ago if you
Were going to see Shoshone
Falls, the road was not, God knows, slicked
Up for the wheeled hordes of Nature-
Lovers gawking in flowered shirts
From Hawaii, and little bas-
tards strewing candy wrappers as
They come. No—rough roads then, gravel
Sometimes and, too, lonesomeness: no
10 Pervasive stink of burnt high-test,
Like the midnight memory of
Some act of shame long forgotten
But now back in sickening sweat.

The thunder, in vacant silence,
First grew like a dream of thunder,
Then external palpitation
Of air, not sound. Then, there it is—
The chasmed roar clambers now up
To smite you, as tons of water,

20 Glinting like steel, if steel could flow,
   Plunge over geologic de-
   bris to darkening depth where crash-
   ing white and foam-stung air prove the
   Great natural depth and shadow—
   While the red sun of August, mis-
   shapen, bloated, sinks to a far
   Mountain heave.

                    The woman went back
   To the car. Noise gave her headaches.

   I watched the chasm darker grow,
30 And deeper while the white crashing
   Momently seemed deeper, deeper,
   But paradoxically loud-
   er. I found myself drawn to the
   Brink, gaze frozen downward. Arms, white,
   Wreathed upward, imploring. I tore
   My eyes from that compulsion, that
   Deepening sound and white fulfill-
   ment. I lifted eyes. Stared west. The
   Sun, rim down now, flamed to the un-
40 winged, utmost, blank zenith of sky.
   I stared till flame color, blood col-
   or, faded to dusking color-
   lessness, and the first star, westward
   And high, spoke. Then, slowly, night. I
   Heard the crash rise merciless, kept
   Eyes on that first star. But sudden-
   ly, glare of the car's headlights bursts.

   Directly on me bursts. Then the
   Scream. Then: "Look!" I turned to look and
50 There it was. On the slant of a
   Skyward-broken stratum, among
   Sparse scrub, it crouched, the great shoulder
   Muscles bunched separate and high,
   The noble head outthrust but mas-
   sive jaws just clear of earth, upper
   Lip drawn slightly back to expose
   White glitter of fangs. The eyes, catch-
   ing headlight glare, glared at me as
   Vented from a skull with blown coals
60 Packed. The tail, in shadow, slow swung
   From side to side. My blood was ice.

   But no reason. With insolent,
   Contemptuous dignity, its
   Curiosity about this
   Strange and defenseless beast now at

Last satisfied, it wheeled and took
One leap that, in slow grace, looked more
Like flight into blank darkness past
Lip of the chasm. That was all.

70 Back in my seat, the brake released,
I let the car coast out on the
Road such as it was. Turned switch. The
Motor snapped to life. My heart was
Slow again. We had seen what we
Had come to see, Nature's beauty,
But not what in the uncoiling
Of Time, Time being what it is,
We would come to see. Now under
White gaze in high darkness of in-
80 different stars, unknowing, word-
less, we lower swung, lower past
Tormented stone of crags, then in
Black maw of conifer forest:

And there, what beast might, waiting, be.

What beast with fang more white, with claw
More scimitar, with gaze of blaze
More metaphysical, patient
As stone in geological
Darkness, waits, waiting, will wait
90 Where and how long?—While we,
By other crag, by moonlit field,
By what star-tumbling stream, or through
What soundless snow which wipers groan
To cope with, roads poor-mapped, will move
Toward what foetal, fatal truth
Our hearts had witlessly concealed
In mere charade, hysterical

Or grave, of love.

Cocktail Party

Beyond the haze of alcohol and syntax and
Flung gage of the girl's glance, and personal ambition,
You catch some eye-gleam, sense a faint
Stir, as of a beast in shadow. It may be Truth.

Into what distance all gabble crawls away!
You look, and thirty lips move without sound
As though something had gone wrong with the TV,
And you see, of a sudden, a woman's unheard laugh exposing

*

Glitter of gold in the mouth's dark ghetto like unspeakable
10   Obscenity, but not sound. You try
To speak, an urgency like hard phlegm
In your throat, but no sound comes. You quiver, thinking

Of the horror of Truth. It lies in wait—ha, ha!—
A pun—or rises, diaphanous, like
Smoke from the red-stained cigarette butt
Half-crushed in a carved gold ashtray.

In wait, it lies. Or like a tumor grows
Somewhere inside your brain. Oh, doctor, please, oh,
Remove it! Expense be damned, I only
20   See lips moving. I move my lips, but no

Sound comes, not even a lie. Yes, operate, then I
Can hear them—and tell them I love them. At least,
If we are all to be victims of Truth,
Let us be destroyed together in normal communication.

Or maybe I'm only a little drunk. Oh, waiter!

The Cross

Once, after storm, I stood at the cliff-head,
And up black basalt the sea's white claws
Still flung their eight fathoms up to have my blood.
In the blaze of new sun they leap in cruel whiteness,
Not forgiving me that their screaming lunges
Had nightlong been no more than a dream
In the tangle and warmth and breathless dark
Of love's huddle and sleep, while stars were black
And the tempest swooped down to snatch our tiles.

10   By three, wind down and sun still high,
I walked the beach of the little cove
Where scavengings of the waves were flung—
Old oranges, cordage, a bottle of beer
With the cap still tight, a baby doll
But the face smashed in, a boom from some mast,
And most desperately hunched by volcanic stone
As though trying to cling in some final hope,
But drowned hours back you could be damned sure,
The monkey, wide-eyed, bewildered yet
20   By the terrible screechings and jerks and bangs,
And no friend to come and just say *ciao.*

*

I took him up, looked in his eyes,
As orbed as dark aggies, as bright as tears,
With a glaucous glint in deep sightlessness,
Yet still seeming human with all they had seen—
Like yours or mine, if luck had run out.

So, like a fool, I said *ciao* to him.

Under wet fur I felt how skin slid loose
On the poor little bones, and the delicate
30 Fingers yet grasped, at God knew what.
So I sat with him there, watching wind abate.
No funnel on the horizon showed.
And of course, no sail. And the cliff's shadow
Had found the cove. Well, time to go.

I took time, yes, to bury him,
In a scraped-out hole, little cairn on top.
And I enough fool to improvise
A cross—

Two sticks tied together to prop in the sand.

40 But what use that? The sea comes back.

Language Barrier

Snow-glitter, snow-gleam, all snow-peaks
Scream joy to the sun. Green
Far below lies, shelved where a great *cirque* is blue, bluest
Of waters, face upward to sky-flaming blue. Then
The shelf falters, fails, and downward becomes

Torment and tangle of stone, like Hell frozen, where snow
Lingers only in shadow. Alone, alone,
What grandeur here speaks? The world
Is the language we cannot utter.
10 Is it a language we can even hear?

Years pass, and at night you may dream-wake
To that old altitude, breath thinning again to glory,
While the heart, like a trout,
Leaps. What,
Long ago, did the world try to say?

It is long till dawn.
The stars have changed position, a far train whistles
For crossing. Before the first twitter of birds

You may again drowse. Listen—we hear now
20 The creatures of gardens and lowlands.

It may be that God loves them, too.

Antinomy: Time and What Happened

(1)

Alone, alone, I lie. The canoe
On blackness floats. It must
Be so, for up to a certain point
All comes back clear. I saw,
At dock, the canoe, aluminum, rising ghost-white on blackness.
This much is true. Silent,
As entering air, the paddle, slow, dips. Silent,
I slide forth. Forth on,
Forth into,
10 What new dimension? Slow
As a dream, no ripple at keel, I move through
The stillness, on blackness, past hope or despair
Not relevant now to illusion I'd once
Thought I lived by. At last,
Shores absorbed in the blackness of forest, I lie down. High,
Stars stare down, and I
See them. I wonder
If they see me. If they do, do they know
What they see?

(2)

20 Do I hear stars speak in a whisper as gentle as breath
To the few reflections caught pale in the blackness beneath?
How still is the night! It must be their voices.
Then strangely a loon-cry glows ember-red,
And the ember in darkness dims
To a tangle of senses beyond windless fact or logical choices,
While out of Time, Timelessness brims
Like oil on black water, to coil out and spread
On the time that seems past and the time that may come,
And both the same under
30 The present's darkening dome.

(3)

A dog, in the silence, is barking a county away.
It is long yet till day.

*

(4)

As consciousness outward seeps, the dark seeps in.
As the self dissolves, realization surrenders its burden
And thus fulfills your fictionality.
Night wind is no more than unrippling drift.
The canoe, light as breath, moves in a dignity
As soundless as a star's mathematical shift
Reflected light-years away
40 In the lake's black parodic sky.

I wonder if this is I.

(5)

It is not long till day.

(6)

Dawn bursts like the birth pangs of your, and the world's, existence.
The future creeps into the blueness of distance.
Far back, scraps of memory hang, rag-rotten, on a rusting barbed-wire fence.

(7)

One crow, caw lost in the sky-peak's lucent trance,
Will gleam, sun-purpled, in its magnificence.

Auto-da-fé

Beautiful the intricacy of body!
Even when defective. But you have seen
Beauty beyond such watchmaker's craft,
For eyes unshutter in darkness to gleam out
As though to embrace you in holiness.

"...though I give my body to be burned,
And have not..." You know the rest,
And how the "I" is not the "body."
At least, according to St. Paul's text.

10 Beautiful in whatever sense
The body be, it is but flesh,
And flesh is grass, the season short.
Is a bag of stercory, a bag
Of excrement, the worm's surfeit,
But a bag with movement, lusts, strange
Ecstasies, transports, and strange dreams.
But, oh!—not "I" but "body" screams
When flame licks like a lover. That

Is the pure language of body, purer
20   Than even the cry, ecstatic, torn out
At the crisis of body's entwinement. That voice
From flame has a glory wilder than joy
To resound forever in heart, mind,
And gut, with thrilled shock and soprano of Truth.

All history resounds with such
Utterance—and stench of meat burned:
Dresden and Tokyo, and screams
In the Wilderness as flame on the wounded
Encroached, and the soft-bellied citizen,
30   With swollen ego as he tests
The new Cadillac and, half-drunk, piles on-
to the goddam overpass buttress. Then flame.
You can be quite sure he screams. But

Some have not. Witches sometimes,
And saints and martyrs, no doubt in number.
Take Latimer or, evasion all past,
White-bearded Cranmer, who, in slow drizzle,
Outraces the pack, ragtag and bobtail—
Though old, first to the blessèd stake.
40   Climbs up. Waits. Composed, austere.
Faggots lighted, white beard prickling sudden in
Wisps of brightness, he into fire thrusts
The recreant hand. No, no, not his!—
That traitor in the house.

                    Or that
Cracked Maid, and her Voices that she, at the last,
Could not betray, though foreknowing the end.
Through dazzle and shimmer of flame-dance, she raptly
Fixed eyes on the tied-stick cross a brutish
Soldier held up. Her cry was a prayer.

50   Such evidence can scarcely attest
Sure meaning.

                    But executioners
Might choke flame to smoke to suffocate
Clients quickly. Or sometimes gunpowder in packets,
To belly affixed, made a human grenade
Timed short for the job. This, perhaps,
From some fumbling thought of the holiness or

Beauty of body.

Passers-By on Snowy Night

Black the coniferous darkness,
White the snow track between,
And the moon, skull-white in its starkness,
Watches upper ledges lean,

And regards with the same distant stare,
And equal indifference,
How your breath goes white in steel air
As you trudge to *whither* from *whence.*

For from somewhere you rose to go,
10 Maybe long before daylight withdrew,
With the dream of a windowpane's glow
And a path trodden to invite you.

And, indeed, there may be such place,
Perhaps at next corner or swerve,
Where someone presses a face
To the frost-starred glass, though the curve

Shows yet only mocking moonlight.
But soon, but soon!—Alone,
I wish you well in your night
20 As I pass you in my own.

We each hear the distant friction,
Then *crack* of bough burdened with snow,
And each takes the owl's benediction,
And each goes the way he will go.

Chthonian Revelation: A Myth

Long before sun had toward the mountain dipped,
There downward at crag-fall, bare-footed, bare-hided but for
Beach-decency's minimum, they
Painfully picked past lava, past pumice, past boulders
High-hung and precarious over the sea-edge, awaiting
Last gust or earth-tremor. Below,
Lay the sand-patch, white
As the lace-fringe that, languid and lazy,
Teased from the edge of the sun-singing sea.

10 Few know what is there:
Sea and sand finger back into cave-shade where
Gothic, great strata,
Once torn in the shudder of earth and earth-agony, had
Down-reached to find footing in depth. Now deep
In arched dusk from the secret strand, the eye
Stares from that mystic and chthonian privacy
To far waters whose tirelessly eye-slashing blue
Commands the wide world beyond that secret purlieu.

After sun, how dark! Or after sun-scimitar, how
20 Gentle the touch of the shade's hypothetical hand. Farther on,
Farther in!—and on the soft sand he is sure
Of the track. Then looks back
Just once through the dwindling aperture
To the world of light-tangled detail
Where once life was led that now seems illusion of life
And swings in the distance with no more identity than
A dream half-remembered. He turns. His face lifts
To the soaring and scarcely definable nave,
From which darkness downward and endlessly sifts.

30 Eyes lower: and there,
In that drizzle of earth's inner darkness, she
Stands, face upward, arms up as in prayer or
Communion with whispers that wordlessly breathe—
There in columnar gracility stands, breasts,

In that posture, high. Eyes closed. And in
Such world of shadows, she,
From the light of her own inner being, glows.

Slowly, the lifted arms descend, fingers out,
Slightly parted. His eyes find the light of her eyes,
40   And over immeasurable distance,
Hands out, as though feeling his way in the act,
On the soundless sand he moves in his naked trance.
At last, fingertips make contact.

When in hermetic wisdom they wake, the cave-mouth is dim.
Once out, they find sun sinking under the mountain-rim,
And a last gleam boldly probes
High eastward the lone upper cloud. Scraps of nylon
Slip on like new skin, though cold, and feet
Find the rustle and kitten-tongue kiss of the foam creeping in.

50   A kilometer toward the headland, then home: they wade out,
And plunge. All wordless, this—
In a world where all words would be
Without meaning, and all they long to hear
Is the gull's high cry
Of mercilessly joyful veracity
To fill the hollow sky.

Side by side, stroke by stroke, in a fading light they move.
The sea pours over each stroke's frail groove.
Blackly, the headland looms. The first star is declared.
60   It is white above the mountain mass.
Eyes starward fixed, they feel the sea's long swell
And the darkling drag of nameless depth below.
They turn the headland, with starlight the only light they now know.

At arch-height of every stroke, at each fingertip, hangs
One drop, and the drops—one by one—are
About to fall, each a perfect universe defined
By its single, minuscule, radiant, enshrinèd star.

Looking Northward, Aegeanward: Nestlings on Seacliff

Chalky, steel-hard, or glass-slick, the cliff
That you crawl up, inch up, or clamber, till now,
Arms outspread, you cling to rotting scrub roots, and at last
See what you'd risked neck to see, the nub
Of rock-shelf outthrust from the shaded recess where,
From huddle of trash, dried droppings, and eggshell, lifts
The unfeathered pitiless weakness of necks that scarcely uphold
The pink corolla of beak-gape, the blind yearning lifeward.

*

In sun-blast, around and above, weave
10 The outraged screams that would net your head,
And wings slash the air with gleaming mercilessness,
While for toehold, or handhold, downward you grope,
Or for purchase to pause on and turn to the sun-crinkled sea,
To watch it fade northward into the
Horizon's blue ambiguity. You think
How long ago galleys—slim, black, bronze-flashing—bore
Northward too, and toward that quarter's blue dazzle of distance.
Or of a tale told.

And then think how, lost in the dimness of aeons, sea sloshed
20 Like suds in a washing machine, land heaved, and sky
At noon darkened, and darkness, not like any metaphor, fell,
And in that black fog gulls screamed as the feathers of gull-wing
From white flash to flame burst. That was the hour
When rooftree or keystone of palaces fell, and
Priest's grip drew backward the curls of the king's son until
Throat-softness was tightened, and the last cry
Was lost in the gargle of blood on bronze blade. The king,
In his mantle, had buried his face. But even
That last sacrifice availed naught. Ashes
30 Would bury all. Cities beneath sea sank.

In some stony, high field, somewhere, eyes,
Unbelieving, opened. They saw, first,
The sky. Stared long. How little
They understood. But, slowly, began,
In new ignorance, the nature of Time.

You think of necks, unfeathered and feeble, upholding
The pink corolla of beak-gape—that blind yearning lifeward.

Going West

Westward the Great Plains are lifting, as you
Can tell from the slight additional pressure
The accelerator requires. The sun,
Man to man, stares you straight in the eye, and the
Ribbon of road, white, into the sun's eye
Unspools. Wheat stubble long behind,
Now nothing but range land. But,
With tire song lulling like love, gaze riding white ribbon, forward
You plunge. Blur of burnt goldness
10 Past eye-edge on each
Side back-whirling, you arrow
Into the heart of hypnosis.

*

This is one way to write the history of America.

It was that way that day—oh, long
Ago. I had to slap
The back of my neck to stay awake,
Eyes westward in challenge to sun-gaze, lids
Slitted for sight. The land,
Beyond miles of distance, fled
20 Backward to whatever had been,
As though Space were Time.
Now do I see the first blue shadow of foothills?
Or is that a cloud line?
When will snow, like a vision, lift there?

I do not see, sudden out of
A scrub clump, the wing-burst. See only
The bloody explosion, right in my face,
On the windshield, the sun and
The whole land forward, forever,
30 All washed in blood, in feathers, in gut-scrawl.

It is, of course, a fool pheasant.

Hands clamping the wheel with a death grip
To hold straight while brakes scream, I,
With no breath, at the blood stare. The ditch
Is shallow enough when the car, in the end, rolls in.

Clumps of old grass, old newspaper, dry dirt—
All this got the worst off. Slowly
Red sunset now reddening to blood streaks,
Westward the car moved on. Blood
40 Fried on the glass yet stove-hot. For the day,
It had sure been a scorcher. Later,
Handfuls of dry dirt would scrape off the fried blood.
Eventually, water at a gas station.

Even now, long afterwards, the dream.

I have seen blood explode, blotting out sun, blotting
Out land, white ribbon of road, the imagined
Vision of snowcaps, white in their purity.

Rumor Verified

Since the rumor has been verified, you can, at least,
Disappear. You will no longer be seen at the Opera,
With your head bowed studiously, to one side a little,
Nor at your unadvertised and very exclusive
Restaurant, discussing wine with the sommelier,
Nor at your club, setting modestly forth your subtle opinion.

Since the rumor has been verified, you can try, as in dream,
To have lived another life—not with the father
Of rigid self-discipline, and x-ray glance,
10 Not with the mother, overindulgent and pretty,
Who toyed with your golden locks, slipped money on the side,
And waved a witch's wand for success, and a rich marriage.

Since the rumor has been verified, you may secretly sneak
Into El Salvador, or some such anguished spot,
Of which you speak the language, dreaming, trying to believe
That, orphaned, you grew up in poverty and vision, struggling
For learning, for mankind's sake. Here you pray with the sick, kiss lepers.

Since the rumor has been verified, you yearn to hold
A cup of cold water for the dying man to sip.
20 You yearn to look deep into his eyes and learn wisdom.
Or perhaps you have a practical streak and seek
Strange and derelict friends, and for justification lead
A ragtag squad to ambush the uniformed patrol.

Well, assuming the rumor verified—that may be
The only logical course: at any price,
Even bloodshed, however ruthless, to change any dominant order
And the secret corruption of power that makes us what we seem.
Yes, what is such verification against a strength of will?

But even in the face of the rumor, you sometimes shudder,
30 Seeing men as old as you who survive the terror
Of knowledge. You watch them slyly. What is their trick?
Do they wear a Halloween face? But what can you do?
Perhaps pray to God for strength to face the verification
That you are simply a man, with a man's dead reckoning, nothing more.

Mountain Mystery

On the mountain trail, all afternoon,
Gravel, uncertain, grinds under hoof.
On left side, with scrub growth, the cliff hangs.
On right, hypnotic emptiness.

*

Far down, in distance, a stream uncoils,
Like nothing more than a glittering wire
Tangled in stone-slots, lost on the plain,
In distance dissolved, or down canyon, gone.

You stop. You turn and know what already
10 You know: snow commanding west ranges, sun
Yet high. Again, eastward turn, and the sun's
Hot hand, fingers spread, is pressed against your shoulders.

Soaring in sunlight, eastward, the eagle
Swings to a height invisible
Except when light catches a bright flash of wing.
You open your lips in infinite thirst for

The altitude's wine. All, all of the past
Is gone. Yet what is the past but delusion?
Or future? In timeless light the world swims.
20 Alone, alone, you move through the timeless

Light. Toward what? The ranch in the valley,
Some ten miles away—what but delusion?
Alone, but not alone, for if
You lift your eyes, you see, some forty

Feet off, her there—unless, of course,
The track now rounds an abutment, and she
Has ceased to exist, and you are alone
In the world's metaphysical beauty of light.

Only alone do you then think of love.
30 Eyes shut, you think how, in saddle, that narrow
Waist sways. You think how, when soon the trail straightens,
She will lean back to smile. Her eyes will be bright.

You pass the abutment. Beyond, the great mesa
Sinks blue. The world falls away, falls forever.
But she sways in the saddle, turns, smiles, and your heart
Leaps up. Then cries out: *Oh, what is enough?*

That night you will lie in your bed, not alone—
But alone. In dark paradox, you lie
And think of the screaming gleam of the world
40 In which you have passed alone, lost—

And in dark, lost, lain, hearing frailty of breath beside.

Vermont Ballad: Change of Season

All day the fitful rain
Had wrought new traceries,
New quirks, new love-knots, down the pane.

And what do I see beyond
That fluctuating gray
But a world that seems to be God-abandoned—

Last leaf, rain-soaked, from my high
Birch falling, the spruce wrapped in thought,
And the mountain dissolving rain-gray to gray sky.

10   In the gorge, like a maniac
In sleep, the stream grinds its teeth,
As I lay a new log at the fireplace-back.

It is not that I am cold:
But that I think how the flux,
Three quarters now of a century old,

Has faithfully swollen and ebbed,
In life's brilliantly flashing red
Through all flesh, in vein and artery webbed.

But now it feels viscous and gray
20   As I watch the gray of the world,
And that thought seems soaked in my brain to stay.

But who is master here?
The turn of the season, or I?
What lies in the turn of the season to fear?

If I set muzzle to forehead
And pull the trigger, I'll see
The world in a last flood of vital red—

Not gray—that cataracts down.
No, I go to the windowpane
30   That rain's blurring tracery claims as its own,

And stare up the mountain track
Till I see in the rain-dusk, trudging
With stolid stride, his bundle on back,

A man with no name, in the gloom,
On an errand I cannot guess.
No sportsman—no! Just a man in his doom.

In this section such a man is not an uncommon sight.
In rain or snow, you pass, and he says: "Kinda rough tonight."

Dead Horse in Field

In the last, far field, half-buried
In barberry bushes red-fruited, the thoroughbred
Lies dead, left foreleg shattered below knee,
A .30-30 in heart. In distance,
I now see gorged crows rise ragged in wind. The day
After death I had gone for farewell, and the eyes
Were already gone—that
The beneficent work of crows. Eyes gone,
The two-year-old could, of course, more readily see
10 Down the track of pure and eternal darkness.

A week later I couldn't get close. The sweet stink
Had begun. That damned wagon mudhole
Hidden by leaves as we galloped—I found it.
Spat on it. As a child would. Next day
The buzzards. How beautiful in air!—carving
The slow, concentric, downward pattern of vortex, wing-glint
On wing-glint. From the house,
Now with glasses, I see
The squabble and pushing, the waggle of wattle-red heads.

20 At evening I watch the buzzards, the crows,
Arise. They swing black in nature's flow and perfection,
High in sad carmine of sunset. Forgiveness
Is not indicated. It is superfluous. They are
What they are.

How long before I go back to see
That intricate piece of
Modern sculpture, white now,
By weather and sun, intricate, now
Assuming in stasis
30 New beauty! Then,
A year later, I'll see
The green twine of vine, each leaf
Heart-shaped, soft as velvet, beginning
Its benediction.

It thinks it is God.

Can you think of some ground on which that may be gainsaid?

The Corner of the Eye

The poem is just beyond the corner of the eye.
You cannot see it—not yet—but sense the faint gleam,

Or stir. It may be like a poor little shivering fieldmouse,
One tiny paw lifted from snow while, far off, the owl

Utters. Or like breakers, far off, almost as soundless as dream.
Or the rhythmic rasp of your father's last breath, harsh

As the grind of a great file the blacksmith sets to hoof.
Or the whispering slither the torn morning newspaper makes,

Blown down an empty slum street in New York, at midnight,
10 Past dog shit and garbage cans, while the full moon,

Phthisic and wan, above the East River, presides
Over that last fragment of history which is

Our lives. Or the foggy glint of old eyes of
The sleepless patient who no longer wonders

If he will once more see in that window the dun-
Bleached dawn that promises what. Or the street corner

Where always, for years, in passing you felt, unexplained, a pang
Of despair, like nausea, till one night, late, late on that spot

You were struck stock-still, and again remembered—felt
20 Her head thrust to your shoulder, she clinging, while you

Mechanically pat the fur coat, hear sobs, and stare up
Where tall buildings, frailer than reed-stalks, reel among stars.

Yes, something there at eye-edge lurks, hears ball creak in socket,
Knows, before you do, tension of muscle, change

Of blood pressure, heart-heave of sadness, foot's falter, for
It has stalked you all day, or years, breath rarely heard, fangs dripping.

And now, any moment, great hindquarters may hunch, ready—
Or is it merely a poem, after all?

What Voice at Moth-Hour

What voice at moth-hour did I hear calling
As I stood in the orchard while the white
Petals of apple blossoms were falling,
Whiter than moth-wing in that twilight?

What voice did I hear as I stood by the stream,
Bemused in the murmurous wisdom there uttered,
While ripples at stone, in their steely gleam,
Caught last light before it was shuttered?

What voice did I hear as I wandered alone
10 In a premature night of cedar, beech, oak,
Each foot set soft, then still as stone
Standing to wait while the first owl spoke?

The voice that I heard once at dew-fall, I now
Can hear by a simple trick. If I close
My eyes, in that dusk I again know
The feel of damp grass between bare toes,

Can see the last zigzag, sky-skittering, high,
Of a bullbat, and even hear, far off, from
Swamp-cover, the whip-o-will, and as I
20 Once heard, hear the voice: *It's late! Come home.*

Another Dimension

Over meadows of Brittany, the lark
Flames sunward, divulging, in tinseled fragments from
That height, song. Song is lost
In the blue depth of sky, but
We know it is there at an altitude where only
God's ear may hear.

Dividing fields, long hedges, in white
Bloom powdered, gently slope to the
Blue of sea that glitters in joy of its being.

10 Once I lay on the grass and looked upward
To feel myself redeemed into
That world which had no meaning but itself,
As I, lying there, had only the present, no future or past.

*

Yes—who was the man who on the midnight street corner,
Alone, once stood, while sea-fog
Put out last lights, electric or heavenly?
Who knows that history is the other name for death?
Who, from the sweated pillow, wakes to know
How truth can lie? Who knows that jealousy,
20 Like a chinch-bug under the greenest turf, thrives?
Who learned that kindness can be the last cruelty?

I have shut my eyes and seen the lark flare upward.
All was as real as when my eyes were open.
I have felt earth breathe beneath my shoulder blades.
I have strained to hear, sun-high, that Platonic song.

It may be that some men, dying, have heard it.

English Cocker: Old and Blind

With what painful deliberation he comes down the stair,
At the edge of each step one paw suspended in air,
And distrust. Does he thus stand on a final edge
Of the world? Sometimes he stands thus, and will not budge,

With a choking soft whimper, while monstrous blackness is whirled
Inside his head, and outside too, the world
Whirling in blind vertigo. But if your hand
Merely touches his head, old faith comes flooding back—and

The paw descends. His trust is infinite
10 In you, who are, in his eternal night,
Only a frail scent subject to the whim
Of wind, or only a hand held close to him

With a dog biscuit, or, in a sudden burst
Of temper, the force that jerks that goddamned, accurst
Little brute off your bed. But remember how you last saw
Him hesitate in his whirling dark, one paw

Suspended above the abyss at the edge of the stair,
And remember that musical whimper, and how, then aware
Of a sudden sweet heart-stab, you knew in him
20 The kinship of all flesh defined by a halting paradigm.

Have You Ever Eaten Stars?

A Note on Mycology

Scene: A glade on a bench of the mountain,
Where beech, birch, and spruce meet
In peace, though in peace not intermingled,
Around the slight hollow, upholstered
In woods-earth damp, and soft, centuries old—
Spruce needle, beech leaf, birch leaf, ground-pine belly-crawling,
And fern frond, and deadfall of birch, grass blade
So biblically frail, and sparse in that precinct where
The sunray makes only its brief
10   And perfunctory noontide visitation.
All, all in that cycle's beneficence
Of being are slowly absorbed—oh, slowly—into
What once had fed them. And now,
In silence as absolute as death,
Or as vision in breathlessness,
Your foot may come. Or mine,
As when I, sweat-soaked in summer's savagery,
Might here come, and stand
In that damp cool, and peace of process,
20   And hear, somewhere, a summer-thinned brook descending,
Past stone, and stone, its musical stair.

But late, once in the season's lateness, I,
After drouth had broken, rain come and gone,
And sky been washed to a blue more delicate,
Came. Stood. Stared. For now,
Earth, black as a midnight sky,
Was, like sky-darkness, studded with
Gold stars, as though
In emulation, however brief.
30   There, by a deer trail, by deer dung nourished,
Burst the gleam, rain-summoned,
Of bright golden chanterelles.
However briefly, however small and restricted, here was
A glade-burst of glory.

Later, I gathered stars into a basket.

Question: What can you do with stars, or glory?
I'll tell you, I'll tell you—thereof
Eat. Swallow. Absorb. Let bone
Be sustained thereof, let gristle
40   Toughen, flesh be more preciously
Gratified, muscle yearn in
Its strength. Let brain glow
In its own midnight of darkness,
Under its own inverted, bowl-shaped

Sky, skull-sky, let the heart
Rejoice.

What other need now
Is possible to you but that
Of seeing life as glory?

Afterward

After the promise has been kept, or
Broken. After the sun

Has touched the peak westward and you suddenly
Realize that Time has cut another notch

In the stick with your name on it, and you wonder
How long before you will feel the need

For prayer. After you have stumbled on the obituary
Of a once-girl, photograph now unrecognizable,

Who, at night, used to come to your apartment and do everything but
10 It. Would fight like a tiger. Then weep.

Never married, but, as the paper says,
Made a brilliant career, also prominent in good works. After

You have, in shame, lain awake trying to account for
Certain deeds of vanity, weakness, folly, or

Neurosis, and have shuddered in disbelief. After
You have heard the unbearable, lonely wolf-howl of grief

In your heart, and walked a dark house, feet bare. After
You have looked down on the unimaginable expanse of polar

Icecap stretching in light of gray-green ambiguousness,
20 And, lulled by jet-hum, wondered if this

Is the only image of eternity. —Ah, menhirs, monoliths, and all
Such frozen thrusts of stone, arms in upward anguish of fantasy, images

By creatures hairy and humped, on heath, on hill, in holt
Raised! Oh, see

How a nameless skull, by weather uncovered or
The dateless winds,

*

In the moonlit desert, smiles, having been
So long alone. After all, are you ready

To return the smile? Try. Sit down by a great cactus,
30 While other cacti, near and as far as distance, lift up

Their arms, thorny and black, in ritual unresting above
Tangles of black shadow on white sand, to that great orb

Of ever out-brimming, unspooling light and glow, queenly for good or evil, in
The forever sky. After you have sat

In company awhile, perhaps trust will grow.
Perhaps you can start a conversation of mutual comfort.

There must be so much to exchange.

Fear and Trembling

The sun now angles downward, and southward.
The summer, that is, approaches its final fulfillment.
The forest is silent, no wind-stir, bird-note, or word.
It is time to meditate on what the season has meant.

But what is the meaningful language for such meditation?
What is a word but wind through the tube of the throat?
Who defines the relation between the word *sun* and the sun?
What word has glittered on whitecap? Or lured blossom out?

Walk deeper, foot soundless, into the forest.
10 Stop, breath bated. Look southward, and up, where high leaves
Against sun, in vernal translucence, yet glow with the freshest
Young tint of the lost spring. Here now nothing grieves.

Can one, in fact, meditate in the heart, rapt and wordless?
Or find his own voice in the towering gust now from northward?
When boughs toss—is it in joy or pain and madness?
The gold leaf—is it whirled in anguish or ecstasy skyward?

Can the heart's meditation wake us from life's long sleep,
And instruct us how foolish and fond was our labor spent—
Us who now know that only at death of ambition does the deep
20 Energy crack crust, spurt forth, and leap

From grottoes, dark—and from the caverned enchainment?

from Chief Joseph of the Nez Perce

[Little Bear Paws and Joseph's Surrender]

Joseph, at last, to the Little Bear Paws comes.
He believes himself safe by the "Old Lady's Skirts":

> I sat down in a fat and beautiful country. I had won my freedom and
> the freedom of my people. There were many empty places in the
> lodges and the council, but we were in a land where we could not be
> forced to live in a place we did not want.

Clearly defensible, in the alluvial gulch
Of Snake Creek, beside good water, they
Set themselves down, protected from wind
By bluffs, farther by mountains, tepees now set
In a circle, good hunting handy. Women
Could here dry winter meat, and livestock
Graze widely. But in precaution at each
10 Tepee a mount was staked. No scouts out, however.
For this was a land of peace. They had peace.

In dawn light this was the pastoral scene Miles saw—
And saw, or thought he saw, how the slope,
Wide, rolling, slightly atilt,
Invited cavalry's thunder. No Howard!
His heart leaped. One charge—and the star!

But Fate, the slut, is flirtatious. What
Miles, in hypnotic passion, did not
See was a network of small, brush-grown coulees,
20 And a great coulee, moatlike, east and west,
Draining down to the Snake, and top growth
At that distance looked like the leveling plain.
This, Miles could not see, but clear to his sight,
If not to his brain, there was, beyond,
A long ridge, now brown with autumn-bit sage to give
Perfect deception for braves to lie in,
Barrel steady, trigger-finger looped, eye squinting.

*

How calm the plain looked. In saintly peace
Miles stood in God's love. He knew that God loved him.
30   For at the debouchment of Bear Paws there was
No perspective to show, in the dip, swell and dip,
That the last east-west cross-ridge, southward,
That looked so easy, lied.
The easiest yet, it looked,
For eastward
It sinks. Ah, how in his dream could he know
That on the far side, on the north,
Before the flat of the village, it dropped sharp
To hoof-trap and haunch-grind that, sudden,
40   Would crumple the cavalry eastward, and spill it,
Tangled and cramped, directly under
The rifle-pricked ridge beyond,
And the closer spite of the fanged coulee?

That is what the land-lay today indicates.

Miles saw in his head the victory form like a crystal—
With Companies *A, D,* and *K* of Custer's
Old favorite Seventh, with Cheyenne scouts,
Who could not now for scouting be used
For fear of alarm,
50   As the cutting edge of attack.

His breath comes hard. How slow the bastards find place!
Already the Cheyennes, now slick-skinned and naked
To breech-clout and moccasins, hold back
Pawing mounts, though they pant to ride
For the kill, to make *coup,*
To dab cheek with the blood of a brother.
They yelp in the snow-swirl. Captain Hale jokes:
"My God, have I got to go out and get killed
In such weather?" It was a good joke. But no laughter.

60   No Howard yet! Miles lifts his arm.
He takes the deep breath. He shouts, "Attack!"

He thought of the half-wits down there, scarce more
Than a hundred. *What were they thinking down there?*

There was only silence down there.

Now is the rhythm of hoof. First, trot:
Down slope, down dip, up ridge-swell,
Then down. Then bursts the hoof-thunder!—
And then the blind surge when the last
Ridge divulges its dire,
70   Deadly secret, compresses the ranks, swerves horsemen, and spills
The mass to the open before the moat-coulee. Blaze

Now has burst, bursts first
At two hundred, a hundred and fifty, a hundred, then fifty
Long paces, but not long for lead, and the charge,
Like sea-froth at cliff-foot, in blood-spume
Shatters:

Horses rearing in death, the death scream, saddles
Blown empty, lines broken, all officers down, pure panic.
Now Death probes out for the backbone, for shoulders,
80   At Enfield—at Winchester—at Sharps range,
Snow red, then redder,
And reddening more, as snow falls
From the unperturbed gray purity of sky.

Captain Hale was'a prophet: dead in such weather.

> I never went up against anything like the Nez Perces in all my life, and
> I have been in a lot of scraps.
>
> *James Snell, Scout for Miles*

Miles's infantry made out some better; took losses, of course,
But in dying laid down a ring of investment, which promised a siege.
So the siege settled down,
With slow, systematic shelling of all in the village,
And hunger began its long gut-gnaw.

90   For Miles, what bastardly luck! A siege—and how long?

But luck held for Miles. Under the fire
Of cannon buried howitzerwise, what else
But negotiation? It came—with Miles
Violating a flag of truce to hold Joseph.
But the braves were alert. They, too, grabbed a hostage.
So terms were arranged, Miles's terms mysteriously generous.

Now Howard stands, suddenly, there.

Stood there, commander, enduring the only
Outlet of rage and hatred Miles
100   Could give vent to: ironical courtesy, cold,
Gray as snot. But Howard,
Whose sweat had soaked sheets in wrestling with God,
Laid his remaining hand on the steel-stiff shoulder
That quivered beneath it. Howard, almost
As soft as a whisper, promises him the surrender.

And hearing his own words, he knew a pure
And never-before-known bliss swell his heart.

*

Miles laughed with the laughter of friend or brother.
But if Howard smiled, the smile was inward—
110 A fact unnoticed by Miles, who already
Was deep in his head's dizzy darkness composing
The rhetoric of his official communiqué:

> We have had our usual success. We made a very direct and rapid
> march across country, and after a severe engagement and being
> kept under fire for three days, the hostile camp under Chief Joseph
> surrendered at two o'clock today.

How now would the newspapers blaze! Sherman smile!
And let old Sturgis—a colonel yet—bite his nails.
To hell with his son—all soldiers die.

> I felt the end coming. All for which we had suffered and lost!
> Thoughts came of Wallowa, where I grew up ... Then with a rifle
> I stand forth, saying in my heart, 'Here I will die.'
>
>   *Yellow Wolf*

But did not. Lived on. In history.

Five inches of snow now, sky gray, and yonder
One buffalo rug, black on white,
And kept black until Howard, Miles, and the staff
120 Would arrive when the hour struck.
It would strike.

For terms now are firm: rifles stacked
With bandoliers twined. No need now for rifles,
For hunting or honor. They'd go to Keogh
And eat white man's bread, with only the promise
Of Miles that in spring they'd go west to high land
Where mountains are snow-white and the Great Spirit
Spills peace into the heart of man.
Wallowa—no! But another land of pure air,
130 Blue distance, white peaks, their own lives to live,
And again their own guns, to hunt as man must.
And there they might think of the eyes of the fathers
Yet on them, though across all
The mountains, the distance, the noble disaster.

> I believed General Miles or I never would have surrendered.
>
>   *Chief Joseph*

At late afternoon, light failing, Howard
Is called, with his brass, to the buffalo robe that
Lies black against snow. Up from the dry
Brown gravel and water-round stones of the Eagle,
Now going snow-white in dryness, and up
140 From the shell-churned
Chaos of camp-site, slowly ascends
The procession. Joseph, not straight, sits his mount,
Head forward bowed, scalp lock with otter-skin tied.

Black braids now framed a face past pain.
Hands loose before him, the death-giving rifle
Loose-held across, he comes first.
The bullet scar is on his brow.
Chief Hush-hush-kute, beside him, on foot,
Moves, and that chief speaks, and the head
150 Of Joseph is bowed, bowed as in courtesy
To words of courage and comfort. But
The head may be bowed to words by others unheard.

Joseph draws in his mount. Then,
As though all years were naught in their count, arrow-straight
He suddenly sits, head now lifted. With perfect ease
To the right he swings a buckskinned leg over. Stands.
His gray shawl exhibits four bullet holes.

Straight standing, he thrusts out his rifle,
Muzzle-grounded, to Howard. It is
160 The gesture, straight-flung, of one who casts the world away.

Howard smiles as a friend. But
Peremptory or contemptuous,
Indicates Miles. Upon that steel symbol,
The hand of Miles closes. We do not know
What ambiguities throttle his heart.
Miles is sunk in his complex tension of being,
In his moment of triumph and nakedness.

Joseph steps back. His heart gives words.
But the words, translated, are addressed to Howard.

Tell General Howard I know his heart. What he told me before I have
in my heart. I am tired of fighting. Our chiefs are killed. Looking
Glass is dead. The old men are killed. It is the young men who say
yes or no. He who led the young men is dead. It is cold and we have
no blankets. Our little children are freezing to death. I want time to
look for my children and see how many of them I may find. Maybe I
shall find them among the dead. Hear me, my chiefs, I am tired. Heart
is sick and sad. From where the sun now stands, I will fight no more
forever.

170 Then Joseph drew his blanket over his head.

[Joseph at Grant's Funeral]

He is famous now. Great men have come
To shake his hand in his poverty.
Generals who chased him, ten to one,
With their fancy equipment, Gatling guns,
Artillery. Histories name him a genius.
And even Sherman, who never had fought him
But gave more death than ever his subordinate generals—
Yes, slime-green waters of Leavenworth—wrote:

> The Indians throughout displayed a courage and skill that elicited
> universal praise; they abstained from scalping; let captive women go
> free; and did not commit indiscriminate murders of peaceful families
> ... they fought with almost scientific skill.

Frontiersmen, land-grabbers, gold-panners were dead.
10 Veterans of the long chase skull-grinned in darkness.
A more soft-handed ilk now swayed the West. They founded
Dynasties, universities, libraries, shuffled
Stocks, and occasionally milked
The Treasury of the United States,
Not to mention each other. They slick-fucked a land.

But as their wealth grew, so Joseph's fame.
As the President's guest, in the White House,
He had shaken Roosevelt's hand. With Miles,
No longer a mere brigadier, he broke
20 Bread among crystal and silver. Back West
Artists came to commemorate for the future
That noble head. In bronze it was cast:

In gallery 224 of the American wing of the Metropolitan Museum of
Art, accession number 06.313, may be found the bronze portrait of
'Joseph, Chief of the Nez Perce Indians. His Indian name, Hin-mah-
toó-yah-lat-kekht, is said to mean Thunder Rolling in the Mountains
... This medallion was taken from life in 1889. Bronze, diameter
17-1/2 in. Signed Olin L. Warner... '

American Sculpture Catalogue
of the Collection of the Metropolitan
Museum of Art, page 42

Great honor came, for it came to pass
That to praise the red man was the way
Best adapted to expunge all, all, in the mist
Of bloodless myth. And in the predictably obscene
Procession to dedicate Grant's Tomb, which grandeur
Was now to hold the poor, noble dust of Appomattox,
Joseph, whose people had never taken
30 A scalp, rode beside Buffalo Bill—
Who had once sent his wife a yet-warm scalp,
He himself had sliced from the pate
Of a red man who'd missed him. Joseph rode
Beside Buffalo Bill, who broke clay pigeons—
One-two-three-four-five—just like that.

Joseph rode by the clown, the magician who could transform
For howling patriots, or royalty,
The blood of history into red ketchup,
A favorite American condiment. By his side
40 Joseph rode. Did Joseph know
Of the bloody scalp in love's envelope, know
That the dead Grant had once, in the White House,
In his own hand, certified the land
Of the Winding Waters to Joseph's people—
"Forever"—until some western politico, or such,
Jerked him by the nose, like a bull with a brass
Ring there for control?

Not right, not left,
Joseph looked, as hoofs on the cobbles clacked
50 In the dolor of that procession. He
Was only himself, and the distances
He stared into were only himself.

from Altitudes and Extensions

Three Darknesses

I.

There is some logic here to trace, and I
Will try hard to find it. But even as I begin, I
Remember one Sunday morning, festal with springtime, in
The zoo of Rome. In a natural, spacious, grassy area,
A bear, big as a grizzly, erect, indestructible,
Unforgiving as God, as rhythmic as
A pile-driver—right-left, right-left—
Slugged at an iron door. The door,
Heavy, bolted, barred, must have been
10 The entrance to a dark enclosure, a cave,
Natural or artificial. Minute by minute, near, far,
Wheresoever we wandered, all Sunday morning,
With the air full of colored balloons trying to escape
From children, the ineluctable
Rhythm continues. You think of the
Great paws like iron on iron. Can iron bleed?
Since my idiot childhood the world has been
Trying to tell me something. There is something
Hidden in the dark. The bear
20 Was trying to enter into the darkness of wisdom.

II.

Up Black Snake River, at anchor in
That black tropical water, we see
The cormorant rise—cranky, graceless,
Ungeared, unhinged, one of God's more cynical
Improvisations, black against carmine of sunset. He
Beats seaward. The river gleams blackly west, and thus
The jungle divides on a milk-pale path of sky toward the sea.
Nothing human is visible. Each of us lies looking
Seaward. Ice melts in our glasses. We seem ashamed

10 Of conversation. Asia is far away. The radio is not on.
   The grave of my father is far away. Our host
   Rises silently, is gone. Later we see him,
   White helmet in netting mystically swathed,
   As he paddles a white skiff into the tangled
   Darkness of a lagoon. There moss hangs. Later,
   Dark now, we see the occasional stab of his powerful
   Light back in the darkness of trunks rising
   From the side lagoon, the darkness of moss suspended.
   We think of the sound a snake makes
20 As it slides off a bough—the slop, the slight swish,
   The blackness of water. You
   Wonder what your host thinks about
   When he cuts the light and drifts on the lagoon of midnight.
   Though it is far from midnight. Upon his return,
   He will, you know,
   Lie on the deck-teak with no word. Your hostess
   Had gone into the cabin. You hear
   The pop of a wine cork. She comes back. The wine
   Is breathing in darkness.

III.

   The nurse is still here. Then
   She is not here. You
   Are here but are not sure
   It is you in the sudden darkness. No matter.
   A damned nuisance, but trivial—
   The surgeon has just said that. A dress rehearsal,
   You tell yourself, for
   The real thing. Later. Ten years? Fifteen?
   Tomorrow, only a dry run. At
10 5 A.M. they will come. Your hand reaches out in darkness
   To the TV button. It is an old-fashioned western.
   Winchester fire flicks white in the dream-night.
   It has something to do with vice and virtue, and the vastness
   Of moonlit desert. A stallion, white and flashing, slips,
   Like spilled quicksilver, across
   The vastness of moonlight. Black
   Stalks of cacti, like remnants of forgotten nightmares, loom
   Near at hand. Action fades into distance, but
   You are sure that virtue will triumph. Far beyond
20 All the world, the mountains lift. The snow peaks
   Float into moonlight. They float
   In that unnamable altitude of white light. God
   Loves the world. For what it is.

Mortal Limit

I saw the hawk ride updraft in the sunset over Wyoming.
It rose from coniferous darkness, past gray jags
Of mercilessness, past whiteness, into the gloaming
Of dream-spectral light above the last purity of snow-snags.

There—west—were the Tetons. Snow-peaks would soon be
In dark profile to break constellations. Beyond what height
Hangs now the black speck? Beyond what range will gold eyes see
New ranges rise to mark a last scrawl of light?

Or, having tasted that atmosphere's thinness, does it
10 Hang motionless in dying vision before
It knows it will accept the mortal limit,
And swing into the great circular downwardness that will restore

The breath of earth? Of rock? Of rot? Of other such
Items, and the darkness of whatever dream we clutch?

Immortality Over the Dakotas

It is not you that moves. It is the dark.
While you loll lax, semisomnolent, inside the great capsule,
Dark hurtles past. Now at the two-inch-thick plane-window glass,
You press your brow, see the furious
Futility of darkness boil past. It can't get in.
It is as though you were at last immortal.

You feel as though you had just had a quick dip
In the Lamb's mystic blood. You laugh into manic darkness.
You laugh at the tiny glow that far, far down
10 Shines like a glowworm beside an unseeable stone.
It would be a little Dakota town where
Population has not been dipped in the mystic blood.

On a July afternoon you once gassed up
At a town like that: movie, eatery, Baptist church
(Red brick), tourist court, white shotgun bungalows,
Wheat elevator towering over all.
Farms, of course, bleeding out forever.
Most likely the mercury stood at a hundred and one.

Now suddenly through glass, through dark fury, you see
20 Who must be down there, with collar up on the dirty sheepskin,
Snow on red hunter's cap, earflaps down.
Chores done. But he just can't bring himself to go in.
The doctor's just said he won't last till another winter.

*

She's sitting inside, white bun of hair neat as ever,
Squinting studiously down through bifocals at what she's knitting.
He knows her fire's getting low, but he can't go in.
He knows that if he did he might let something slip.
He couldn't stand that. So stares at the blackness of sky.
Stares at lights, green and red, that tread the dark of your immortality.

Arizona Midnight

The grief of the coyote seems to make
Stars quiver whiter over the blankness which
Is Arizona at midnight. In sleeping-bag,
Protected by the looped rampart of anti-rattler horsehair rope,
I take a careful twist, grinding sand on sand,
To lie on my back. I stare. Stars quiver, twitch,
In their infinite indigo. I know
Nothing to tell the stars, who go,
Age on age, along tracks they understand, and
10   The only answer I have for the coyote would be
My own grief, for which I have no
Tongue—indeed, scarcely understand.
Eastward, I see
No indication of dawn, not yet ready for the scream
Of inflamed distance,
Which is the significance of day.
But dimly I do see
Against that darkness, lifting in blunt agony,
The single great cactus. Once more I hear the coyote
20   Wail. I strain to make out the cactus. It has
Its own necessary beauty.

Hope

In the orchidaceous light of evening
Watch how, from the lowest hedge-leaf, creeps,
Grass blade to blade, the purpling shadow. It spreads
Its spectral ash beneath the leveling, last
Gold rays that, westward, have found apertures
From the magnificent disaster of the day.

Against gold light, beneath the maple leaf,
A pale blue gathers, accumulates, sifts
Downward to modulate the flowery softness
10   Of gold intrusive through the blackening spruce boughs.
Spruces heighten the last glory beyond by their stubbornness.
They seem rigid in blackened bronze.

*

Wait, wait—as though a finger were placed to lips.
The first star petals timidly in what
Is not yet darkness. That audacity
Will be rewarded soon. In this transitional light,
While cinders in the west die, the world
Has its last blooming. Let your soul

20 Be still. All day it has curdled in your bosom
Denatured by intrusion of truth or lie, or both.
Lay both aside, nor debate their nature. Soon,
While not even a last bird twitters, the last bat goes.
Even the last motor fades into distance. The promise
Of moonrise will dawn, and slowly, in all fullness, the moon

Will dominate the sky, the world, the heart,
In white forgiveness.

New Dawn

To John Hersey and Jacob Lawrence

I. Explosion: Sequence and Simultaneity

Greenwich Time	11:16 P.M.	August 5	1945
New York Time	6:16 P.M.	August 5	1945
Chicago Time	5:16 P.M.	August 5	1945
San Francisco Time	3:16 P.M.	August 5	1945
Pearl Harbor Time	1:16 P.M.	August 5	1945
Tinian Island Time	9:16 A.M.	August 6	1945
Hiroshima Time	8:16 A.M.	August 6	1945

II. Goodbye to Tinian

Now that all the "unauthorized items" are cleared from the bomber, including
The optimistic irrelevance of six packs
Of condoms, and three pairs of
Pink silk panties. Now that
The closed briefing session of midnight
Is over, with no information from Colonel Tibbets, commander, on the
Secret, obsessive question of every crewman—What
Is the cargo? From Tibbets only
That it is "very powerful." Now that
10 The crew, at the end of the briefing,
Have taken what comfort they can from the prayer
Of their handsome chaplain, a man's man of

Rich baritone—"Almighty Father,
Who wilt hear the prayer of them that love Thee,
We pray Thee to be with those
Who brave the heights
Of Thy heaven..."

And now that around the bomber the klieg lights
Murdering darkness, the flashbulbs, the barking
20   Of cameramen, the anonymous faces preparing to be famous,
The nag of reporters, the handshakes, the jokes,
The manly embraces,
The scrape of city shoes on asphalt, the tarmac,
The news
From weather scouts out that clouds hovering over
The doomed world will, at dawn,
Probably clear. And,

Now down to brass tacks, Lewis,
The flawless co-pilot,
30   Addresses the crew, "...just don't
Screw it up. Let's do this really great!"

III. Take-off: Tinian Island

Colonel Tibbets, co-pilot beside him,
Lays hand to controls of the plane, which he
Has named for his mother, Enola Gay.

Pocketed secretly in Tibbets' survival vest,
Under the pale green coverall, is the
Metal container of twelve capsules of cyanide,
These for distribution to command if facing capture.

Though a heavy-caliber sidearm would serve.

The tow jeep strains at the leash. Wheels,
10   Under the weight of 150,000 pounds,
Overweight 15,000, crunch
Off the apron, bound for the runway. Position taken.

"This is Dimples Eighty-two to
North Tinian Tower. Ready for
Takeoff instructions."

So that is her name now. At least in code. Dimples.

"Tower to Dimples Eighty-two. Clear
To taxi. Take off Runway A, for Able."

*

At 2:45 A.M., August 6, Tinian Time,
20 Tibbets to Lewis:
"Let's go!"

All throttles full,
She roars down the runway, flicking past
Avenues of fire trucks, ambulances, overload
The last gamble, the runway
Now spilling furiously toward
Black sea-embrace.

Who would not have trusted the glittering record of Tibbets?

But even Lewis cries out. Grabs at controls. Tibbets,
30 Gaze fixed, hears nothing. Time
Seems to die. But
Iron hands, iron nerves, tighten at last, and
The control is drawn authoritatively back. The carriage
Rises to show
The air-slick belly where death sleeps.

This at cliff-verge.

Below, white, skeletal hands of foam
Grope up. Strain up.

Are empty.

IV. Mystic Name

Some 600 miles north-northwest to Iwo Jima, where,
In case of defect developing in the *Enola Gay,*
Tibbets will land, transfer cargo to
The waiting standby plane,
And take over. If not necessary,
No landing, but he will rendezvous
With weather planes and two B-29's
To fly with him as observers.

At 3 A.M., well short of Iwo Jima, code lingo
10 To Tinian Tower: "Judge going to work"—
To announce innocently the arming
Of the cargo. The cargo,
Inert as a sawed-off tree trunk ten feet long,
Twenty-eight inches in diameter, four and a half tons in weight, lies
In its dark covert.

*

It is
So quiet, so gentle as it rocks
In its dark cradle, in namelessness. But some
Name it "The Beast," and some,
20   With what irony, "Little Boy." Meanwhile,
It sleeps, with its secret name
And nature.

Like the dumb length of tree trunk, but literally
A great rifle barrel packed with uranium,
Two sections, forward one large, to rear one small, the two
Divided by a "tamper" of neutron-resistant alloy.
All harmless until, backed by vulgar explosive, the small will
Crash through to
The large mass
30   To wake it from its timeless drowse. And that
Will be that. Whatever
That may be.

V. When?

When can that be known? Only after
The delicate and scrupulous fingers of "Judge"
Have done their work. After:

    1. Plugs, identified by the color green,
       Are installed in waiting sockets

    2. Rear plate is removed

    3. Armor plate is removed

    4. Breech wrench frees breech plug

    5. Breech plug is placed on rubber mat

10   6. Explosive charge is reinserted,
       Four units, red ends to breech

    7. Breech plug is reinserted, tightened home

    8. Firing line is connected

    9. Armor plate is reinstalled

    10. Rear plate is reinstalled

    11. Tools are removed

    12. Catwalk is secured

In that dark cramp of tunnel, the precise
Little flashlight beam
20   Finicks, fastidious, over all.

*

Soft feet withdraw.

Later, 6:30 A.M. Japanese Time, last lap to target, green plugs
On the log, with loving care, tenderly, quietly
As a thief, will be replaced by plugs marked
Lethally red.

VI. Iwo Jima

Over Iwo Jima, the moon, now westering, sinks in faint glimmer
Of horizon clouds. Soon
The heartbreaking incandescence of tropic dawn,
In which the *Enola Gay* loiters for contact
With weather scouts and the two B-29's
Which rise to attend her: observers.

Weather reports good from spotters.
Three options: Nagasaki, Kokura, Hiroshima.

But message of one spotter:
10 "Advise bombing primary"—i.e.,
Hiroshima.

Already preferred by Tibbets.

What added satisfaction it would have been to know that
At 7:31 A.M. Japanese Time, the
All Clear signal sounds over Hiroshima.

VII. Self and Non-Self

Tibbets looks down, sees
The slow, gray coiling of clouds, which are,
Beyond words, the image
Of sleep just as consciousness goes. He looks up, sees
Stars still glaring white down into
All the purity of emptiness. For an instant,
He shuts his eyes.

Shut
Your own eyes, and in timelessness you are
10 Alone with yourself. You are
Not certain of identity.
Has that non-self lived forever?

Tibbets jerks his eyes open. There
Is the world.

VIII. Dawn

Full dawn comes. Movement begins
In the city below. People
May even copulate. Pray. Eat. The sun
Offers its circular flame, incomparable,
Worship-worthy.

IX. The Approach

Speed 200 miles per hour, altitude
31,060 feet, directly toward the
Target control point of Aioi Bridge. On time. On
Calculation. Polaroid glasses
(Against brilliance of expected explosion)
Ordered on. Color
Of the world changes. It
Changes like a dream.

X. What *That* Is

What clouds remain part now, magically,
And there visible, sprawling supine, unfended, the city.
The city opens itself, opening
As in breathless expectancy.

Crossed hairs of bombsight approach
Aioi Bridge as specified, on time
For the target. Ferebee, bombardier, presses
Forehead devoutly to the cushion of bombsight.
Says,"I've got it."

10   The bomb is activated:
Self-controlled for the six-mile earthward
Plunge—and at that instant the plane,
Purged of its burden, leaps upward,
As though in joy, and the bomb
Will reach the calculated optimum of distance
Above ground, 1,890
Feet, the altitude determined
By the bomb's own delicate brain.

There,
20   The apocalyptic blaze of
New dawn

*

Bursts.

Temperature at heart of fireball:
50,000,000 degrees centigrade.

Hiroshima Time: 8:16 A.M., August 6, 1945.

XI. Like Lead

Of that brilliance beyond brilliance, Tibbets
Was later to report: "A taste like lead."

XII. Manic Atmosphere

Now, after the brilliance,
Suddenly, blindly, the plane
Heaves, is tossed
Like a dry leaf in
The massive and manic convulsion of
Atmosphere, which, compressed, from
Earth, miles down,

Bounces.

The plane recovers.

10 Again, then, the heave, the tossing.

With recovery.

XIII. Triumphal Beauty

Now, far behind, from the center of
The immense, purple-streaked, dark mushroom that, there, towers
To obscure whatever lies below,
A plume, positive but delicate as a dream,
Of pure whiteness, unmoved by breath of any wind,
Mounts.

Above the dark mushroom,
It grows high—high, higher—
In its own triumphal beauty.

XIV. Home

Later, home. Tinian is man's only home—
The brotherly hug, the bear-embrace, the glory, and
"We made it!"

The music, then solemn
Silence of the pinning of the medal,
The mutual salute. At last,
The gorging of the gorgeous feast
To the point of vomit, the slosh
Of expensive alcohol
10 In bellies expensively swollen.

XV. Sleep

Some men, no doubt, will, before sleep, consider
One thought: I am alone. But some,
In the mercy of God, or booze, do not

Long stare at the dark ceiling.

True Love

In silence the heart raves. It utters words
Meaningless, that never had
A meaning. I was ten, skinny, red-headed,

Freckled. In a big black Buick,
Driven by a big grown boy, with a necktie, she sat
In front of the drugstore, sipping something

Through a straw. There is nothing like
Beauty. It stops your heart. It
Thickens your blood. It stops your breath. It

10 Makes you feel dirty. You need a hot bath.
I leaned against a telephone pole, and watched.
I thought I would die if she saw me.

How could I exist in the same world with that brightness?
Two years later she smiled at me. She
Named my name. I thought I would wake up dead.

Her grown brothers walked with the bent-knee
Swagger of horsemen. They were slick-faced.
Told jokes in the barbershop. Did no work.

*

Their father was what is called a drunkard.
20   Whatever he was he stayed on the third floor
Of the big white farmhouse under the maples for twenty-five years.

He never came down. They brought everything up to him.
I did not know what a mortgage was.
His wife was a good, Christian woman, and prayed.

When the daughter got married, the old man came down wearing
An old tail coat, the pleated shirt yellowing.
The sons propped him. I saw the wedding. There were

Engraved invitations, it was so fashionable. I thought
I would cry. I lay in bed that night
30   And wondered if she would cry when something was done to her.

The mortgage was foreclosed. That last word was whispered.
She never came back. The family
Sort of drifted off. Nobody wears shiny boots like that now.

But I know she is beautiful forever, and lives
In a beautiful house, far away.
She called my name once. I didn't even know she knew it.

Last Walk of Season

For the last time, for this or perhaps
Any year to come in unpredictable life, we climb,
In the westward hour, up the mountain trail
To see the last light. Now
No cloud in the washed evening lours,
Though, under drum-tight roof, while each minute's
Mouse-tooth all night gnawed,
The season's first rain had done duty. Dams and traps,
Where the old logging trucks had once made tracks, now gurgle. That
10   Is the only voice we hear. We do not ask
What burden that music bears.

Our wish is to think of nothing but happiness. Of only
The world's great emptiness. How bright,
Rain-washed, the pebbles shine! A few high leaves
Of birch have golden gone. Ah, the heart leaps
That soon all earth will be of gold:
Gold birch, gold beech, gold maple. That
Is its own delight. Later, nothing visible
Except black conifers will clamber
20   Up the first white of ridge, then the crag's blank sun-blaze of snow.
Can it be that the world is but the great word
That speaks the meaning of our joy?

*

We came where we had meant to come. And not
Too late. In the mountain's cup, moraine-dammed, the lake
Lies left by a glacier older than God. Beyond it, the sun,
Ghostly, dips, flame-huddled in mist. We undertake
Not to exist, except as part of that one
Existence. We are thinking of happiness. In such case,
We must not count years. For happiness has no measurable pace.
30 Scarcely in consciousness, a hand finds, on stone, a hand.

They are in contact. Past lake, over mountain, last light
Probes for contact with the soft-shadowed land.

Last Meeting

A Saturday night in August when
Farm folks and tenants and black farmhands
Used to crowd the street of a market town
To do their "traden," and chew the rag,

And to hide the likker from women hung out
Behind the poolroom or barbershop—
If you were white. If black, in an alley.
And the odor of whiskey mixed with the sweat

And cheap perfume, and high heels waggled
10 On worn bricks, and through the crowd
I saw her come. I see her now
As plain as then—some forty years back.

It's like a flash, and still she comes,
Comes peering at me, not sure yet,
For I'm in my city clothes and hat,
But in the same instant we recognize

Each other. I see the shrunken old woman
With bleary eyes and yellow-gray skin,
And walking now with the help of a stick.
20 We hug and kiss there in the street.

"Ro-Penn, Ro-Penn, my little tadpole,"
She said, and patted my cheek, and said,
"Git off yore hat so I'll see yore haid."
And I did. She ran her hands through thinning hair.

"Not fahr-red, like it used to be."
And ran her fingers some more. "And thinner,
And sandy color some places too."
Then she rocked her arms like cuddling a child,

*

And crooned, and said,"Now big and gone
30　Out in the wide world—but 'member me!"
I tried to say "I couldn't forget,"
But the words wouldn't come, and I felt how frail

Were the vertebrae I clasped. I felt
Tears run down beside her nose,
And a crazy voice, like some half-laugh,
Said, "Chile, yore Ma's dead, yore Pappy ole,

"But I'm hangen on fer what I'm wuth."
So we said goodbye, with eyes staring at us
And laughter in some corner, somewhere.
40　That was the last time we ever met.

All's changed. The faces on the street
Are changed. I'm rarely back. But once
I tried to find her grave, and failed.
Next time I'll promise adequate time.

And find it. I might take store-bought flowers
(Though not a florist in twenty miles),
But a fruit jar full of local zinnias
Might look even better with jimson weed.

It's nigh half a lifetime I haven't managed,
50　But there must be enough time left for that.

Muted Music

As sultry as the cruising hum
Of a single fly lost in the barn's huge, black
Interior, on a Sunday afternoon, with all the sky
Ablaze outside—so sultry and humming
Is memory when in barn-shade, eyes shut,
You lie in hay, and wonder if that empty, lonely,
And muted music was all the past was, after all.
Does the past now cruise your empty skull like
That blundering buzz at barn-height—which is dark
10　Except for the window at one gable, where
Daylight is netted gray with cobwebs, and the web
Dotted and sagged with blunderers that once could cruise and hum?

What do you really know
Of that world of decision and
Action you once strove in? What
Of that world where now
Light roars, while you, here, lulled, lie
In a cunningly wrought and mathematical

*

Box of shade, and try, of all the past, to remember
20　*Which* was *what, what, which.* Perhaps
That sultry hum from the lone bumbler, cruising high
In shadow, is the only sound that truth can make,
And into that muted music you soon sink
To hear at last, at last, what you have strained for
All the long years, and sometimes at dream-verge thought

You heard—the song the moth sings, the babble
Of falling snowflakes (in a language
No school has taught you), the scream
Of the reddening bud of the oak tree

30　As the bud bursts into the world's brightness.

Why Boy Came to Lonely Place

Limestone and cedar. Indigo shadow
On whiteness. The sky is flawlessly blue.
Only the cicada speaks. No bird. I do not know
Why I have these miles come. Here is only *I.* Not *You.*

Did I clamber these miles of distance
Only to quiver now in identity?
You are yourself only by luck, disaster, or chance,
And only alone may believe in your reality.

What drove you forth?—
10　Age thirteen, ignorant, lost in the world,
Canteen now dry and of what worth
With the cheese sandwich crumbling, and lettuce brown-curled?

Under the ragged shadow of cedar
You count the years you have been in the world,
And wonder what heed or
Care the world would have had of your absence as it whirled

In the iron groove of its circuit of space.
You say the name they gave you. That's all you are.
You move your fingers down your face,
20　And wonder how many years you'll be what you are.

But what is that? To find out you come to this lonely place.

Youthful Picnic Long Ago: Sad Ballad on Box

In Tennessee once the campfire glowed
With steady joy in its semi-globe
Defined by the high-arched nave of oaks against
Light-years of stars and the
Last scream space makes beyond space. Faces,

In grave bemusement, leaned, eyes fixed
On the fingers white in their delicate dance
On the strings of the box. And delicate
Was the melancholy that swelled each heart, and timed
10 The pulse in wrist, and wrist, and wrist—all while
The face leaned over the box
In shadow of hair that in fire-light down-gleamed,
Smoother than varnish, and black. And like
A silver vine that upward to darkness twines,
The voice confirmed the sweet sadness
Young hearts gave us no right to.

No right to, yet. Though some day would,
As Time unveiled,
In its own dancing parody of grace,
20 The bony essence of each joke on joke.

But even back then perhaps we knew
That the dancing fingers enacted
A truth far past the pain declared
By that voice that somehow made pain sweet.

Would it be better or worse, if now
I could name the names I've lost, and see,
Virile or beautiful, those who, entranced, leaned.
I wish I knew what wisdom they had there learned.

The singer—her name, it flees the fastest!
30 If only she'd toss back that varnished black screen
Of beautiful hair, and let
Flame reveal the grave cheek-curve, eye-shine,
Then I'd know that much.
If not her name.

Even now.

Last Night Train

In that slick and new-fangled coach we go slam-banging
On rackety ruin of a roadbed, past caterpillar-
Green flash of last light on deserted platforms,
And I watch the other passenger at this
Late hour—a hundred and eighty pounds of
Flesh, black, female, middle-aged,
Unconsciously flung by roadbed jerks to wallow,
Unshaped, unhinged, in
A purple dress. Straps of white sandals
10 Are loosened to ease the bulge of color-contrasting bare instep.
Knees wide, the feet lie sidewise, sole toward sole. They
Have walked so far. Head back, flesh snores.
I wonder what she has been doing all day in N.Y.

My station at last. I look back once.
Is she missing hers? I hesitate to ask, and the snore
Is suddenly snatched into eternity.

The last red light fades into distance and darkness like
A wandering star. Where that brief roar just now was,
A last cricket is audible. That lost
20 Sound makes me think, with quickly suppressed
Nostalgia, of
A country lane, late night, late autumn—and there,
Alone, again I stand, part of all.
Alone, I now stand under the green station light,
Part of nothing but years.

I stare skyward at uncountable years beyond
My own little aura of pale-green light—
The complex of stars is steady in its operation.
Smell of salt sedge drifts in from seaward,
30 And I think of swimming, naked and seaward,
In starlight forever.

But I look up the track toward Bridgeport. I feel
Like blessing the unconscious wallow of flesh-heap
And white sandals unstrapped at bulging of instep.

I hear my heels crunch on gravel, making
My way to a parked car.

Question at Cliff-Thrust

From the outthrust ledge of sea-cliff you
Survey, downward, the lazy tangle and untangle of
Foam fringe, not on sand, but sucking through
Age-rotten pumice and lava like old fruitcake lost in an angle of
A kitchen closet, the fruit long since nibbled away
By mouse-tooth. This is a day
Of merciless sun, no wind, and
Of distance, slick as oil, sliding infinitely away
To no far smudge of land.
10 You stare down at your cove beneath.
No blackness of rock shows,
Only the gradual darkening green as depth grows.
In that depth how far would breath
Hold? Down through gull-torn air
You lean forward and stare
At the shelving green of hypnosis.

Who would guess
It would be as easy as this?

A pebble companions your white downward flash.
20 You do not hear what must be its tiny splash
As, bladelike, your fingertips
Into the green surface slash
And your body, frictionless, slips
Into a green atmosphere,
Where you can hear
Only the nothingness of sound, and see
Only the one great green and unforgiving eye of depth that steadily
Absorbs your being in its intensity.
You take the downward strokes, some two or three.
30 Suddenly your lungs, aflame, burn.
But there is the beckoning downwardness
That you must fight before you turn, and in the turn
Begin the long climb toward lighter green, and light,
Until you lie in lassitude and strengthlessness
On the green bulge of ocean under the sight
Of one gull that screams from east to west and is

Demanding what?

INDEX OF TITLES AND FIRST LINES